Cracking the MCAS

Grade 10 English Language Arts

The Princeton Review

Cracking the MCAS

Grade 10 English Language Arts

by Gloria Levine

Random House, Inc.
New York

www.randomhouse.com/princetonreview

The Independent Education Consultants Association recognizes The Princeton Review as a valuable resource for high school and college students applying to college and graduate school.

Princeton Review, L.L.C.
2315 Broadway
New York, NY 10024

E-mail: comments@review.com

Published in the United States by Random House, Inc., New York.

ISBN 0-375-75587-X

Editor: Oona Schmid
Designer: Evelin Sanchez O'Hara

Manufactured in the United States of America

9 8 7 6 5 4 3 2

First Edition

Acknowledgments

I can't thank Russell Kahn and Oona Schmid enough for their help in getting the MCAS book into a new and much-improved form. I'd also like to thank everyone else at the Princeton Review who worked on the book: Sherri Muller, Sarah Hague, Kristen Azzara, Greta Englert, and Matthew Callan.

Contents

Part I

Introduction

Chapter 1

About the MCAS Exams

The Mystery Exams: About the MCAS Exams

If you're reading this right now, chances are you already know something about the Massachusetts Comprehensive Assessment System (MCAS) exams. For starters, you probably know that passing them will be a requirement for graduation from high school in Massachusetts beginning with the Class of 2003. In other words, 10th grade students must pass the grade 10 exams (in Math and English Language Arts) as one condition for getting a high school diploma. (Future classes will probably have to pass additional MCAS exams to graduate.) There's a lot of pressure on teachers and schools to see that students do well, but don't worry. Whether you're a student, teacher, or parent, you've come to the right place for help.

You probably bought this book because you will be taking the MCAS exams yourself or because you're helping your students or children get ready for them. Congratulations. This is the best guide you can use to prepare for the MCAS exams.

We're going to start by taking the mystery out of the MCAS.

What Exactly Are the MCAS Exams?

What Exactly Are the MCAS Exams?

The MCAS exams are given to all Massachusetts public school students in grades 3 through 8 and 10 to measure performance on the state learning standards in four content areas: English Language Arts (ELA), Mathematics, Science and Technology, and History and Social Science. These standards are called the Massachusetts Curriculum Frameworks.

A History of the Exam

So whose big idea was this, anyway? In the early 1990s many politicians, educators, parents, and members of the general community felt that students were getting diplomas without learning what they needed from high school. These people felt that creating tough state standards—spelling out exactly what Massachusetts students need to learn—would improve student academic performance. And so the Massachusetts Comprehensive Assessment System was born.

What Else is the MCAS For?

Not only do these exams measure individual students' aptitudes, but they also serve as a basis of accountability for schools and districts. Nobody outside of the public school system will see your score and, after 5 years, the record will be destroyed.

Who is The Princeton Review?

The Princeton Review is the nation's leader in test preparation. With offices in more than fifty cities across the United States and many outside the country, we help more than 2 million students every year with courses, books, online services, and software. We prepare students for the SATs, the PSATs, the ACT, and a wide range of statewide tests. The Princeton Review strategies that we share with you in this book have proven to be hugely successful in helping thousands of students achieve their goals.

We're Here to Help

There's no doubt that familiarity with the MCAS exams can help to reduce your stress level when you take them. By reviewing the content of the exam and giving you exposure to the exam format, we'll help you perform to the best of your ability. Plus, you will learn a lot of test-taking strategies that will also help you tackle the many other tests that are undoubtedly in your future.

If you'd like more information on the MCAS exams, you can go to the Massachusetts Department of Education's Web page at www.doe.mass.edu/mcas.

Whereas the SAT and ACT are college entrance exams, the MCAS exams are high school exit exams. If present trends continue, you'll soon have to take a test just to pass from one day to the next! *You passed the test? Good, you can move on to Thursday. You didn't pass the test? Sorry, you have to stay in Wednesday.* Okay, so maybe it's not *that* bad. But we do understand that all these exams can seem a bit overwhelming. That's why we've written this book.

What's So Special About This Book?

Our research and development teams have spent hours upon hours making sure that the guide contains all you need to know to ace the MCAS exams. We have the inside scoop on the MCAS exams, and we're going to let you in on what we know.

We have gone through and made sure that all skills and content listed in the Massachusetts Curriculum Framework for English Language Arts are reviewed and practiced in this book. Basically, this book was written with two goals in mind: First, we want to help you review all the information that may be on the exam. Second, we want to make sure that you know the exam like the back of your hand so that you are calm, cool, and collected on exam day.

Samuel Adams didn't have to take the MCAS exams, and he turned out okay...True enough. But, of course, Samuel Adams and his contemporaries had their own challenges. One of your generation's challenges, unfortunately, is to maintain your sanity as you take an ever-increasing number of examinations.

Frequently Asked Questions

When and where do I take the exams?

The Grade 10 MCAS exams are given in the spring at school during the regular school day. Students who fail an exam will be allowed to retake it—but when (and how often) has yet to be determined.

How long does it take to finish all the exams?

Most of the 10th grade exams are stretched out over one three-week period in May. (The Long Composition portion of the ELA is currently scheduled for a day in April about a month before the rest of the MCAS exams.) Two testing sessions are generally held each day. The MCAS exams will be given in sessions of about 45 minutes each. The key is that yuou can get an extension (probably 5-20 minutes); you won't be rushed the way you are on the SAT or ACT exams.

What's the breakdown of the Grade 10 MCAS exams as a collective whole?

There will be four exams, and a passing grade on the English and Math exams will be mandatory for graduation for the class of 2003 or beyond.

English (Language/Literature & Composition): 5 sessions of about 45 minutes each (2 sessions of Composition ; 3 sessions of Language and Literature)

Math: 3 sessions of about 45 minutes each

Science and Technology: 3 sessions of about 45 minutes each

History and Social Science: 3 sessions of about 45 minutes each

Does everybody have to take the exam?

Yes, every student in all Massachusetts public schools in grades 3 through 8 and 10 have to take the MCAS exams in selected subjects. If you're in public school, your parents cannot legally refuse to have you take the exams. (As of right now, though, private school and home-schooled students do not have to take the MCAS, but they will be allowed to take the exams in the future, if they want to.)

What if I have a disability?

For students with disabilities, appropriate testing accommodations (such as smaller testing rooms) are allowed. There aren't any exemptions from the exam, but the exam will take a different shape for two groups of students:

- A student whose disabilities are such that the student's Individualized Education Plan (IEP) team determines that the student won't be able to take the regular exam. (In this case, the student's education team will develop an alternate assessment, based on the student's individual needs.)

- A student with limited English proficiency who has been in a U.S. public school for three years or less and who is ineligible for the Spanish-language version of MCAS. (In this situation, the Department of Education is currently designing an alternative exam.)

What if I'm out the day of an exam?

You will have to take a makeup exam. If you don't show up that day—like any day—your absence must be authorized, or else you will be subject to penalties for truancy.

What do I need to take with me to the exam?

You should have a couple of pencils for the ELA exam, plus you'll be allowed to use a dictionary while writing the long composition.

What do the questions on the MCAS exams look like?

All of the exams have multiple-choice questions (with four choices each) and open-response questions (requiring a one- or two-paragraph response—or sometimes a graphic). In addition, the Math exams have some short-answer questions, and the English Language Arts (ELA) exams have a writing prompt, requiring students to write a long composition, often related to a reading passage.

What do the exam results look like—and who's going to see them?

The results for individual students—as well as for schools and districts—are reported as one of the following:

- Advanced (Students at this level can really understand and think about the subject in depth.)

- Proficient (Students' understanding at this level is solid.)

- Needs Improvement (Students at this level only "get" the subject somewhat.)

- Failing (These students just don't get it.)

Students' individual scores are sent home and become part of a students' permanent school record. Nobody outside of the public school system will see your score, so it will not figure into any college admissions decisions.

How are the exams scored?

I hope this isn't a big shock, but a huge computer scores your multiple-choice responses. Each correct response is assigned 1 point, and each incorrect response is given 0 points. Each open-response is scored on a 0 to 4 scale, with a score of 4 given to a thorough, complete response with the right answer. For long compositions, two separate scorers assigns the writing two scores, one for topic development (1–6 points) and one for standard English conventions (1–4 points)—for a total score of between 2 and 20 points.

To make it easier to compare results across content areas and grade levels, students' "raw scores" (actual points earned) are converted to scaled scores. For each content area, a student's MCAS scores are reported on a scale between 200–280.

Here's the breakdown by performance level:

Advanced   260–280

Proficient   240–259

Needs Improvement   220–239

Failing   200–219

As you can see, you need a 220 or higher to pass.

Who are the scorers?

Massachusetts teachers are trained as scorers for the long compositions. The state hired a contractor, Advanced Systems in Measurement and Education, Inc., who in turn hires professional scorers—all of whom have experience in the subject area being scored—to score open response questions. And, of course, the big machines score the multiple-choice questions.

Does everyone take the same exams?

Everyone gets about 80% of the questions on the exam in common, while the other problems will vary from booklet to booklet. Only the questions that everyone takes count toward individual exam scores. The other problems, called field test items, won't count on your score and are only used for research purposes for future tests. Unfortunately, you won't know which questions are the ones that count for your score, so you'll just have to answer all the questions as if they all matter.

How many questions are on the exam?

Different content area exams have different numbers of questions. Here's how many common items there were on each of the exams in May 2000.

Exam	Multiple Choice	Open Response	Short Answer	Writing Prompt	Total Items	Total Scoreable Items
ELA	48	6	0	1	55	41
Math	39	7	5	0	51	42
Sci. & Tech.	44	7	0	0	51	42
Hist. & S.S.	48	9	0	0	57	38

In addition to the 41 common items on the 1998 ELA exam, there were 11 field test items (8 multiple choice, 2 open response, and 1 writing prompt.) The practice tests in this book will contain 52 items, to get you used to the length of the "real thing." You won't know which items are field test (unscored) items, so do your best on every question.

How do the MCAS Exams Compare with Other Standardized Tests?

There are some pretty big differences between the MCAS exams and other standardized tests, such as the SAT. Questions on the MCAS exams do *not* progress from easy to hard to nearly impossible. All items are *not* multiple-choice (they're a mix of multiple-choice and open-ended questions). All students are *not* taking exactly the same exams. It is *not* designed simply to measure your aptitude for learning; it is a cumulative test of knowledge.

The whole idea is: "This is the stuff that every Massachusetts student should know—so now show that you know it!" *There is no mystery about that content of the exam.* It is clearly outlined in the Curriculum Framework, and we will make sure you have the skills necessary by the time you've completed this book!

How do I prepare for the tests?

Well, of course, you'll want to use this book. Other than that, it goes without saying that you should try to do your best in school. But on a more concrete level, you can find sample questions from released exams on the Internet at the Massachusetts Department of Education's Web site (www.doe.mass.edu/mcas). Take these for extra practice to supplement the priceless book in your hands.

How This Book is Organized

In the following chapter, we go into detail about the structure, format, and scoring of the exam. We'll give you a "tool kit" that you can use not only for the MCAS exams but also for other multiple-choice tests on your educational and career horizon.

And Finally...

We know that the MCAS exams can be pretty challenging. But if you are willing to work with us by going through this book, you *will* do well. We'll even help you have some fun along the way!

We congratulate you on taking the first step in preparing for the Grade 10 MCAS exam in English Language Arts by choosing this guide—it's the best one there is! Good luck, although we know you won't need it!

How do we know what's tested on the MCAS exams? We have carefully studied the Massachusetts Standards, past MCAS exam questions, and information put out by the Massachusetts Department of Education about the exams.

Chapters 3 through 6 will review the subject material covered on the 10th grade English Language Arts exam. We will also cover the different types of questions and learn how to tackle each one. Throughout the subject review, we will offer sample questions to show you how these topics are tested on the MCAS exams.

Finally, we have constructed two full-length English Language Arts Grade 10 practice tests. You will find detailed explanations for every question, and some sample essays. It is important to approach these exams as if they were the real thing. Read the explanations—even if you got the right answers—and look at how various sample essays were scored. That way you will learn good test-taking techniques, see which subject areas you need to focus on, and get an idea of how to polish your writing for a top score.

Chapter 2

Structure and Strategies

Chapter One gave an overview of Massachusetts's MCAS exams. Since you bought this particular book, your main concern is the ELA (English Language Arts) Grade 10 MCAS exam, so let's get down to business and focus on that exam.

In this chapter we'll tell you which skills and content are tested, and how. We'll show you what the exam looks like, how it's formatted and organized, and how it's scored. And we'll show you what you'll need to do to ace this exam by filling up your "MCAS tool kit" with techniques you can use on the exam.

What is the ELA Grade 10 MCAS?

The ELA Grade 10 MCAS exam consists of five sessions, each lasting 45 minutes. At the end of 45 minutes, you are allowed some extra time if you need it. You'll probably complete two sessions each day, but some schools may administer more sessions if they choose to. The two Composition sessions are given on the same day with a short break between the composing and revising sessions. You can have 20 minutes or so for an optional practice test.

Each student gets a Student Answer Booklet in which to place all their answers for the multiple-choice and open-response questions—you'll be using the same Answer Booklet for your English (ELA) exam as for your other MCAS exams, such as the Science and Technology and Math exams. You'll get a separate ELA Long Composition Booklet for writing your long composition, which you would've done a few weeks earlier. Make sure you've filled out all the identification information correctly and completed the grids (bubbles) properly!

What Should I Expect?

The English Language Arts exam is structured in two parts: the Composition exam and a Language and Literature exam (also called the "Reading exam"). Two of the five ELA sessions are devoted to the Composition exam, and three to the Language and Literature exam.

The Composition Exam

For the Composition exam, you're given a topic ("prompt") for creating an essay, sometimes based on a short reading passage that accompanies it. You respond to the prompt by writing a composition in the ELA Long Composition Answer Booklet. You'll have two 45-minute sessions, separated by a short break, in which to write that composition. If you need more time, you can ask and you're supposed to be given a "reasonable" amount of additional time, which can be anywhere from five to thirty extra minutes.

The Language and Literature (Reading) Exam

Remember: It doesn't matter whether you get the field-test (also called "matrix") problems right. These questions do not affect your score. However, since you won't be able to tell which ones they are, try to do your best on all questions!

The second part of the ELA exam, the ELA Language and Literature (Reading) exam is given about a month after the ELA Composition sessions. The exam is spread out over three testing sessions. During each session, you are presented with reading passages (fiction, nonfiction, and poetry), followed by multiple-choice and open-response questions. You are given a Student Answer Booklet where you record answers.

To give you an idea of how many of each type of question you're likely to find on the exam, note that on the 1999 ELA Grade 10 exam, there were thirty-six multiple-choice questions, four open-response questions, and one Composition, plus some field-test questions.

What Kinds of Stuff Are They Going to Ask?

So, what exactly is on this exam? As you may recall from chapter 1, the content of all the MCAS exams corresponds to a list of learning goals known as the Massachusetts Curriculum Framework. Specifically, the ELA exam questions are drawn from the 28 "standards" that the Curriculum Framework set up—but let's be honest: There's no way anyone has the time or inclination to be this exhaustive.

First, the ELA exam has to exclude material because some things simply can't be measured on a paper-and-pencil test. Things like speaking skills and group work are *not* factors on this exam. Second, even though there are 28 standards in all, some of these are considered much more important. We'll come right out and tell you which "standards," or areas of study, are critical. And, we'll spend extra time reviewing these skills. For example, since your long composition accounts for about a quarter of the possible score points, we'll devote an entire chapter (chapter 6) to the Composition.

What Other Areas Are Emphasized?

To give you the overall picture of what sorts of skills the ELA exam emphasizes, and hence, the type of information that forms the core of this book, we'll go over four of the standards. Don't get frightened by any jargon here, we'll translate each into plain English.

Learning Standard 9: "Students will identify the basic facts and essential ideas in what they have read, heard, or viewed."

TPR Translation: You should understand the basics of what's being communicated. We'll give you the straight dope and plenty of tips in chapters 3 and 4, so you can answer questions about what you've read.

Learning Standard 13: "Students will identify, analyze, and apply knowledge of the structure, elements, and meaning of nonfiction or informational material and provide evidence from the text to support their understanding."

TPR Translation: You may be asked to pull apart a piece of nonfiction and figure out how it's put together—and what it means. We'll go into nonfiction in detail in chapter 5, so that you'll be well prepared to answer any questions about nonfiction texts.

Learning Standard 15: "Students will identify and analyze how an author's choice of words appeals to the senses, creates imagery, suggests mood, and sets tone."

TPR Translation: When you read poetry and fiction, you should be able to answer a whole series of questions about the type of writing it is and what kinds of feelings it invokes. We'll make sure you know a bunch of literary devices such as the simile, oxymoron, and irony that will help you ace this part of the exam. Didn't we tell you not to worry? We go over these terms very carefully in chapters 3 and 5.

Learning Standard 19: "Students will write compositions with a clear focus, logically related ideas to develop it, and adequate detail."

TPR Translation: You'll be asked to express and support your ideas clearly in writing. Chapter 6 is all about the specific techniques and tricks that will help you write open-response answers and the composition.

What Do the Questions Look Like?

Now that you know what the exam looks like overall and what skills are tested, let's focus on the three formats of questions that appear on the ELA exam: *Multiple-choice questions, open-response questions,* and *writing prompts.* For now, we're just showing you how these questions are going to look like on the exam. Later in this chapter, we'll go over the best ways to crack these questions.

What's a Multiple-Choice Question?

Selected readings are followed by four or five questions about each reading. The questions are followed by four choices: *A, B, C,* and *D* and you'll need to pick one of these *multiple choices.* For example, you might be asked:

1. What does the last sentence in paragraph 2 mean?
    A. The ugly duck was very ugly.
    B. The ugly duck wasn't always ugly.
    C. The ugly duck became pretty as it got older.
    D. The ugly duck was actually very beautiful inside.

2. In paragraph 3, what does the word "dank" mean?
    A. wet
    B. dark
    C. depressed
    D. kind

We'll go over in detail how to tackle multiple-choice questions later in this chapter, as well as in chapters 3, 4, and 5.

What is an Open-Response Question?

The multiple-choice answers are scored by a dumb machine. That machine recognizes pencil marks. Period. It certainly can't tell that you *meant* that little squiggle just outside one bubble to be your answer or that you *didn't mean* that half-erased pencil smudge on the other bubble to count. In other words, neatness counts!

After the multiple-choice questions following each passage, there may be one or two *open-response questions.* For these, you need to write an organized response, with plenty of support from the text. A concise paragraph or two (5–7 sentences) should be enough. Chapter 6 specifically describes how you'll do this on the exam.

3. Describe the entrance of Hamlet's ghost in this scene. Include a physical description of the scene and the effect it had on those present. Use specific details from the passage to support your answer.

Here's a pretty good answer that the scorers would probably give a four:

Darkness has fallen and Horatio is talking with two guards, Bernardo and Marcellus, in front of the castle when the ghost of the former king marches in. The ghost of Prince Hamlet's father moves like he's in the army, and, according to Horatio, wears the same armor the king had on when he fought in Norway. Without a word, the armed ghost soon stalks off as if mad when challenged by Horatio to speak. Marcellus and Bernardo had seen the ghost twice before while on their watch, and are pleased that it decided to make an appearance before the skeptical Horatio. Horatio, on his part, is confused by and scared of this figure, although he admits he can no longer doubt its existence.

What is the Composition?

This is the part of the ELA exam where you actually have to *show* that you can write by *writing something*. Makes sense, right? You may be given a reading passage followed by a writing assignment; you may be given an idea and asked to apply it to a piece of literature you choose (like the belief that "revenge is sweet" or that "things are not always what they seem").

For example, you might be given the following exam question:

4. BACKGROUND FOR WRITING

Read the following opening paragraph from a short story by Saki from the book Beasts and Superbeasts. *When you are done reading, respond to the writing assignment below.*

"The Lumber Room"
by Saki

The children were to be driven, as a special treat, to the sands at Jagborough. Nicholas was not to be of the party; he was in disgrace. Only that morning he had refused to eat his wholesome bread-and-milk on the seemingly frivolous ground that there was a frog in it. Older and wiser and better people had told him that there could not possibly be a frog in his bread-and-milk and that he was not to talk nonsense; he continued, nevertheless, to talk what seemed the veriest nonsense, and described with much detail the colouration and markings of the alleged frog. The dramatic part of the incident was that there really was a frog in Nicholas' basin of bread-and-milk; he had put it there himself, so he felt entitled to know something about it. The sin of taking a frog from the garden and putting it into a bowl of wholesome bread-and-milk was enlarged on at great length, but the fact that stood out clearest in the whole affair, as it presented itself to the mind of Nicholas, was that the older, wiser, and better people had been proved to be profoundly in error in matters about which they had expressed the utmost assurance.

WRITING ASSIGNMENT

A writer often "sets the stage" for the rest of the story in the opening paragraphs. In a well-organized essay, tell us what you know about Nicholas, based on clues you found in the opening paragraph and what you think of him. To support your ideas, you might analyze the author's diction, choice of viewpoint, characterization, use of imagery, establishment of setting and mood.

Here's an example of a competent answer:

When Saki introduces us to the naughty boy in the first paragraph, he offers several clues about what will happen to the main character.

The little boy put a frog in his wholesome snack and then had the nerve to admit it. Nicholas, it seems to me, is unrepentant. He's a little bit of an imp because he describes the frog's colors in order to insist people look for the frog he placed in his own cereal bowl.

The narrator's tone is ironic because the narrator seems to question who's the smart one in the story—Nicholas or the "older, wiser, and better people" who make mistakes. That tone gives the reader an idea how the adults around Nicholas act and what he thinks of them. Some adult in the household apparently thinks that bread-and-milk is "wholesome" but Nicholas does not have the same high opinion. While that adult believes Nicholas is "talking nonsense" when he complains about the frog in his food, the adult is wrong; Nicholas knows more. The adult assumes that she is "older, wiser, and better" than Nicholas, but obviously she is not, since she didn't recognize the truth about the frog.

I think in the end, Nicholas will get the better of the adult who harps upon "the sin of taking a frog from the garden and putting it into a bowl of wholesome bread-and-milk." In other words, the narrator's attitude indicates that Nicholas will prevail and the adult will get her "just desserts." In fact, the opener not only says that Nicholas will have the last laugh on that humorless adult, but makes the reader eager to see that moment come.

We can safely say that a lot of students don't look forward to the composition portion of the exam. Writing under exam conditions isn't much fun, but some of the pressure will be lessened in this case because, as we said, you can *take as much time as you need*, within reason. As with any stressful situation, however, practice makes a huge difference and we're going to give you a lot of examples and practice in this book.

How well you state and support your main idea will largely determine your score. We will go over how to write a well-organized composition about a piece of literature. In chapter 6, we go into a lot of detail about strategies for building your composition and we will give you practice answering MCAS examlike prompts.

At least one dictionary is provided per classroom for use during the Composition sessions of the exam. No other tools or reference books are allowed during other ELA testing sessions, that is, during the reading portion.

How is the Exam Scored?

As we explained in chapter 1, the scale score on MCAS is derived from your raw score, the number of correct multiple-choice answers combined with the number of points earned by open-response answers, plus the long composition. We've mentioned that a machine will score the multiple-choice section of the exam. Teachers and other professionals will score your open responses and long compositions. Assuming that your exam will be similar to the Spring 1999 MCAS, here is the scoring breakdown of your exam:

Maximum points you could earn for each type of question

Multiple choice	Open-response	Writing Prompt
36	16 (4 questions, 4 points each)	20 (10 points from each scorer)

The chart above shows that on the 1999 exam, you could get a maximum of 36 points from the multiple-choice questions (from 36 questions worth 1 point each), plus a maximum of 16 points from the open-response questions, and a maximum of 20 points for a Long Composition. These points are converted into a scale score between 200 and 280 and you will need a scale score of 220 or higher to pass. For your long composition, at least two scorers read your paper and each comes up with a score.

How Am I Going to Handle All of This?

You're off to a great start because you've bought this book. The goal of our book is to give you some aides and help with the exam. Think of us as arming you with a "MCAS tool kit." We describe tools that you can use to tackle problems you face on this exam and others. What strategies will end up in your kit?

Process of Elimination (POE)

Try the following question:

1. What is the adverb in this sentence: "Drivers who ram other cars and smash into barriers in the virtual world of auto-racing video games are more likely to drive aggressively in real life, too"?

What? You can't remember what the heck an adverb is?

Lucky for you, all the MCAS multiple-choice questions come with four alternatives to choose from. Take a look:

A. ram

B. smash

C. drive

D. aggressively

Say you really don't have any idea what an adverb is (although we'll review all those grammar terms and rules in chapter 3), but you *do* remember that a verb is an action word. You might look at your choices and realize that three of these are verbs (action words): *A, B,* and *C*. You can eliminate these, then, because if they're verbs, they're not adverbs. All that's left is the right answer choice, *D*!

You may have heard this strategy (coming up with the right answer choice by eliminating the wrong ones) called *process of elimination* (POE for short). It is often easier to detect the wrong choices than the right ones. We suggest that you literally cross out those wrong choices first. That way, you narrow down your choices, and it's easy to see what's left to choose from.

Even if you can't eliminate three out of the four answer choices right off the bat as we did with the sample item, you still improve your odds with each choice you throw out. It's better to guess among two or three choices than among four, so narrow down the field as much as you can and then make your best guess.

Now you have the first tool for your kit: POE. We'll mention it throughout the book, because we think it is one of the most useful test-taking strategies you will ever learn. Try it the next time you lose your keys.

Aggressive Guessing

Try another item:

2. The headline, "Bam Bam Bigelow Beats Diamond Dallas" uses what literary device?

You may know that the answer is "alliteration" before even looking at your choices, but don't sweat it if you don't. We'll go over that kind of thing in chapter 5. Okay, now look at the answer choices:

      A. simile

      B. irony

      C. alliteration

      D. hyperbole

Sure enough, look at your four choices and—there it is, *C*! If you had carefully checked each answer choice *before* guessing aggressively, the wrong answer choice might have confused you.

Of course, you can't always make an aggressive guess before looking at the four alternatives. For example:

3. Based on what this author says in his Nobel Prize acceptance speech, which of the following bumper stickers do you think he'd agree with?

There's no point in trying to guess what the answer is before checking the choices out, is there? There are zillions of bumper sticker slogans, and therefore zillions of possible choices.

> **Remember:** you're not penalized for guessing, so don't leave any questions blank. And use POE to improve your odds for each guess.

To sum up: When you can, guess aggressively for the answer, then look for it among the answer choices. It's like eating at the mall. You could just go to the food court and look at all your choices and then decide what you want. But if you're hungry and want to save time and energy, you should decide what you want and then head straight for the appropriate restaurant.

"Most Important" Lists

Have you ever noticed how fond of lists many English teachers are?

Which of the following lists have your English teachers shared with you?

- Important purposes for writing

- Important literary devices

- Important patterns for organizing your writing

- Important grammar rules

If your response is "All of the above!", you should thank those teachers, because you're a step ahead in the MCAS game. In addition to POE and aggressive guessing strategies, we're sharing "most important" lists that will help you on the MCAS. And for the tenth time... Don't worry! We'll refresh your memory in the upcoming chapters.

General Test-Taking Tips

Finally, there are some tips that you've heard before, but they really make a difference:

- Get a good night's sleep before the exam days (but don't overdo it so you wake up feeling sluggish).

- Eat a good breakfast (but that doesn't mean steak and eggs if you're used to a breakfast bar).

- Bring at least three sharpened #2 pencils.

- Remind yourself that you are in control. You've gone through this book, you've done the practice tests, you know the exam like the back of your hand and you are ready!

So, here's a list of some tools you'll have for "cracking" the MCAS ELA exam:

- Process of Elimination (POE)

- Aggressive Guessing

- Grammar and Literary Terms

- "Most Important" Lists

Let's get cracking and tackle some vocabulary!

Keep in mind that you *can write in the exam booklet.* Yes! You can and should mark it up as you cross out wrong choices, underline key words, and find answers in the passages. And in the first Composition exam session, you should jot down ideas, organize and reorganize your ideas on the draft paper, as directed by the exam proctor. Just make sure that when you sit down for the second Composition session after the break, you neatly write your finished composition in your Long Composition booklet.

Part II

Subject Review

Chapter 3

The Language Part of the Language and Literature Exam

In this chapter, we'll walk you through English language questions on vocabulary and grammar. We'll emphasize the material you need to know for the ELA Grade 10 exam and give you practice with the MCAS exam format. In addition, we'll share our proven strategies for picking the correct choices even if you don't know the right answers. By the time you finish this chapter, you'll have completed about one third of what you'll need to know for the ELA Grade 10 MCAS exam. So, let's get cracking!

Vocabulary

Words comprise the basic building block of English, and *vocabulary* is another way to describe how many words you know. You already know thousands of words, but the MCAS will test you on some new ones. Fortunately, even if you've never seen a word before, you can still get the answer right (and dumb wild luck is not the reason why.). This section focuses on simple things you can do to ferret out good answers to questions on vocabulary. To emerge victorious from your showdown with difficult vocabulary, you'll need only three skills: figuring words in *context*, using their *parts*, and understanding *derivations*.

Context

The words on your ELA Grade 10 exam will always appear in a *context*. In other words, you will never be asked to define a word that hasn't been used in a sentence or two, surrounded by information. These texts contain valuable clues. Picture an obliging bloodhound named Clover. She's sniffing around the word in a sentence to help you find hints that point to its meaning. Sometimes those clues are really big ones, such as when the sentence actually defines the word for you.

Let's illustrate what we're telling you with a few examples. Look at this sentence:

Geckos, lizards found in the tropics, have a half-million microscopic hairs on each foot, called setae.

We're guessing you don't know what a *gecko* is, let alone *setae!* So if you faced this question, what would you do?

1. *Geckos* are

    A. lizards.

    B. tropics.

    C. feet.

    D. hairs.

2. *Setae* are

    A. numbers.

    B. microscopes.

    C. feet.

    D. hairs.

Look at this sentence and smell out a trail from the mystery words (*geckos, setae*) in the passage to the definitions nearby. In this case, the definitions are easy to find because they are set off by commas: "lizards found in the tropics," and "hairs on each foot." *Geckos* are lizards and *setae* are hairs.

> Tip: Commas that set off a phrase around an unfamiliar word —the way they set off "lizards found in the tropics" here—often point to a definition clue.

Sometimes the clues aren't as obvious. For instance, you and Clover might find words near a mystery word that tell what it does *not* mean. Try this sentence:

The quarterback was nervous whenever he had to do any public speaking, but he was intrepid on the football field.

Clover sniffs out the word *but*, a tipoff that what comes next contrasts with what came before. Clover and you can reason that to be *intrepid* means the opposite of nervous, right? The word *but* is a good clue that the quarterback is *not* jittery on the field. He's confident and bold. With Clover's aid, you discover that *intrepid* means *bold.*

Word Parts

In addition to Clover, the clever context hound, there's a second important tool for getting unfamiliar words to give up their meanings. *Word parts*, the pieces that make up polysyllabic words, assist you with intimidating vocabulary. What? You don't know what the word polysyllabic means? If you know that *poly* means *many* (that's why *poly*nomials in math have *many* sides), you can figure out that the *poly*syllabic words have *many* syllables.

> Once you recognize basic word parts, you can use them again and again to unlock the meanings of alien words.

Breaking tough words into little pieces can make them surprisingly easy to define. Ever heard of *nasology?* In the word *nasology,* there are two parts. There's the *nas* first part; there's the *ology* second part. Did the word *nasology* remind you of biology or geology? That's because *ology* means the *study of.* The *ology* is a *suffix,* and it's something that you can attach to the end of a word. The first part, *nas,* is the *root. Naso,* as you might imagine, means *nose.*

Sometimes the suffix *ology* hooks up with different roots, to form new words like bi*ology,* ge*ology,* and nas*ology.* Other times the root attaches itself to different suffixes, so instead of *nas*ology, you might see words like *nas*al and *nas*ogastric.

Prefixes

In addition to roots and suffixes, you can attach *prefixes* to the beginning of words. Ever watch the *pre*game show, the show that comes before the game? *Pre* is a prefix that means before.

> Pencil in any additional examples you think of that might aid you. Or if one example on the list "clicks" for you, circle it.

Prefixes that indicate direction

ac (also: ad) = to, toward	*ac*cessorize, *ad*mit, *ad*vocate
circum = around	*circum*ference, *circum*spect, *circum*vent
co = with	*co*operate, *co*ordinate, ac*co*mpany
dis = take away	*dis*agree, *dis*credit, *dis*tract

en = in, in	*en*slave, *en*gulf, *en*shrine
epi = upon, beside	*epi*demic, *epi*sode, *epi*gram
ex = out, from	*ex*pel, *ex*clude, *ex*it
extra = outside of	*extra*terrestrial, *extra*curricular, *extra*vert
hyper = over, excessive	*hyper*active, *hyper*critical, *hyper*bole
hypo = under	*hypo*active, *hypo*critical, *hypo*dermic
in (also: em, im) = inside	*in*habit, *em*bed, *im*pel,
inter = between, among	*inter*action, *inter*cept, *inter*fere
intra = within	*intra*departmental, *intra*venous, *intra*mural
intro = within, inwardly	*intro*duce, *intro*spective, *intro*ject
para = beside	*para*llel, *para*lysis, *para*phrase
peri = about, around	*peri*scope, *peri*phery, *peri*patetic
pro = forward	*pro*gress, *pro*ceed, *pro*mote
retro = backward	*retro*active, *retro*grade, *retro*spective
sub = under	*sub*marine, *sub*conscious, *sub*merge
super = above, beyond	*super*abundant, *super*b, *super*heated
syn = with, together	*syn*c, *syn*onym, *syn*chronize
trans = across	*trans*atlantic, *trans*action, *trans*portation

Prefixes that indicate amount or degree

arch = chief	*arch*bishop, *arch*enemy, *arch*angel
bi = two	*bi*cycle, *bi*noculars, *bi*ennial
de = removal, negation	*de*tract, *de*humanize, *de*horn
di = two, double	*di*vorce, *di*oxide, *di*lemma
in (also: un) = not	*in*active, *in*vert, *un*able
mono = one	*mono*poly, *mono*tone, *mono*gamist
multi = many	*multi*ple, *multi*tude, *multi*media

non = not	*non*sense, *non*stop, *non*profit
omni = all	*omni*bus, *omni*scient, *omni*range
pan = all	*pan*demic, *pan*orama, *pan*human
re = again, back	*re*ject, *re*pay, *re*marry
semi (also: demi, hemi) = half	*semi*circle, *hemi*sphere, *demi*monde
tri = three	*tri*angle, *tri*dent, *tri*cycle
ultra = excessive, extreme	*ultra*modern, *ultra*marine, *ultra*conservative
uni = one	*uni*ty, *uni*sex, *uni*cycle
vice = deputy, next in rank	*vice* president, *vice*roy, *vice* deputy

Prefixes that indicate time

ante = before	*ante*, *ante*bellum, *ante*rior
meso = middle	*meso*derm, *meso*sphere, *meso*morph
pre = before	*pre*dict, *pre*fix, *pre*vention
proto = first	*proto*col, *proto*type, *proto*plasm

Prefixes that indicate badness or goodness

contra = against	*contra*dict, *contra*band, *contro*versy
anti = against	*anti*freeze, *anti*toxin, *anti*pathy
mal = bad, wrongful	*mal*adjusted, *mal*administer, *mal*adroit
mis = wrong, bad	*mis*fit, *mis*hap, *mis*representation

If you can create an association between a word and its prefix, you will possess the key to mastering this material. Try this: Anytime you see a word with *syn*, think of 'N Sync, a band that sings *together*. Now what if you get the words *syn*copate or *syn*chronize on your MCAS exam? Okay, you have no clue what these words mean, but you'll remember the band of "Bye, Bye, Bye" sings *together,* and that syncopate and synchronize relate to things that happen together. Even if you don't know exactly what these words mean, that may be all the information you need to get the right answer! To create your own associations, circle the example word that seems most obvious to you. Write in your own word(s), like 'N Sync.

Roots

Did you notice that some of the example words sound redundant, such as invert and extravert? These words share a *root—vert*, which means *to turn*. Something inverted is *turned inward*, someone who's extraverted is *turned outward*.

Just as knowing a few prefixes give you a leg up on the MCAS exam, knowing root words will similarly give you a big advantage.

Root	What it means	Common examples
anthro = man		*anthro*pology, phil*anthro*pist, mis*anthro*pe
aqua = water		*aqua*rium, *aqua*tic, *aqua*marine
chron = time		*chron*ic, *chron*icle, ana*chron*ism
cognos (also: gnosi) = know		*cogn*itive, re*cogn*ize, in*cogn*ito
cred = believe		*cred*it, in*cred*ible, dis*cred*ited
derm = skin		*derm*atology, epi*derm*is, taxi*derm*y
dict = say		*dict*ate, contra*dict*, pre*dict*ion
dorm = sleep		*dorm*itory, *dorm*ant, *dorm*ancy
fin = end		*fin*al, in*fin*ity, *fin*ale
flex (also: flect) = bend		*flex*ible, re*flect*, in*flect*ion
fort (also: forc) = strong		*fort*ress, en*forc*e, e*fort*less
gen = race, kind		*gen*etic, *gen*eration, *gen*erate
germ = vital part		*germ*inate, *germ*, *germ*ane
gram = written		*gram*mar, dia*gram*, tele*gram*
graph = write		*graph*ic, geo*graph*y, photo*graph*
habit = live		in*habit*, *habit*at, *habit*
jac (also: ject) = throw, lie		pro*ject*, re*ject*ion, ob*ject*
jur (also: jud, jus) = law		*jur*or, *jud*ge, *jus*tice
liber = free		*liber*ty, *liber*ator, *liber*al
lic (also: licit) = permit		*lic*ense, il*licit*, so*licit*

log = word	*log*ic, ana*log*, *log*istics
man = by hand	*man*ual, *man*icure, e*man*cipation
mar = sea, pool	*mar*ine, *mar*sh, aqua*mar*ine
mit (also: miss) = send	*miss*ion, per*mit*, trans*mit*
mort (also: mors) = death	*mort*al, *mort*uary, re*mors*eful
navi = ship	*nav*y, *navi*gate, *navi*gator
numer = number	*numer*al, *numer*ous, in*numer*able
pac = peace	*pac*ifist, *pac*ify, *pac*t
ped (also: pod) = foot	*ped*al, *ped*estrian, *pod*iatrist
plac = please	*plac*id, com*plac*ent, *plac*ate
pend = hang, suspend	*pend*ant, sus*pend*, ap*pend*ix
puls = drive, push	*puls*e, im*puls*ive, ex*puls*ion
scrib (also: scrip) = write	*scrib*ble, *scrip*t, trans*crip*t
soph = wisdom	*soph*omore, philo*soph*y, *soph*isticated
spec = look, see	*spec*tacle, in*spec*t, *spec*tator
sphere = ball	*sphere*ical, strato*sphere*, hemi*sphere*
spond (also: spons) = answer	re*spond*, corre*spond*, re*spons*e
struct = build	*struct*ure, in*struct*, de*struct*ive
tact = feel	in*tact*, *tact*ile, con*tact*
tang = touch	*tang*o, *tang*ent, *tang*ible
temp = time	con*temp*orary, *temp*o, *temp*orary
ten = stretch, strain	*ten*don, in*ten*sify, at*ten*tion
tract = pull	*tract*or, con*tract*, sub*tract*
val = strength, worth	*val*ue, *val*iant, in*val*id
ver (also: veri) = true, genuine	*ver*dict, a*ver*, *veri*fiable
vict (also: vinc) = conquer	*vict*im, con*vict*, in*vinc*ible
vis = see	*vis*ual, in*vis*ible, *vis*ionary

On the 1999 ELA Grade 10 MCAS exam, there were a lot of unfamiliar words in both reading passages and in questions that specifically asked for definitions. If we were omniscient and knew the specific words on your test, we'd just list those words. But we aren't all-knowing (that's what *omniscient* means) and you could be tested on any of a number of words. That's a big burden unless you're Noah Webster or Data from *Star Trek*. No? Then these lists are the next best thing to being a cyborg.

And don't forget about our 'N Sync trick. Make an association between each root and one of our (or your) samples.

Here's a second example of an association: Picture a *pend*ulum, hanging from a clock. Any time you see *pend* such as *pending, suspension* and *pendency,* visualize your clock. These words relate to *pend*, meaning to hang; *pend*ing and *pend*ency describe things hanging over you that still need to be done, and sus*pens*ion means dangling, like a suspension bridge.

Suffix

Okay, there's one more list to go. In addition to mix'n'matching prefixes and roots, you can tack on *suffixes* to the ending of words. If you decide to go to college, you'll discover a lot more words that end with *ology*—such as entym*ology*, cyt*ology*, and psych*ology*—that represent areas college students can *study*. Here are some more suffixes:

Suffix What it Means	Common Examples
Adjectives	
able (also: ible, ble) = able, can	invis*ible*, innumer*able*, solu*ble*
al = makes the root an adjective	reg*al*, equ*al*, tempor*al*
an (also: ian) = of, pertaining to root	Americ*an*, Republic*an*, Elizabeth*an*
ant (also: ent) = makes the root an adjective (can also be a n.)	depend*ent*, pleas*ant*, superabund*ant*
ar = of the nature of	pol*ar*, stell*ar*, titul*ar*
acy = quality, state	pir*acy*, fall*acy*, leg*acy*
ary = connected with	honor*ary*, vision*ary*, contempor*ary*
ate = makes the root an adjective* (* can also be used for n. or v.)	sed*ate*, moder*ate*, separ*ate*

ative = makes the root an adjective	rel*ative*, impuls*ive*, respons*ive*
ous = full of	joy*ous*, wondr*ous*, nerv*ous*
er = comparative adj. * (* or adv.)	slow*er*, hard*er*, low*er*
escent = makes the root an adjective	convale*scent*, incande*scent*
esque = in the style or manner	Roman*esque*, burl*esque*, grot*esque*
ese = nationality, language, style * (* also can be n.)	Chin*ese*, Burm*ese*, legal*ese*
ial = adjective form	fil*ial*, imper*ial*, judic*ial*
ic = adjective form	poet*ic*, metall*ic*, iron*ic*
ical = adjective form	polit*ical*, econom*ical*, rhetor*ical*
ile = ability	ag*ile*, doc*ile*, tact*ile*
ine = of the nature of	crystal*line*, equ*ine*, mar*ine*
ious = adjective form	od*ious*, relig*ious*, malic*ious*
ish = belonging to, resembling	Brit*ish*, baby*ish*, redd*ish*
ive = showing the tendency of	correc*tive*, construc*tive*, attrac*tive*
ous = full of	joy*ous*, nerv*ous*, glori*ous*
ory = having the function of	compuls*ory*, declarat*ory*, mandat*ory*
y = inclined to	butter*y*, grouch*y*, dream*y*

A word's suffix often indicates its part of speech—such as whether it's an adjective or a verb. When we do sample exercises, you'll see that this ammunition can help you get rid of answer choices in multiple-choice questions and help you navigate the MCAS exam.

Nouns

ance = makes the root a noun	brilli*ance*, appear*ance*, buoy*ance*
ancy = state or quality	brilli*ancy*, buoy*ancy*, dorm*ancy*
ant (also: ent) = makes root a noun* (* can also be used for adj.)	accid*ent*, tang*ent*, pend*ant*
ard = makes the root a noun	cow*ard*, drunk*ard*, wiz*ard*
ation = makes the root a noun	separa*tion*, modera*tion*, inflec*tion*
cy = makes the root a noun	democra*cy*, accura*cy*, expedien*cy*

ee = one who is the object	employ*ee*, assign*ee*, refer*ee*
eer/ier = one connected with	auction*eer*, engin*eer*, brigad*ier*
ence = makes the root a noun	abstin*ence*, differ*ence*, depend*ence*
ency = makes the root a noun	consist*ency*, depend*ency*, exig*ency*
er = person concerned with	employ*er*, enforc*er*, southern*er*
ery/ry = business, actions, conditions	bak*ery*, scen*ery*, trick*ery*
escence = action or process	conval*escence*, lumin*escence*
ese = nationality, language, style* (* can also be an adj.)	Chin*ese*, legal*ese*, Japan*ese*
ess = female	host*ess*, lion*ess*, count*ess*
et (also: ette) = little one	isl*et*, midg*et*, cigar*ette*
ia = indicates a noun	malar*ia*, anem*ia*, milit*ia*
ion = action or condition	crea*tion*, fus*ion*, not*ion*
ist = one who practices	hypnot*ist*, real*ist*, podiatr*ist*
ment = action, state, product	impedi*ment*, refresh*ment*, frag*ment*
or = who or that which does something	profess*or*, credit*or*, elevat*or*
ose = full of	joc*ose*, verb*ose*, bellic*ose*
osis = process, condition	halit*osis*, metamorph*osis*, tubercul*osis*
osity = noun form	gener*osity*, verb*osity*, lumin*osity*
sis = process, state	homeosta*sis*, the*sis*
tude = noun form	lati*tude*, alti*tude*, plati*tude*
ty = quality, state	uni*ty*, enmi*ty*, dispari*ty*
ure = action, instrument	press*ure*, legisla*ture*, liga*ture*
y = actions	inqui*ry*, carpentr*y*, infam*y*

Verbs

esce = verb ending *	conval*esce*, coal*esce*
(* can also be a noun)	
fy = to make	simpli*fy*, beauti*fy*, lique*fy*
ize = following a line of action	vapor*ize*, maxim*ize*, colon*ize*

We did not print these lengthy lists to bore you; we created them to help you spot similarities in vocabulary. Some words will remind you of others, even if we didn't define its word parts here (Yes, that's possible.). When you see an unfamiliar word, ask yourself if it reminds you of any others. These relationships will help you ace vocabulary you've never seen before, just as associations helped you with 'N Sync and the clock's pendulum.

Word Parts Drill

That's a lot of material on vocabulary, so let's put this knowledge to work. The drill that follows doesn't use the MCAS exam question format, but it will beef up your vocabulary.

Use the word part charts above to define each of the words below (Keep in mind: Some have prefixes. Some have suffixes. Some have both.).

First, divide each word into its parts. *Inadequate* might break up like this: in-ad-equ-ate. What does it mean? Look at the segments. The prefix *in* means not, so a first guess might be *not adequate*. Did you spy the word *equate* here? You might reason that *inadequate* refers to something that doesn't equate, or something that falls short.

Try these other words on your own. Check your answer choices against the Answer Key on page 34.

Word Parts	Definition
1. extrasensory	
2. intramolecular	
3. epidermis	
4. omnipotent	
5. superannuated	
6. misanthropic	
7. extracurricular	
8. verbose	

Answers

Word Parts	Definition
1. extra/sensor/y	going beyond what can usually be sensed, telepathic, clairvoyant
2. intra/molecul/ar	within molecules
3. epi/dermis	outer skin
4. omni/potent	all powerful
5. super/annuated	above old or very old, obsolete
6. mis/anthrop/ic	not liking people or contemptuous of mankind
7. extra/curricul/ar	outside of school

Did you look for *curricular* on our lists—and it wasn't there? Did you wonder how you're supposed to know this? Word parts are only one example of an association. Say you just saw the word *extracurricular* on the MCAS exam. What would you do? First look for familiar word parts: *extra,* a prefix, means *outside.* But maybe you hit a brick wall with *curricular.* What other words come to mind? Curriculum? Curriculum has something to do with classes and courses. You can guess that *extracurricular* means *outside of courses* or *outside of school.*

8. verb/ose	wordy, using too many words

Again, our lists didn't include v*erb.* But what does the word verb remind you of? Maybe *verb* and *verbal.* You're looking for an adjective (the *ose* suffix indicates an adjective) about words. *Verbose* means *very wordy.* Just so you know for future reference, this sentence is especially, incredibly, absurdly, pointlessly verbose.

Vocabulary Drill

Let's try a new drill, one that synthesizes work on word parts with your ability to find context clues. POE (process of elimination) and aggressive guessing will also help you with this drill.

As we mentioned earlier, words won't appear in isolation on the MCAS exam. Questions will come with a reading passage, and you'll have four choices to choose from. Let's get cracking on some drills that more closely resemble the material on your ELA Grade 10 MCAS exam.

We'll practice with some poems called limericks from Edward Lear's *The Book of Nonsense*. We'll do the first one together.

> There was an Old Person of Gretna
>
> Who rushed down the crater of Etna;
>
> When they said, "Is it hot?"
>
> He replied, "No it's not!"
>
> That mendacious Old Person of Gretna.

1. In line 5, what does the word *mendacious* mean?

    A. cautious

    B. rapidly

    C. beggar

    D. deceitful

What the heck does *mendacious* mean? Don't worry; take the question slowly.

Turn first to POE. By using the Process of Elimination, we can cross off the choices that just don't make sense. How do you start eliminating choices? Read this poem very carefully, and smell out any clues. Does *Etna* ring a bell? What about a *crater*? You probably know that craters are big holes and you may remember that Mt. Etna is a whopper volcano. In any case, craters are generally something careful people stay away from. Zap *A* because someone who'd rush into a crater wouldn't be "cautious."

Use your knowledge of word parts. *Mendacious* ends with a suffix, *ious*, and you know whatever this word means, it is adjective. Nix answer choices that aren't adjectives. Send *B* (*rapidly* is an adverb) and *C* (*beggar* is a noun) packing. Could someone be rapidly old or beggar old? These answer choices don't make sense.

POE leaves you with one answer choice. To be safe, test the remaining choice, *D*. Might you describe someone who denies that it's hot after leaping into a volcano—with all that hot lava—*deceitful*? Makes sense to us.

Maybe you knew that *mendacious* meant dishonest before you ever read the poem. In that case, eliminate the choices that don't match the definition, (*A*, *B*, and *C*), and select the one that does (*D*). Either way, you get the right answer choice.

See how context clues and word parts help you figure out word meanings? Here are a few more limericks by Edward Lear to practice with. The answers are on page 38.

There was an old person of Bangor

Whose face was distorted with anger;

He tore off his boots,

And subsisted on roots,

That borascible person of Bangor

2. In line 5, what does the made-up word, *borascible* probably mean?

   A. elderly

   B. cranky

   C. overweight

   D. patience

There was an Old Man of Cape Horn,

Who wished he had never been born;

So he sat on a chair,

Till he died of despair,

That dolorous man of Cape Horn.

3. In line 5, what does the word *dolorous* mean?

   A. relaxation

   B. joyous

   C. sad

   D. angry

There was a young lady of Turkey,

Who wept when the weather was murky;

When the day turned out fine,

She ceased to repine,

That capricious young lady of Turkey.

4. In line 4, what does the word *repine* mean?

   A. laugh

   B. grieve

   C. enjoy

   D. shiver

There was a young lady from Portugal,

Whose ideas were excessively nautical;

She climbed up a tree,

To examine the sea,

But declared she would never leave Portugal.

5. In line 2, what does the word *nautical* mean?

   A. having to do with the ocean

   B. the process of deciding

   C. adventure

   D. complex

Answers

2 B   Look closely (or have Clover look) at the text. The man had an *angry face* and *tore off his boots*; he's pretty grouchy. Use POE to eliminate *C*, because there's nothing in the poem about being heavy and *D*, because he seems the opposite of patience. (Or you might eliminate *D* because the suffix *-ible* indicates an adjective, not a noun.) The man is old, so *A* (elderly) seems possible, but "*iras*cible," meaning irritable, is a relative of the word *borascible* that means *cranky* (*B*).

3 C   Did you notice the phrases *wished he had never been born* and *died of despair*? This man is beyond sad. The *-ous* ending indicates you need an adjective, so that eliminates *A* (a noun). POE also gets rid of *B* (joyous does not describe this man) and *D* (there's no evidence that he's angry).

4 B   Since the young lady *wept when the weather was murky*, you can guess that *repine* means unhappy. Utilizing POE, scratch off positive answer choices like *laugh* and *enjoy*, *A* and *C*. What else can you get rid of? Try using *D*, "shiver," in the context of the poem. Sounds like gibberish, so kick out *D*. The last choice, grieve (*B*), makes more sense in the context of the poem. What word parts in *repine* might give you more clues? The prefix *re* means again. Have you heard the expression that someone pined away for love or lack thereof? Pine means pain; *repine* means *to fret or grieve*.

5 A   Since this lady climbed a tree to examine the sea, you can guess that *nautical* relates to the sea. (And, you may have heard of nautical history, the Nautilus submarine, and nautilus snails.) Use POE to get rid of *B* and *C* because you're looking for an adjective (the *-ical* in *nautical* tells you that). *D* doesn't make sense in the poem, so cross that off. Keep in mind, even if you have to guess, POE improves your odds, putting you in better position.

Derivation

A *derivation* means a word formed from another word. You already understand this principle because you know prefixes, suffixes, and roots. Remember the root for *touch*, *tac*, or *tang*. We gave the examples of *tactile, tango,* and *tangent*, and maybe you thought of *tangible* or *tactful*. Words belong to families, and these five words are relatives—they look similar, their definitions relate, and they derive from the base word, *touch*. (*Tactile* and *tangible* refer to something perceptible by touch; a *tangent* touches—lightly—on something else.) In other words, these five siblings—*tactile, tango, tangent, tangible,* and *tactful*—share an ancestor, an old Latin word, *tangere*, which means *to touch*. Linguists say these five words are derivations of a base word, *tangere*.

The MCAS exam may ask you about the relationships between words by testing you on derivations and base words. They'll ask you to demonstrate your knowledge of root words and derivations in one of two kinds of questions: *reading a dictionary entry* and matching a *base word with its derivation*.

Dictionary entry

Have you wondered how we know which words are related to each other? There's a simple way to discover the family any word belongs to, the dictionary. Give this a try: Go to a dictionary and look up the word for *enumerate*. You might see something like this:

enu•mer•ate \i-'n(y)u-me-ra-ter\ *vt* **-at•ed; -at•ing** [L *enumeratus*, pp. of *enumerare*, fr. *e-* + *numerare* to count]

I know you can't tell where this word comes from yet, but give us a second and all secrets will be revealed! The derivation of a word is always listed in brackets []. To save space, dictionary makers use abbreviations, indicating the various places from which the English language has pirated its base words.

The four most important abbreviations are:

G = German

Gk = Greek

L = Latin

ME = Middle English

So where did the word *enumeration* come from? Easy! It came from a Latin word, *enumerare,* which means *to count.* What does *enumerate* mean in English? Easy! It means to *count* or to *list.*

> The dictionary entry always gives a word's history backwards. In other words, the first abbreviation refers to its most recent usage and then traces the word to its origin.

Some words have more complicated derivations—maybe there are several base words from several cultures. For example, look at the word *nabob*'s derivation:

[Urdu *nawwab,* fr. Ar *nuwwab,* pl. of *na'ib* governor]

Urdu is the official language of Pakistan, but the good people living in Pakistan did not invent their word for governor, *nawwab,* rather they borrowed this base word from an ancient Arabic word. (Don't worry that you don't know what the abbreviations mean. At the beginning of every dictionary is a list of abbreviations.) In English a *nabob* refers to any person of *great wealth or prominence.*

Although there were no dictionary entry questions on the 1999 ELA Grade 10 MCAS, there was one on the 1998 exam. Just remember the four abbreviations above, which indicate the source for the overwhelming majority of English words, and use your common sense on any oddballs you might get.

Base word match

In addition to the dictionary entry question, you might get a question that asks you to relate a base word (probably a Latin root word) to its derivation. Frankly, these questions may be the more difficult multiple-choice questions that you'll have to answer. The good news is that the 1999 MCAS exam only had one derivation question; let's hope you get even fewer. But—just in case—we want you to be prepared if you get a question that looks like this:

1. Which underlined word in the following excerpts derives from the Latin word *abducere*, which means to lead away?

> "When alien rodents _abduct_ Santa Claus, in this movie, schnauzers come to the rescue."
>
> "These canines demonstrate their _ability_ to outwit extraterrestrials."
>
> "St. Nick tightens the belt around his _abdomen_ and watches the fur fly.
>
> "He is a well-known children's _advocate_ and staunchly defends their right to play."

A. abduct

B. ability

C. abdomen

D. advocate

Let's find the correct answer choice using POE, word parts, and common sense. First, find the words parts. You'll need to identify what you're comparing to the root word. You may get:

A. ab-duct

B. ab-il-ity

C. ab-domen

D. ad-vocate

Notice right away that *B* and *D* don't look anything like the root word. Since derivations and root words look similar, cross off *B* and *D*. Derivations match in meaning, too. You and Clover can examine the text, to define any words you're not familiar with and to deduce which answer choice is the best one. An abdomen is a part of the body, not something related to lead away. Cross off *C*. To *abduct* means *to take away by force.* The only answer choice that isn't crossed off your list is *A, abduct,* and its meaning matches the meaning of the root word.

Here's another question we can do together.

2. Which underlined word in the following excerpts derives from the Latin word *imbibere*, which means "to drink"?

> "No one wants to appear like an *imbecile* on a first date."
>
> " The waiter will undoubtedly remind you that diners under 21 are not permitted to *imbibe* yeast-based beverages."
>
> "Miss Mannerly's column offers some basic advice to keep teens from *embarrassing* their dates and themselves at dinner."
>
> "No matter how thick-skinned a companion may seem, nobody is entirely *immune* to criticism."

A. imbecile

B. imbibe

C. embarrass

D. immune

Use your knowledge about word parts, and toss out *C* and *D* because they don't match the Latin word. Besides, they have nothing to do with drinking. Even if you get stumped between *A* and *B*, you've increased your odds of correctly guessing. You may know that *A, imbecile,* means silly, which is unrelated to drinking. That leaves *imbibe* which happens to means *to drink* or *to absorb liquid!* Here are more practice questions. This time, try them by your-self and check your answers on pages 42 and 43.

Remember: A derivation not only looks like the original word. It shares a related meaning as well.

3. Which underlined word in the following excerpts derives from the Latin word *adversus*, or *hostile*?

> "The potato chip company is paying millions to *advertise* their new fat-free product."
>
> "A physician's *advice* to an obese patient might well include avoiding snack foods altogether."
>
> "The infomercial details one teen's battle of the bulge—how she faced *adversity* and conquered it."
>
> "'Love handles' are really just *adipose* tissue, more commonly known as 'flab.'"

   A. advertise

   B. advice

   C. adversity

   D. adipose

4. Which underlined word in the following excerpts derives from the Greek word, *eikon*, an image or figure?

> "Turn on your computer and click on the *icon* depicting a magnifying glass."
>
> "You'll want to design a Web page that projects the *image* you want."
>
> "Including *figures* and diagrams helps make the text more reader-friendly."
>
> " That site is recommended for anyone who wants to learn about *ikebanna*."

   A. icon

   B. image

   C. figure

   D. ikebanna

Answers

3 **C** Look at the word parts and eliminate *D* immediately. The other three still seem possible. Compare the meanings of the words to *adversus, hostility. A* means advertise, or to sell to someone. Cross it off. What about *B, advice*? A recommendation or advice has nothing to do with hostility. This leaves you with *C, adversity*, something acting against you, such as hostility.

4 A Contrast these word parts and scratch out *B* and *C*, which simply can't come from this root word because they don't look anything like it. You may recall that an icon on your computer is a little image that stands for something bigger. Can you guess this word probably comes from the Greek word for *figure*? Look closely at the context. Both these words have to do with *figures* and *images*. *A*, an *icon*, derives from *eikon*. Although these questions can be tough, POE can significantly improve your score.

Longer Passage

You might view the ELA Grade 10 MCAS exam as an open-book exam, with each reading passage being an "open book" you can consult. Sometimes the questions are simple and the answers are right there. In other cases, you'll need to read between the lines. Still, the text will provide clues; you and Clover just need to track them down.

The ELA Grade 10 MCAS exam will ask you to define words and derivations in poetry (like the limericks above) and in longer prose passages (writing that is not like poetry). Some exams have had passages over a whole page. But don't look at length as a bad thing. More text means more information to help you; these long passages are gifts.

Plan of Attack

Every time you come to a new passage on the MCAS, follow the seven steps listed below.

1. Give the passage a quick once-over. Glance at the whole passage for an idea of the subject. Notice anything that sticks out—like captions or big space breaks—to get a sense of what the parts are.

2. Read and translate the questions carefully. Read the questions so you know what information you'll need to look for in the passage. Put the question in your own words so you can understand what you're being asked. You probably do this all the time in real life; like when you hear, "Isn't it time we see other people?", your translation might be, "Shouldn't we call it quits?"

3. Read the passage, keeping the questions in mind. That way, answers will leap out at you. You might underline answers, so you can find them again later. You will also need to build answers to the harder questions.

4. Put your finger on the answer to the first question. If the question inquires about a detail in the passage, you need to find the reference in the text. Place your finger on it— Gotcha!

5. Answer the question in your own words. Before you look at the answer choices, come up with an answer of your own, if you can. If you can guess aggressively at this point, do it, but don't worry if you can't.

6. Use POE. Zap any answer choices that you're certain are wrong. Literally cross them out. Depending on how many you eliminate, you'll have only the correct answer choice left, or you'll be able to make a better guess.

7. Repeat Steps 4, 5, and 6 until all questions are answered. When you've completed all the questions that go with a particular passage, take a moment to celebrate. Then move on to the next passage and set of questions.

Let's try it out. Read the text and questions below, and then apply our seven steps to find the correct answer choice. (You might want to mark this page since you'll be returning to the passage several times throughout the chapter.)

Practice

The Winnepeg Wolf

from *Animal Heroes*

by Ernest Thompson Seton

1 It was during the great blizzard of 1882 that I first met the Winnipeg Wolf. I had left St. Paul in the middle of March to cross the prairies to Winnipeg, expecting to be there in twenty-four hours, but the Storm King had planned it otherwise and sent a heavy-laden eastern blast. The snow came down in a furious, steady torrent, hour after hour. Never before had I seen such a storm. All the world was lost in snow—snow, snow, snow—whirling, biting, stinging, drifting snow—and the puffing, monstrous engine was compelled to stop at the command of those tiny feathery crystals of spotless purity.

2 Many strong hands with shovels came to the delicately curled snowdrifts that barred our way, and in an hour the engine could pass—only to stick in another drift yet farther on. It was dreary work—day after day, night after night, sticking in the drifts, digging ourselves out, and still the snow went whirling and playing about us.

3 "Twenty-two hours to Emerson," said the official; but nearly two weeks of digging passed before we did reach Emerson, and the poplar country where the thickets stop all drifting of the snow. Thenceforth the train went swiftly, the poplar woods grew more thickly. We passed for miles through solid forests, then perhaps through an open space. As we neared St. Boniface, the eastern outskirt of Winnipeg, we dashed across a little glade fifty yards wide, and there in the middle was a group that stirred me to the very soul.

4 In plain view was a great rabble of dogs, large and small, black, white, and yellow, wriggling and heaving this way and that way in a rude ring; to one side was a little yellow dog stretched and quiet in the snow; on the outer part of the ring was a huge black dog bounding about and barking, but keeping ever behind the moving mob. And in the midst, the center and cause of it all, was a great, grim, wolf.

5 Wolf? He looked like a lion. There he stood, all alone—resolute—calm—with bristling mane, and legs braced firmly, glancing this way and that, to be ready for an attack in any direction. There was a curl on his lips—it looked like scorn, but I suppose it was really the fighting snarl of tooth display.

Led by a wolfish-looking dog that should have been ashamed, the pack dashed in, for the twentieth time no doubt. But the great gray form leaped here and there, and chop, chop, chop went those fearful jaws, no other sound from the lonely warrior; but a death yelp from more than one of his foes, as those that were able again sprang back, and left him statuesque as before, untamed, unmaimed, and contemptuous of them all.

6 How I wished for the train to stick in a snowdrift now, as so often before, for all my heart went out to that gray-wolf; I longed to go and help him. But the snow-deep glade flashed by, the poplar trunks shut out the view, and we went on to our journey's end.

7 This was all I saw, and it seemed little; but before many days had passed I knew surely that I had been favored with a view, in broad daylight, of a rare and wonderful creature, none less than the Winnipeg Wolf.

8 His was a strange history—a wolf that preferred the city to the country, that passed by the sheep to kill the dogs, and that always hunted alone. In telling the story of *le Garou*, as he was called by some, although I speak of these things as locally familiar, it is very sure that to many citizens of the town they were quite unknown. The smug shopkeeper on the main street had scarcely heard of him until the day after the final scene at the slaughter-house, when his great carcass was carried to Hine's taxidermist shop and there mounted, to be exhibited later at the Chicago World's Fair, and to be destroyed, alas, in the fire that reduced the Mulvey Grammar School to ashes in 1896.

1. In paragraph 5, what does the word *statuesque* mean?

    A. unreal and strange

    B. vicious and mean

    C. large and dignified

    D. stony and artificial

Let's try answering this question with our seven steps:

1. Give the passage a quick once-over.

This is a story about a wolf, followed by a vocabulary question: *statuesque*

2. Read and translate questions.

What does it mean to be *statuesque*?

3. Read the passage, keeping the questions in mind

As you read the passage from start to finish, look out for the word *statuesque*.

4. Put your finger on the answer to the first question.

Now go back to paragraph 5. A mental red flag should have gone up when you came across *statuesque*. Put your finger on it.

5. Answer the question in your own words.

What does *statuesque* mean here? Picture the scene. You have a big wolf standing proudly, surrounded by a ring of yapping dogs. Look at its word parts: statue-esque. Remember that *esque* means *in the style of.* Guess aggressively about what it means.

6. Use POE.

Maybe the choices were hard, and you couldn't guess aggressively. Try eliminating wrong answer choices. *A* and *D* don't make any sense in the context, because the wolf is realistic and vibrant (or full of life). Now your choices are between *B* and *C*. Check the text closely. The wolf appears regal and "contemptuous of them all." Choice *C*, *dignified*, makes a lot of sense here.

7. Repeat Steps 4, 5, and 6 until all questions are answered.

If this were an actual MCAS exam, the passage would be followed by three or four questions in all. So try two more questions on your own and check the answers on page 47.

2. Which word is closest to the meaning of *resolute* in paragraph 5?

   A. doubtful

   B. quiet

   C. determined

   D. fierce

3. Which word is derived from the Old English word for to attempt, *peiran*?

> "The snow came down in a *furious*, steady torrent…"
>
> "…but I suppose it was really the *fighting* snarl of tooth display."
>
> "But the great gray *form* leaped here and there, and chop, chop, chop went those *fearful* jaws…."

   A. furious

   B. fighting

   C. form

   D. fearful

4. In paragraph 5 what does the word *unmaimed* mean?

    A. against nature

    B. with ferocity

    C. badly hurt

    D. not injured

5. Which of the following words is derived from *rudus*, a Latin word that means rabble?

> "…to cross the *prairies* to Winnipeg…"
>
> "In plain view was a great *rabble* of dogs, large and small… wiggling and heaving this way and that way in a *rude* ring;"
>
> "…I knew I had been favored with a view, in broad daylight, of a *rare* and wonderful creature…"

    A. prairies

    B. rabble

    C. rude

    D. rare

Answers

2 **C** This question's tricky, because POE only quickly knocks out *A* (since this tough wolf is anything but *doubtful*). Think of words related to *resolute*. Resolve and resolution are related to making decisions, or maybe you notice the root word *solve* and think of solving problems. *B* and *D*, (*quiet* and *fierce*) are unrelated to decisions. So, you can guess that *resolute* means *C*, *determined* or *decisive*.

3 **D** By looking at the word parts, you must have crossed off *B* and *C*, as neither could be derived from the word *peiran*. Between *A* and *D*, you may be leaning toward *D*, which sounds a little more like the base word. Check the meanings of the words. Something *furious* is angry or livid, and has nothing to do with *attempting,* but something *fearful* seems as if it could relate to trying new endeavors. Put a line through *A* and choose *D*, the right answer choice.

4 **D** Did you take a good look at the passage around the word *unmaimed?* You should have uncovered some juicy hints in the context: *untamed, unmaimed, and contemptuous of them all*. All three reiterate the description of the wolf. Answer in your own words. The wolf is proud and unhurt. By POE you can knock out *A, B*, and *C*. You might have also

noticed the parts inside the word *unmaimed* include the prefix, *un,* which means not. *D* is the only choice that includes a not, *not injured.*

5   **C**   Did you guess aggressively on this one? Probably you picked C immediately because *rude* sounds like *rudus.* How did you check your answer? *Prairie* (*A*) or *rare* (*D*) have to be wrong because derivations look like their base words. *B* seems possible, but look closely at the context. *B* has something to do with animals. (A rabble is disorganized collection of people or animals.) If someone's *rude* they have *coarse elemental manners*, not unlike rabble.

Figurative Meanings

You've heard about the vocabulary on the ELA Grade 10 MCAS exam, and you know about using context, word parts, and derivations. So far, our examples (like your questions on limericks and *The Winnipeg Wolf*) covered literal meaning, or what the vocabulary really means. But there are instances when words don't mean what we think they do. *Huh?* Don't worry, this isn't as weird as you suspect.

> The words *like* or *as* should send up flags that you may be looking at a simile. "My love is like a red, red rose" utilizes a simile because the love and rose are being compared by using the word *like.*

If someone says, "Go fly a kite," they aren't telling you they think you should fly a kite. They mean, "Go away!" This expression uses *figurative meaning.*

We use these figures of speech all the time (See, there's one!) They're really a breeze to understand (There's another!) If I don't stop this, I'm going to eat my hat (Ha! There's a third.) Linguists call these expressions idioms, or phrases that are not meant to be taken verbatim or literally, but rather intended to be read figuratively.

Simile

Besides idioms, there are other examples of figurative speech. In particular, the MCAS exam focuses on two kinds of figurative speech. The first of these is the *simile.* In a simile, two unrelated things are compared to one another using the words *like* or *as.*

Metaphor

An author may compare two things without using the word *like* or *as* by using a *metaphor*. A metaphor is another type of figurative speech but the comparison does not use either *like* or *as*. Paul Simon's song, "I Am A Rock," does not refer to a person who turned into stone. It's an example of a metaphor, in which the singer compares himself to a cold, unfeeling object. Similarly, Emily Dickinson used a metaphor in her poem, "The Iron Horse," in which she likens a train to a ferrous horse, a horse made of iron.

On the MCAS exam, you need to be able to identify examples of figurative speech and to point out what's a simile and what's a metaphor. Because metaphors are often implied, they can be difficult to spot. But we'll give you a lot of practice finding metaphors and similes and you'll be a pro soon.

> The difference between a simile and a metaphor is important! The 1999 ELA exam asked six questions about identifying simile and metaphors in texts. That's a lot of points! Review this section if you get *any* of our practice questions wrong.

Practice

Remember *The Winnipeg Wolf* on page 44? You may be asked questions like the following on the MCAS exam. We'll do the first one together.

1. In paragraph 1, the "crystals of spotless purity" refer to

   A. train.

   B. snow.

   C. pristine nature.

   D. wolf.

1   B Go back to the first paragraph. The entire paragraph describes "the great blizzard," in which snow comes down all over. Snow makes logical sense here. To double-check, substitute each answer choice for "crystals of spotless purity," and see what's plausible. *A, C,* and *D* have to be eliminated; they make no sense. The only choice left is *B*.

Try another question on this passage and then two more questions on a new poem on your own. Review your answers on page 51.

> You can locate figurative speech by asking yourself if the author means what she or he wrote literally. If literal reading sounds silly or just impossible, you're looking at some kind of figurative speech—perhaps you're looking at a metaphor or a simile.
> Let's try finding figurative speech in a reading sample you're not yet familiar with.

2. When Ernest Seton says the wolf "looked like a lion," he is using which device?

   A. metaphor

   B. alliteration

   C. rhyme

   D. simile

The Sonnet (In Answer to a Question)

by Richard Watson Gilder

from *Lyrics and Other Poems*

WHAT is a sonnet? 'Tis the pearly shell

That mummers of the far-off murmuring sea;

A precious jewel carved most curiously;

It is a little picture painted well.

What is a sonnet? 'Tis the tear that fell

From a great poet's hidden ecstasy;

A two-edged sword, a star, a song—ah me!

Sometimes a heavy-tolling funeral bell.

This was the flame that shook with Dante's breath;

The solemn organ whereon Milton played,

And the clear glass where Shakespeare's shadow falls:

A sea this is—beware who ventureth!

For like a fjord the narrow floor is laid.

Deep as mid-ocean to the sheer mountain walls.

3. When Gilder answers his own question "What is a Sonnet?" with the words "A two-edged sword, a star, a song," what literary device does he use?

   A. pun

   B. paradox

   C. metaphor

   D. simile

4. Gilder calls a poem "the pearly shell/That mummers of the far-off murmuring sea." What word best describes the relationship Guilder is depicting?

   A. simile

   B. metaphor

   C. waves

   D. rhyme

Answers

2 **D** This is a classic simile because it uses the word *like*. But you can reason out this answer as well. You know you're reading an example of figurative speech because the author doesn't mean the wolf turned into a lion. He's comparing the wolf to the lion. Once you realize this, you need only identify the author as using a simile or a metaphor, so check whether he uses the words *like* or *as*. There's the word *like!* This must be a simile.

3 **C** Because a sonnet does not literally become a weapon or a celestial body, you're looking at figurative speech. To determine whether it's a simile or a metaphor, examine the text for the words *as* or *like*. Neither is used! Choose metaphor.

4 **B** Again, Gilder compares two things, a "pearly shell" and a form of poetry. A poem isn't actually a seashell, so we're reading figurative speech. Because the poet doesn't use the words *like* or *as*, he's creating a metaphor.

Grammar

So far we've reviewed vocabulary and figurative language, so now you know how to answer exam questions that ask about meanings, word definitions, and figurative understandings. In the second part of this chapter, we're moving on to a whole new kind of review—a recap of grammar!

You use grammar every day. Every time you talk with your friends or leave a note for your parents, you use the rules of grammar that you've heard since you first went to school. *Grammar* relates to how we assemble words to make sense. If you spew out random words—bubblegum telephone jumped crazy rope—no one will have any idea what you mean, even if you have the most advanced vocabulary on Earth. There are many grammar rules, but we've sorted out the valuable information to highlight rules that the MCAS exams have covered on the past. Review this section to refresh your memory about specific grammar rules, especially the material most important for doing well on the exam.

Parts of Speech

Grammar is about jargon, key terms that indicate specific *parts of speech*. It's like playing basketball. Your coach calls a "foul" and gives you a "free throw." You need to know what these terms mean in order to play. Similarly, the MCAS exam writers expect you to understand their terms when they ask you to identify gerunds and adverbs. Gerunds? What the heck are they? Read on…

Noun

A *noun* is a person, place, thing, or an idea. (I've bet you've heard this definition every year you've gone to school.)

A person: Nomar Garciaparra, Allison, wrestler, grandmother, president

A place: Springfield, Connecticut River, high school, street

A thing: popcorn, sweatshirt, credit card, college

An idea: love, excellence, optimism, Boyle's Law

Here are some rules about nouns.

Proper noun

Proper nouns are not especially uptight nouns. They're very specific nouns that indicate particular people or places or ideas like Nomar Garciaparra or the Connecticut River or Boyle's Law. Proper nouns take capitals. Other proper nouns are Massachusetts, Queen Elizabeth, Governor Paul Cellucci, and the Korean War.

Plural nouns

If there's more than one noun, the noun is called *plural*.

Most plural nouns end in *s*: *sodas, dates, stadiums, jokes, diets, podiatrists.*

Quizzes are on Fridays.

Videos are on sale.

Some plural nouns do not end in *s*: *men, women, children, geese, mice*

Flying sheep are easy to count.

Mice scare most people.

Some nouns end in *s* but are not plural: *mathematics, news, politics, statistics*

Mathematics is his worst subject.

A noun may describe more than one person or thing.

Statistics is interesting to her.

Collective Nouns

Some nouns look plural but aren't: *United States, family, committee*. These nouns are called collective nouns, and they indicate several individuals, but are singular—and take singular verbs— because they describe one single group.

The United States is a fairly young country.

My family is nutty enough to be on a sitcom.

Gerund

A noun that ends in *ing* may act as the subject of a sentence when it is called a *gerund*. What are the subjects of the two sentences, below?

Eating bamboo shoots is a panda's favorite activity.

Watching movies is fun.

Remember: Check to make sure your sentence has a subject by making sure it answers

the question, "What is/does..?" or "Who is/does...?"

What is a panda's favorite activity? *Eating*. What is fun? *Watching*.

Pronoun

A pronoun is a word that takes the place of a noun. It's a stand-in. We often use pronouns instead of repeating names and words over and over. Here are some examples: *I, you, it, we, they, who, what, anyone, something*.

Antecedent

The word a pronoun stands in for is called the *antecedent*.

Cathy gave away her dessert.

In this sentence, *her* stands in for *Cathy*'s. So the antecedent is *Cathy*.

If you replace a pronoun with an antecedent, the sentence should still mean the exact same thing. *When Laura and her sister Allison went to the store, they left their Dad home alone.* Try substituting *they* with its antecedent, Laura and Allison. Laura and Allison left their Dad home alone. Same as the first sentence? Yep, you've found the antecedent.

My next-door neighbor, *who* hoarded stuff for Y2K, felt pretty silly in the end.

Who replaces *my next-door neighbor*. The antecedent is *my next-door neighbor*.

I have e-mailed my cousin Alexandria, who lives in Danbury, to invite *her* to my graduation.

Who and *her* replace *my cousin Alexandria*. The antecedent is *my cousin Alexandria*.

Agreement

A pronoun must agree with its antecedent. In other words: Check whether or not a pronoun should be masculine or feminine, singular or plural, by looking back at the word it represents.

Ask yourself, "Is the pronoun masculine (or feminine)?" Check. "Is the pronoun singular (or plural)?" Check.

Jonathan put *his* backpack in the closet.

Masculine pronoun? Yes. Singular pronoun? Yes.

I called my sister, *Jennifer*, who has *her* license, to ask *her* for a ride home.

Is each pronoun feminine? Yes. Is each one singular? Yes.

Verb

Every sentence has a *verb*, which describes what the subject did or was.

Usually verbs express actions. Here are some examples: snore, waken, wash, brush, gobble, burp, invert, reproach.

Some verbs describe states of being. Here are some examples: am, seem, appear, become, remain.

Kareem aced his exams.

Rachel was late the morning after her pajama party.

What did Kareem do? He *aced* his exams. What did Rachel do? She *was* late.

Although there are many subjects about verbs that you may have covered in your classes about verbs, there are only two you'll need to focus on for this exam: tense and voice.

Tense

Tense here has nothing to do with what you're feeling right now (the stressed and uptight kind). Verb *tense* refers to when the verb's action takes place.

Today I snore.	Present Tense
Yesterday I snored.	Past Tense
I have always snored.	Present Perfect Tense
I will snore.	Future Tense
I will have snored.	Future Perfect Tense

> Finding a subject in a sentence is easy. First find the verb (action word) in the sentence. Then, ask yourself "Who or what (is doing the verb)?" The answer is the subject of the sentence.

Voice

In addition to when a verb occurred (its tense), it has a *voice* that the action happened in. Verb voice refers to whether you phrase things in a straightforward, "active" way or whether you put things in a more roundabout way by using a form of "to be."

Active: I *ate* the last ice cream bar.   I *know* the number of calories.

Passive: The last ice cream bar *was eaten* by me.   The number of calories *is known* to me.

Unless you have a good reason to use the passive voice, it's often best to use the simpler, more direct active voice.

Subject

Every sentence has a *subject*. The subject is who or what the sentence is mainly about. Subjects are always nouns or pronouns. See if you can spot the subjects in the two sentences below.

Sentence A: The wrestler won the match.

Sentence B: Her tattoo is unforgettable.

Look for the verb in Sentence A and you find *won*. Ask yourself, "Who won?" The wrestler won. The *wrestler* is the subject.

Look for the verb in Sentence B and you find *is*. Ask yourself, "What is?" Her tattoo is. Her *tattoo* is the subject.

If the subject is missing, you may have an incomplete sentence, also known as a *fragment*. A fragment cannot stand by itself as a sentence.

Ask yourself "Can I describe the noun more specifically?" If there is an adjective, you can answer this question. Can I describe more specifically movies that are hard to sit through? *Excruciating* movies.

Incorrect: Raising both arms in victory.

This sentence is wrong because there's no subject. Who was raising both arms? You can't tell from this group of five words. You could correct this fragment by adding a subject:

Correct: The wrestler was raising both arms in victory.

Adjective

Adjectives describe nouns. They often describe a person or thing's appearance, sound, taste, smell, or feel: *flashing* lights, *stentorian* music, *salty* peanuts, *noxious* odor, *sticky* floor.

Adjectives answer one of three questions:

- What kind?

- Which one?

- How many?

- I love pop music like Britney Spears.
  What kind of music?
  Pop music.
  Pop is an adjective modifying *music*, because it tells us what kind of music.

- I thought I'd pack the blue tie.
  Which one of your ties?
  The *blue* one.
  Blue is an adjective modifying *tie*, because it tells which one you're packing.

- Michael wants two Cokes.
  How many Cokes?
  Two Cokes.
  Two is an adjective modifying *Cokes*, because it tell us how many Cokes Michael wants.

Adverb

Adverbs usually describe verbs—but sometimes, they give more information about adjectives. They often describe to what extent the action takes place, usually by telling us how, when, or where: arrive *late,* dance *flamboyantly,* slip *abruptly,* laugh *loudly,* leave *early*

Be careful not to use an adjective when you need an adverb:

Wrong: *He laughed loud.*

Correct: *He laughed loudly.*

When an adjective needs more definition about how, when, or where, it is modified by an adverb.

> Sally wears *very* big earrings.

How big were Sally's earrings? *Very.*

> My dog wears a *flamboyantly* orange collar so he won't get lost in the dark.

What kind of orange collar does my dog wear? *Flamboyantly.*

Adverbs can even modify adverbs, by telling us more information about how something was done.

> Sam plays the right guard position *very* agressively.
>
> *How agressively* does Sam play? *Very.*

Practice

Remember, we're only reviewing the grammar concepts most likely to appear on the exam. Let's get a feel for how the MCAS exam will check these skills. *The Winnipeg Wolf* passage (on page 44) might be followed by questions like these, if it appeared on your MCAS exam.

1. In paragraph 5, the word "it" (used twice) refers to which antecedent?

    A. curl

    B. snow

    C. lips

    D. narrator

2. The last sentence of paragraph 3 ends: "…and there in the middle was a group that stirred me to the very soul." The word *very* here acts as a

    A. noun.

    B. address.

    C. adverb.

    D. adjective.

3. In the first sentence of paragraph 3, the word *poplar* serves as a(n)

   A. pronoun that replaces "Emerson".

   B. adverb that describes how the thickets drift.

   C. adjective that modifies the noun *country*.

   D. adjective that modifies the adverb *nearly*.

Answers

1 **A** Using POE, you'll know that *C, lips*, must be wrong. It's wrong because lips are plural (there's more than one) and antecedents always agree with their pronouns (*it* refers to something singular). Plug the remaining choices into the place of *it* to identify the right answer choice. *B, snow*, makes no sense. Cross it off. There's no reason to believe that *it* refers to the narrator. Eliminate *D*. So the answer is *A*, the *curl* of the lips. When you substitute this answer choice in the text, the sentence reads the same as it did before—the curl of the lips makes the wolf look proud and contemptuous.

2 **C** First, remember that *very* can't be a verb, noun (an address), or an adjective, so kick out *A, B*, and *C*. Wow! Jackpot. POE leaves you with one choice, *D*. But be careful and test this answer choice. What kind of soul? My *very* soul. Perfect!

3 **C** *Poplar* describes what kind of country we're looking at (one with lots of poplar trees), so it's an adjective (a word describing a noun).

   Only a couple of questions are likely to ask about grammar but you should remember these conventions when you write your Composition, so we'll give you more practice in chapter 6.

Summary

Congratulations! You are becoming an expert at vocabulary; figurative speech like similes and metaphors; and grammar—you're off to a great start on the MCAS exam.

In addition to learning more about these subject areas, you've expanded your inventory of tools to help you crack the multiple-choice questions on the MCAS ELA exam. (Although all this information will also come in handy when you write your open-response answers and your long compositions as well.) Anytime you see a multiple-choice question now you can immediately use:

- Process of elimination (POE)

- Aggressive guessing

- Context clues

- Word parts

- Seven-step process

- Grammar rules

Chapter 4

Reading Comprehension

In chapter 3, we gave you tools for cracking vocabulary questions using your knowledge of context, word parts, and derivations. We introduced the techniques to help you understand the words that might appear on the ELA Grade 10 MCAS exam. In this chapter, we'll use some of the same skills (and a few new ones) to help you with the bigger picture. Specifically, we'll focus on *reading comprehension* and how the MCAS exam will test you on understanding sentences, paragraphs, and passages as a whole.

So, let's get cracking!

Main Idea

The skeleton key of reading comprehension is the *main idea*, the reason or primary focus of the writing. If you can find the main idea in a given passage, you've taken the crucial first step toward solving the questions that follow the text. If you can figure out the main idea, you can answer virtually every other question about the text. Why? Because the main idea dictates the supporting details, the organization, the mood, and the tone of the text. Don't worry if you're not exactly clear on these terms yet; we'll go over each one carefully in this chapter.

How to Find the Main Idea

Finding the main idea in a passage should be as easy as spotting Homer Simpson in the airport—it should be attracting attention, making a ruckus, and acting as the focal point. The title of an excerpt and every paragraph in the passage will point to the main idea. So locating the main idea should be pretty easy, and you can use this two-step process to help you: First, ask yourself what you're reading about. Second, look for clues to the main idea in the text. Ask yourself what main point the author makes about the topic. Every paragraph should reinforce the main idea. If the main idea is that the New England Patriots are a better team than the Miami Dolphins, every single paragraph should specify ways that the Pats rule the Fins.

What main idea questions look like

You may luck out and get an exam question that comes right out and asks you: *What was the main idea?* But there are some other ways that the exam has of asking you to identify the main idea that never uses the words *main idea*. Let's look at a list of these, because if you see these questions, you should know you're looking for an answer choice that is the main idea of the passage.

What is the most important thing the author says about her or his subject?

Which paragraph states a major theme in the essay?

Which idea is most thoroughly developed?

Or: Which idea is most thoroughly illustrated?

Supporting Details

Remember our seven-step process? The first step is to give the reading a quick once-over. When you complete this step, you will be close to the main idea because you have a general idea what the text is about. To review the seven-step process, see page 43.

There are two kinds of sentences in most reading samples—*topic sentences* and *supporting sentences*. To develop a main idea, an author provides support or evidence that helps describe or persuade. Imagine that your best friend saw *Mission: Impossible II*, and you talked about it afterwards. If your friend liked the movie, he might tell you that he thought the movie was awesome and he'd probably enumerate some specific reasons. Maybe he thought Thandie Newton was pretty cute and maybe he thought that Tom Cruise's martial arts were cool. In other words, your friend's main idea— he liked the movie—gets some supporting details—Thandie Newton and Tom Cruise's athleticism.

Practice with the main idea

Look at the following passage and question:

Genetically Engineered Rice

Scientists in Switzerland have at least three good reasons to be happy about their recent success in creating a new form of gene-altered rice. The rice, which combats vitamin A deficiency, could help prevent the deficiency that is the world's leading cause of blindness. It could also prevent an infection that affects 250,000 children annually. Finally, the benefits of the new rice might make people less suspicious of bioengineering.

1. In this passage, what does the author say about gene-altered rice?

   A. The rice could help prevent an infection that strikes 250 children a year.

   B. The rice might make people more skeptical about bioengineered foods.

   C. The rice may reduce disease and improve attitudes toward bioengineering.

   D. The rice can cause blindness due to lack of Vitamin A.

Here's how to crack it:

Use the seven-step technique we showed you earlier. (You can check out the technique on page 43). Give the passage the once-over. Read the question and translate it into your own words. An accurate translation might be: *What is this paragraph about?* or *What is the main idea?* Read the passage, keeping the question—what is the main idea—in your mind. Maybe you thought to yourself, *all the sentences are about gene-altered rice.* Now that you know that the topic is gene-altered rice, you can figure out the main idea. Ask yourself: What is the most important thing the author says about this topic? What is the big point that every other idea in the passage helps explain?

You have a good idea of the answer before you even look at the choices. The most important part of this passage is the first sentence: *Scientists in Switzerland have at least three good reasons to be happy about their recent success in creating a new form of gene-altered rice.* That general statement about happy scientists is followed by specific details. In other words, the *topic sentence* is followed by three *supporting sentences*. These sentences detail the rice's three advantages. You could aggressively guess for the answer at this point. Choice *C* is the best response, because the main idea is that the new rice offers benefits to the world.

Or, you might use POE to eliminate the wrong choices. With main idea questions, incorrect answer choices often state the details in the passage incorrectly—or offer a main idea that just doesn't fit. Choices *A*, *B*, and *D* are false details—details that borrow words from the article, but are slightly incorrect.

> Hint: When you are trying to put your finger on the topic, look for a word or phrase that comes up repeatedly. In this example, the word *rice* comes up three times.

Let's try locating another main idea together. We'll read the following passage and answer a few questions on it together.

Edison, His Life and Inventions

by Frank Lewis Dyer

(Courtesy of Project Gutenberg)

The constructive tendencies of this child of whom his father said once that he had never had any boyhood days in the ordinary sense, were early noted in his fondness for building little plank roads out of the debris of the yards and mills. His extraordinarily retentive memory was shown in his easy acquisition of all the songs of the lumber gangs and canal men before he was five years old. One incident tells how he was found one day in the village square copying laboriously the signs of the stores. A highly characteristic event at the age of six is described by his sister. He had noted a goose sitting on her eggs and the result. One day soon after, he was missing. By-and-by, after an anxious search, his father found him sitting in a nest he had made in the barn, filled with goose-eggs and hens' eggs he had collected, trying to hatch them out.

Let's say this passage was followed on the ELA exam with the following question:

1. According to the author, as a child Edison

    A. loved to create original songs and signs.

    B. demonstrated precocious mental and manual abilities.

    C. made his father wish he would act like an ordinary boy.

    D. had several delusions about being a canal man, sign painter, and goose.

When you translate the question into your own words, you'll identify that this question wants you to locate the main idea of the text. Here's one way to crack it:

First, keep in mind who Edison is—that guy who invented the lightbulb and the telegraph. Look closely at the first sentence, where the main idea is often found, and what do you see? The inventor's father noticed his son's special abilities early on. What does every detail in the paragraph—about how little Tom made model roads and memorized songs and copied signs and tried an egg-hatching scheme—all show? They all provide specific details that Tom was a pretty smart, special little boy (who later became a brilliant inventor, of course). By guessing aggressively, you can go straight to the answer choice that best matches your prediction—*B*. Being *precocious* means showing early talent.

Did the word *precocious* throw you because you weren't sure what it meant? You can also arrive at the answer by POE. *A, C,* and *D* can't be right because while they contain bits and pieces of supporting details from the passage, these fragments are twisted into false statements. Tom didn't create original songs and signs—he memorized and copied them. Edison's apparently proud father says his son didn't have a typical childhood—but he doesn't seem to think that's a bad thing. Tom learned songs from canal men, painted signs, and even tried hatching eggs because he had a sharp mind and good imagination—not because he was crazy.

Purpose

You now should be clear on the distinction between main ideas and supporting details. The MCAS exam may ask you to identify both kinds of information, but it may also test you on whether you understand the author's *purpose* for creating the passage.

Every author has a reason for writing something. As you know, there are numerous reasons for this effort—such as getting rich and famous or passing a class in school. But there are only a few purposes that will be the right answers on the MCAS exam. So let's focus on reasons you're most likely to see on your exam:

Persuasive

You engage in *persuasion* when you try to convince your mom to give you money or your dad to lend you the car. Sometimes authors want things too! Maybe they want you to change your mind on a subject. Maybe they want you to give them money. Persuasive writing examples can take the forms of an editorial, a fundraising letter, or an essay such as Thomas Paine's *Common Sense* tract. If the writer is trying to convince you of anything, it's probably a persuasive passage.

Persuasion that is especially biased is called propaganda, because it doesn't give you all the facts—or sometimes any facts! Thomas Paine wasn't interested in providing American colonists with a balanced picture, just as maybe you don't give your parents all the facts when you want them to let you stay out late. The kind of propaganda that you see most often is in the form of advertising.

Humorous

Humorous writing intends to make you laugh, or at least smile. If you get a *humorous* passage, it may come from a humorist like Mark Twain, James Thurber, or Jonathan Swift.

Mark Twain and Jonathan Swift are famous for writing a specific form of humor called *satire*, which pokes fun at a person, group, or practice in order to point out how silly people are. For example, Jonathan Swift wrote several famous essays in which he lampooned British society, usually the middle class. James Thurber excelled at a particular form of satire known as *parody*—a humorous imitation of a serious piece of literature. If you've ever read the stories at www.theonion.com, you're already well acquainted with parody, because *The Onion* parodies news stories. If you've seen the movie *This Is Spinal Tap*, you know it parodies a heavy metal band.

Narrative

Any writing whose sole aim is to tell a story has a *narrative* purpose. Virtually all fiction is narrative such as J. K. Rowling's *Harry Potter* books and Jane Austen's *Pride and Prejudice*. Some nonfiction is also narrative, such as Sebastian Junger's book about Gloucester's swordfishing economy, *The Perfect Storm*. A lot of history is narrative as well, such as Frederick Downs's account of his Vietnam war tour, *The Killing Zone*.

Informative

If an author intends his writing to provide more information about a subject, he creates an *informative* piece. The function is to provide facts, often to a general audience, on a particular subject. Except for the editorial page of the newspaper (an example of persuasive writing), most news articles are informative. Self-help books, like *Chicken Soup for the Teenage Soul* and *Bobbi Brown Teenage Beauty,* are examples of books that give advice and information. Many articles in magazines are likewise about events, people, new inventions, and fashion—keeping you up-to-date and informed.

Technical

If an author intends their writing to give information only to a specialized group of people, its purpose is *technical*. Technical writing uses a specialized language for a specific field (such as a book about HTML for computer users or the instructions that accompany a video game) that provides insiders information in a clear way—but may not be understandable to the general public (such as computer-illiterate parents).

Organization

How is your CD collection organized? Did you organize by artist or by category? Much like your CDs, authors have a lot of information they need to share and to organize. Instead of a heap of CDs, authors have a main idea, supporting details, maybe a few jokes, and descriptions that they feel are important. You can only read one sentence at a time, however, so authors have to choose which information they want read first. So an author structures his or her ideas based on an organizational style, which we refer to as the book's *organization*.

While there are many ways to organize writing, we'll focus on the styles that you will probably be asked about on the exam.

Chronological

In a piece organized *chronologically*, the details are presented in the order they occurred. Not surprisingly, a lot of nonfiction uses this structure. For example, Susanna Kaysen's memoir, *Girl, Interrupted*, is a chronology, describing events in the order that they happened to her when she was a teenager. She goes to the Frick Museum, she is hospitalized at McLean Hospital, and she begins a long path toward recovery. Many narratives (whose purpose are to tell a story) are set up in a chronological style, because they follow a character such as Dolores Price in *She's Come Undone* or Holden Caulfield in *Catcher in the Rye*.

A lot of informational material is organized step-by-step. We call this particular sort of chronological arrangement *sequential* order. The directions for resetting your watch or getting to Six Flags are all organized sequentially. Information about past events is often put into another sort of chronological order called historical organization. You can predict that an article with a title like "Shoes Throughout the Ages" or "The Bubba Years: A Clinton Chronology" will be organized historically. Presenting information historically helps the reader understand the changes that occurred over time and the relationship between past and present.

Hierarchical

Let's say you want to write an essay about why you think cleaning your room is unnecessary. Organizing your essay chronologically is probably a poor idea because, truth be told, nobody cares if you cleaned your room five years ago. If you want an effective essay, you should opt to structure your thoughts based on specific reasons, such as it's a waste of time, it's a futile task, and you have the right to choose your own lifestyle. If you went ahead and composed this essay, you would probably present these specific reasons in rank of importance, so you would address the least important topic first and move toward your weightiest argument. Or, you might do the opposite and list your most compelling reason first and go on to the least important. In either case, you've used a *hierarchical* arrangement. Hierarchy is an effective way to organize persuasive writing, because you can present your case with increasingly powerful ammunition.

It may help you to jot down examples of the purpose and organization of writing that you're familiar with—even if it's your driver's ed booklet or the instructions to *Quake*. This writing still has a purpose and an organization. Write down anything that helps you. Do your *X-Men* comic books use a chronological narrative? Sure!

Comparison/Contrast

If writing compares and contrasts two different things, we say it's *comparative*. In this organization, two different items are juxtaposed to highlight their similarities and differences, such as the contrasts between quarterbacks Drew Bledsoe and Vinny Testaverde. While Drew Bledsoe is a younger quarterback—and bounces back from injuries a little faster than his Jets counterpart—he also has been criticized as not being enough of a leader. In contrast, Vinnie Testaverde, with nearly ten years on Bledsoe, missed nearly the entire 1999 season because of injuries, but he's a formidable leader of his offense. Comparisons often use the words *similar, different, like*, and *unlike*. So, for example, if you wrote a paper comparing the *Simpsons*' daughter, Lisa, and *Family Guy's* daughter, Meg, you might point out how different their attitudes are toward school—because Lisa loves school and Meg dropped out of high school.

Geographical

Tip: The main idea often relates to the reasons the author wrote the passage (its purpose) and to the work's organization. For example, if the author tried to persuade you, chances are the purpose is persuasive and the organization is hierarchical. A narrative novel (its purpose is to tell a story) lends itself easily to a chronological organization.

If a piece of writing presents information in the order of physical appearance or physical space, we say it's *geographical* or *spatial* in organization. Geographical organization—found commonly in both nonfiction and fiction—usually describes the layout of natural surroundings. Go to your local bookstore and you'll find geographical organization in any travel guide. It's a good bet that a book called *The Beachcomber's Guide to Cape Cod* or *Exploring the Berkshires* will contain some nice descriptions or places organized geographically. Stories in which the terrain or setting are very important may also use this style of organization, such as novels like *Around the World with Phineas Fogg* or *20,000 Leagues Under the Sea*.

Tone and Mood

Main ideas, supporting details, purpose, and structure usually relate to the facts, opinions, and information in the passage—but authors need more than a big pile of well-organized facts! Well, it's really *readers* who need more than a heap of orderly supporting materials—we want flavor, élan, attitude. You can call it whatever you want, we want to be kept awake. Where will this spice come from? Almost always, style comes from emotional devices such as tone and mood, which are tricks that authors employ to make their essays more colorful and less dull or drab.

Tone

How many times have you heard your parents say, "I don't like your tone of voice!" Have you ever realized that something was wrong—based on tone of voice? When your girlfriend says "everything's fine," you might not believe her if she emphasized the word *fine* in a certain way. In fact, you may suspect the exact opposite is true. The *tone* of voice can be more important than the words—because the tone indicates the attitude behind the words. Just as spoken words have a tone of voice, written words likewise have an underlying tone, or attitude, and you may be asked to demonstrate that you can identify what tone is being used in a passage on the MCAS exam.

You judge a writer's tone or mood the same way you judge anyone else's—what they say and how they say it. When we read a piece to ourselves, what "tone of voice" do we hear inside our heads or attribute to the speaker? Is the narrator judging his or her subject? What attitude or opinion might we say the author has toward the events and subjects?

For example, here's an excerpt from a story: "In an address before an emergency session of Parliament Monday, George Clinton said he is prepared to drop Da Bomb on Iraq if Saddam Hussein does not loosen up and comply with U.N. weapons inspectors… Preparations for the military strike, dubbed Operation Supergroovalisticprosifunkstication Storm, are already underway." Do you think the attitude is serious here? Ugh, probably not. This is a pretty funny *Onion* report, whose straightforward words contrast with a playful tone of voice. As we said, tone can give writing more zip and sparkle.

Here are some other words commonly used to describe tone:

> Objective or impartial: this tone is often associated with journalism, such as a news report about a scientific breakthrough.

> Amused or humorous: this tone is usually used by writers trying to make you laugh or smile at something silly.

> Nostalgic or sweet: this tone is a way of making readers think about the past fondly, such as an essay on the way things used to be.

Mood

In contrast to the tone of the words, *mood* is the state of mind the author wants us, the readers, to experience. Have you ever thought that a friend was being moody? This is the same general idea—different books have different emotional states. Some books, like Ann Rice's *Interview With a Vampire*, we would describe as downright moody. The mood or the atmosphere the author creates is based on the author's tone, word choice, and organization. It is often connected both to how the characters are feeling and how readers feel as they read about the characters and places in a story.

In plays, fiction, and poetry, mood can create a frame of mind. For example, in *Harry Potter and the Chamber of Secrets*, R.K. Rowling uses mood to make us experience the dread that Harry suffers when he's ordered to see the caretaker of his magic school:

> "Harry had never been inside Filch's office before; it was a place most students avoided. The room was dingy and windowless, lit by a single oil lamp dangling from the low ceiling. A faint smell of fried fish lingered about the place. Wooden filing cabinets stood around the walls; from their labels, Harry could see that they contained details of every pupil Filch had ever punished."

Everything about this "dingy," "windowless," and fish-reeking office tells us that the Harry is in a low mood, one that may well be lowered further by Mr. Filch's vile punishments. By setting a mood, we feel more of Harry's experiences than if Rowling just said that Mr. Filch punished Harry for tracking mud into the castle. As we said, mood creates a more vivid, less flat story.

Mood is sometimes described by weather words. Just as the weather describes the atmosphere outside, these same words can describe the mood within a piece of writing. Here are some typical mood descriptions:

> An ominous mood indicates pending disaster, such as the mood of a suspense novel.

> A foreboding mood may make you feel intimidated, such as the mood Dickens uses when Pip meets Miss Haversham or when Oliver Twist asks for more porridge.

> A sunny mood might indicate that things are going well, such as when Anne of Green Gables wakes up and sees a cherry tree in full bloom right outside her bedroom window.

Practice with tone and mood

Identifying mood and tone can be pretty important (Maybe you shrug your shoulders at your girlfriend's "everything's fine" and hang up the phone—*big* mistake!). What if you read the story "Clinton Threatens to Drop Da Bomb on Iraq" and you misread the tone? You might tell someone that George Clinton was thinking about bombing Iraq as if it were a fact. People might be confused (did you mean to say Bill instead of George?) or think you're nuts (George Clinton isn't doing anything 'cept jivin' tonight).

Let's give you some practice reading in order to better identify moods and tones. Return to the paragraph on bioengineered rice on page 63, and let's answer a question about this passage together.

1. The tone used in the passage about the bioengineered rice is best described as

    A. effusive.

    B. objective.

    C. cynical.

    D. angry.

> Tip: Most science writing and journalism is objective in tone. Try answering a few questions on your own. You can check your answers immediately afterward so you know if you've got the hang of mood and tone.

You skimmed the title and the passage, and you got the main idea fixed in your mind. This is a paragraph about rice. You've read the question carefully and translated it into your own words—*how would I describe this paragraph?* You've read the text very carefully and started to think about its tone. Even if you couldn't put your finger on one specific word, some words may have caught your attention. The author is giving "three good reasons" and then describing benefits using words like "deficiency" and "prevent." It's pretty dispassionate writing. Did you aggressively guess at this point?

If you're not completely sure how to describe this text, you can always turn to POE. Would you describe this writing as *cynical* (*C*), or *angry* (*D*)? Definitely not! If you know that *effusive* (*A*), means excessive, you could cross that off as well.

The Pit and the Pendulum

by Edgar Allen Poe

What boots it to tell of the long, long hours of horror more than mortal, during which I counted the rushing vibrations of the steel! Inch by inch—line by line—with a descent only appreciable at intervals that seemed ages—down and still down it came! Days passed—it might have been that many days passed—ere it swept so closely over me as to fan me with its acrid breath. The odor of the sharp steel forced itself into my nostrils. I prayed—I wearied heaven with my prayer for its more speedy descent. I grew frantically mad, and struggled to force myself upward against the sweep of the fearful scimitar. And then I fell suddenly calm, and lay smiling at the glittering death, as a child at some rare bauble.

1. The mood throughout most of the passage is best described as

    A. light.

    B. nostalgic.

    C. threatening.

    D. somber.

2. What is the narrator's tone at the end of this passage?

A. optimistic

B. euphoric

C. critical

D. detached

Answers

1 **C** There's a *scimitar* swinging closer and closer to this poor helpless guy. (Did you use the context to help you define the word *scimitar?* It's something steel, sharp, and will bring with it "glittering death." Okay, it's a weapon of some kind and it's pretty scary.) All the nice words (*light* and *nostalgic*) should be off the list. *Somber* is too mild a word for this scenario, so reject *D*. The description of the setting—with phrases like "hours of horror" and "fearful scimitar"—creates a very threatening mood.

2 **D** At the end, the narrator is telling us how he changed from a raving, terrified lunatic into someone calmly smiling at the blade that's going to kill him. He must be in shock or resigned to the helplessness of his situation. His tone here is certainly not *optimistic* or *euphoric*. It's not very *critical* either. The narrator sounds removed from the situation at the end—as if it is someone else he is describing. He's detached, *D*.

Standard (and Nonstandard) English

Why did William Shakespeare and Chaucer get to break grammar rules? The short answer is that they didn't have to take the MCAS exam. (They probably would have flunked it.) Maybe you're bummed that they got off the hook, but then again, you don't have to crank out 37 plays like Shakespeare did.

In chapter 3, we detailed the grammar and conventions that characterize *standard English*, or proper correct English. But maybe you've read Shakespeare or Chaucer or even Elmore Leonard, and you know that authors don't always follow these rules. Rather, it seems as if they are following some different set of rules. They are, but they're following rules set by other styles of English.

The MCAS exam will excerpt passages by different authors and ask you to identify what style these authors use. So, here's the skinny on identifying the most important categories of nonstandard English, those most likely to appear on your exam.

Standard English

Standard English is proper English—the grammatically correct language you use in formal situations. (Your English teachers may say in *all* situations.) Whenever you ask your boss for a raise, give a presentation, write a letter to your senator, or craft an essay for the MCAS examiners, you need to use standard, formal English. Almost all nonfiction you read—*The Boston Globe,* the new biography of Catherine the Great, and Tracy Kidder's book about Northampton, *Home Town,* utilize this English.

Example: He won.

Whether you put sprinkles—or jimmies—on your ice cream is a matter of regional dialect.

Archaic English

Archaic refers to something out of date. *Archiac English*, not surprisingly, describes English that uses out of date words. These phrases weren't out of style when the author first used them—at the time, the expressions were common. It's just that centuries have gone by since they wrote their books. Ever read the first line of Chaucer's *Canterbury Tales,* "When the Apryle raines do soote"? The crazy spelling of the month April and Chaucer's use of a word that we no longer use, "soote," indicate that Chaucer's English is archaic. Maybe you've read *Beowulf,* which is another example of archaic English. If an author employs archaic English now, it suggests an earlier time.

Example: He doth won.

Dialects

People in different parts of the country speak different *dialects*. Someone from New Orleans sounds different from someone from New England. A man in Wales sounds funny to a man raised in London. In other words, dialects are regional. The way people pronounce particular words—and the words they use to refer to the same item—may differ. One eats a to-MAY-to, another eats a to-MAH-to. One drinks a soda, another has a pop. Recreating oral dialect—if done well—lends realism to the conversations in stories. Maybe Huck Finn or Rip Van Winkle come to your mind as examples of protagonists who speak in dialect.

Example: He won, matey.

Practice

Let's see if you can use these terms on an exam question. Read the following passage and answer the questions, using our seven steps.

Authors like Mark Twain, Zora Neale Hurston, and Charles Dickens have their characters speak in natural dialects to make them seem more authentic.

Fantastic Fables

by Ambrose Bierce

(Courtesy of Project Gutenburg)

An old politician and a young politician were traveling through a beautiful country, by the dusty highway which leads to the City of Prosperous Obscurity. Lured by the flowers and the shade and charmed by the songs of birds which invited to woodland paths and green fields, his imagination fired by glimpses of golden domes and glittering palaces in the distance on either hand, the young Politician said, 'Let us, I beseech thee, turn aside from this comfortless road leading, thou knowest whither, but not I. Let us turn our backs upon duty and abandone ourselves to the delights and advan- tages which beckon from every grove and call to us from every shining hill. Let us, if so thou wilt, follow this beautiful path, which, as thou seest, hath a guide-board saying, "Turn in here all ye who seek the Palace of Political Distinction."

It is a beautiful path, my son,' said the Old Politi- cian, without either slackening his pace or turning his head, 'and it leadeth among pleasant scenes. But the search for the Palace of Political Distinc- tion is beset with one might peril." What is that? said the Young Politican. "The peril of finding it," the Old Politician replied, pushing on.

1. The politicians in the story use words like "beseech" and "thou knowest whither" that lend a timeless, almost biblical quality to this story. These words might best be described as

   A. archaic.

   B. slang.

   C. dialect.

   D. nonstandard English.

Did you notice in your once-over that this was a passage about a couple of politicians? Maybe you put the question in your own words and thought, *What would I call words like "beseech" and "thou knowest whither"?* As you read the story, you kept in mind that you'll be asked about the style of language. The passage doesn't say exactly what sort of language this is—but you put your finger on the particular phrases (*beseech* and *thou knowest whither*) that give the answer away. These words sound old-fashioned. Did you aggressively guess that archaic means old-fashioned (answer choice *A*)?

If not, POE can still help you get this question right. Slang is *phat, hip,* and *cool, beseech* is not—so cross off *B*. Dialect is the way that people from a certain region talk—*beseech* isn't regional. Eliminate *C*. Nonstandard English includes the sorts of grammar mistakes that generate red ink on your English compositions, such as using sentence fragments. *Beseech* sounds almost formal, hardly the type of thing that a teacher might mark wrong. Get rid of *D*. You're left with *A*, archaic.

Try a few more questions, and check your answers on the following page when you're finished.

2. In *The Winnipeg Wolf,* a dog team returns to town without its drunken driver, Paul. Renaud, a French-Canadian trapper, investigates the trail and makes this comment:

> "Paul he drop somesin' here, ze packet maybe; ze Voolf he come for smell. He follow so—now he know zat eez ze drunken Paul vot slash heem on ze head."

These lines are best described as an example of

A. standard English.

B. informal English.

C. slang.

D. dialect.

3. The author uses the language in the passage above mainly in order to

A. heighten tension by creating suspense.

B. convey authenticity.

C. emphasize that Paul slurs his words drunkenly.

D. create a sense of foreboding.

Answers

2 **D** The author recreates the way a French Canadian—and others from his part of the country—speak English. In other words, it's specific to a region and it's a dialect.

3 **B** Here—and almost any time an author employs dialect—the writer wants to make the dialogue sound genuine.

Reading Comprehension Practice

On the ELA Grade 10 MCAS exam, you'll probably end up reading a total of eight passages that reflect a range of all the above terms. Each of these selections might have four to eight multiple-choice questions afterwards, testing whether you understand the main ideas, supporting details, purpose, structure, tone, mood, and style of English in the passage.

Try your hand at the following passages. Answer the questions that follow, based on these reading samples. When you're done, check your answer choices against the correct answers that follow.

The Hare and the Tortoise

By Ambrose Bierce

A Hare having ridiculed the slow movements of a Tortoise was challenged by the latter to run a race, a Fox to go to the goal and be the judge. They got off well together, the Hare at the top of her speed, the Tortoise, who had no other intention than making his antagonist exert herself, going very leisurely. After sauntering along for some time he discovered the Hare by the wayside, apparently asleep, and seeing a chance to win pushed on as fast as he could, arriving at the goal hours afterward, suffering from extreme fatigue and claiming the victory." Not so," said the Fox; "the Hare was here long ago, and went back to cheer you on your way."

1. This story is an example of a

    A. folktale.

    B. parody.

    C. survival tale.

    D. fantasy.

2. Bierce would probably say that

    A. in the end most meanies get what they deserve.

    B. those who plan their revenge carefully will be rewarded.

    C. perseverance is rewarded, and you should turn the other cheek.

    D. bullies often win, and seeking revenge against them often isn't worth it.

3. The information in this story is presented

    A. in order of importance.

    B. to persuade.

    C. in chronological order.

    D. geographically.

4. Ambrose Bierce wrote this story in order to

    A. demonstrate his knowledge.

    B. describe the reason the hare returned.

    C. inform us of the race's result.

    D. use humor.

Here's another reading passage with some questions:

How Laws are Made

(Courtesy of the Government Printing Office)

1 Laws may be initiated by either member of Congress, the House of Representatives, or the Senate. For this example, we will track a bill introduced in the House of Representatives: the International Dolphin Conservation Act.

2 When a Representative has an idea for a new law, s(he) becomes the sponsor of that bill and introduces it by giving it to the clerk of the House or by placing it in a box, called the hopper. The clerk assigns a legislative number to the bill, with H.R. for bills introduced in the House of Representatives and S. for bills introduced in the Senate. The Government Printing Office (GPO) then prints the bill and distributes copies to each representative.

3 Next, the bill is assigned to a committee (the House has 22 standing committees, each with jurisdiction over bills in certain areas) by the Speaker of the House so that it can be studied.

4 The standing committee (or often a subcommittee) studies the bill and hears testimony from experts and people interested in the bill. The committee may then release the bill with a recommendation to pass it, or revise the bill and release it, or lay it aside so that the House cannot vote on it. Releasing the bill is called reporting it out, while laying it aside is called tabling.

5 If the bill is released, it then goes on a calendar (a list of bills awaiting action). Here the House Rules Committee may call for the bill to be voted on quickly, limit the debate, or limit or prohibit amendments. Undisputed bills may be passed by unanimous consent, or by a two-thirds vote if members agree to suspend the rules.

6 The bill now goes to the floor of the House for consideration and begins with a complete reading of the bill (sometimes this is the only complete reading). A third reading (title only) occurs after any amendments have been added. If the bill passes by simple majority (281 of 435), the bill moves to the Senate.

7 In order to be introduced in the Senate, a senator must be recognized by the presiding officer and announce the introduction of the bill. Sometimes, when a bill has passed in one house, it becomes known as an act; however, this term usually means a bill has been passed by both houses and becomes law.

8 Just as in the House, the bill then is assigned to a committee. It is assigned to one of the Senate's 16 standing committees by the presiding officer. The Senate committee studies and either releases or tables the bill just like the House standing committee.

9 Once released, the bill goes to the Senate floor for consideration. Bills are voted on in the Senate based on the order they come from the committee; however, an urgent bill may be pushed ahead by leaders of the majority party. When the Senate considers the bill, they can vote on it indefinitely. When there is no more debate, the bill is voted on. A simple majority (51 of 100) passes the bill.

10 The bill now moves onto a conference committee, which is made up of members from each House. The committee works out any differences between the House and Senate versions of the bill. The revised bill is sent back to both houses for their final approval. Once approved, the bill is printed by the U.S. Government Printing Office in a process called enrolling. The clerk from the introducing house certifies the final version.

11 The enrolled bill is now signed by the Speaker of the House and then the vice president. Finally, it is sent for presidential consideration. The president has ten days to sign or veto the enrolled bill. If the president vetoes the bill, it can still become a law if two-thirds of the Senate and two-thirds of the House then vote in favor of the bill.

5. In paragraph 4, what does the word *tabling* mean?

    A. Releasing a bill so that it can be voted on.

    B. Voting for a bill so that it becomes an act.

    C. Putting a bill aside so that it cannot be voted on.

    D. Putting a bill aside so that it can be voted on.

6. The organization of information in this article is best described as

    A. hierarchical.

    B. sequential.

    C. historical.

    D. geographical.

7. When is a bill that was introduced in the House given a complete reading?

    A. As soon as the Representative who sponsored it introduces it to the clerk.

    B. As soon as it has been assigned a legislative number.

    C. After it has been released by the standing committee and gone to the House floor.

    D. After it passes the House by a simple majority.

8. Which of the following might the House Rules Committee do?

    A. It decides that the bill will be voted on right away.

    B. It hears testimony from experts.

    C. It vetoes the bill.

    D. It tables the bill.

9. In paragraph 10, what does the word *enrolling* mean?

    A. Working out differences between two versions of a bill.

    B. Sending a revised bill back to the House and Senate.

    C. Having both houses approve a revised bill.

    D. The printing of a bill approved by the House and Senate.

10. How long does the president have after he receives a bill before he has to sign or veto it?

    A. as long as the House Rules Committee gives the president

    B. as long as the president decides to take

    C. twenty-four hours

    D. ten days

11. The main purpose of this article is to

    A. explain how a bill becomes law.

    B. show that the Senate is more influential than the House in making laws.

    C. explain the President's role in how laws are made.

    D. show how a bill can get "hung up" in many places along the way.

12. This article can best be described as

    A. descriptive writing.

    B. informational writing.

    C. persuasive writing.

    D. essay writing.

Answers

The Hare and the Tortoise

1   **B**   Bierce's story fits the definition of parody. It imitates a well-known story (by Aesop), called *The Tortoise and the Hare*, and gives a humorous twist to the original. Did you notice that he reversed Aesop's title, just as he reverses a few other things later on in the story? Use POE to cross off anything incorrect like *A* (this is not a folktale, because Ambrose's story is a modern one) and *C* (this can't be a survival story, because no one is placed in a life-threatening situation). *D* is a weak choice because there is no magic mentioned in the story.

2   **D**   Ask yourself, "What is the lesson that the Tortoise learns?" That lesson is the theme of the story.

Cross off *A*. Meanies get their just desserts? No! The Hare made fun of the Tortoise—but the bully never got the punishment she deserved, did she? Instead, the Hare won the race, had a nice nap, and got to see the Tortoise tire himself out for nothing.

Eliminate *B*. Those who plan revenge carefully are rewarded? No, the Tortoise had big plans for getting the Hare to exert herself—but they fell through.

Get rid of *C*. Is perseverance rewarded? No, the Tortoise plugged away and still lost the race and his chance to get back at his foe failed, too. Turn the other cheek? Maybe the Tortoise would have been better off if he had ignored the taunting, but the first part of this choice is still weak and the answer choice is wrong.

What about *D*? Does the bully win? Yes. Does the Tortoise find that it isn't worth it to try to get back at her? Yes. This choice is the strongest, on all counts.

3   **C**   Did you aggressively guess that Bierce structured his story in chronological order? You can also eliminate the wrong answer choices: Bierce doesn't give the information by order of importance, in order to persuade, nor does he use a geographical structure.

4   **D**   Paraphrase the question: choose Bierce's purpose for writing the story. Put the answer in your own words—he's being funny. You'd probably choose *humorous*, *D*. Or, use POE. Because the story's purpose is not informative, you know you can cross off *A*, *B*, and *C*.

How Laws Are Made

5   **C**   Skim the article until you find *tabling*. Read the sentences around it— "Releasing the bill is called reporting it out, while laying it aside is called tabling." Your paraphrase of this definition might be: it's being *laid aside*, it's being put off or set to the side. Use this paraphrase as an aggressive guess and search for it among the choices. Right there, *C*.

Or, employ POE. Eliminate *A* and *B* because they're nothing like your guess. Look at the text closely. *D* is wrong, a tabled bill *cannot be* voted on. Cross off *D* and choose *C*.

6   **B**   Zap the wrong choices—there's nothing hierarchical, historical, or geographical about the way the details are organized (see page 68 for definitions). The answer is sequential because the information is presented in the order that things occur.

7   **C**   When you skim the passage for key words in the question (*House, complete reading*), you find the information you need in paragraph six. POE can get rid of other choices. A quick review tells you that the actions described in *A* and *B* come before the complete reading of a bill—and *D* comes afterward.

8   **A**   When you skim the passage for the key words (*House Rules Committee*), you find your answer in paragraph five: "the House Rules Committee may call for the bill to be voted on quickly." Put your finger on the right answer. Use POE to send *B*, *C*, and *D* packing because these describe what other committees do.

9   **D**   When you sniff around the word in the passage, you find that you're given a definition, directly, as a context clue *the bill is printed… in a process called enrolling*. Get rid of *A*, *B*, and *C* by POE since they're not even close to this definition.

10 **D** Skim for the words *president*, *sign*, and *veto*. Paragraph eleven states that *The president has ten days to sign or veto*. Don't be fooled by the other choices just because they sound good based on something you've heard elsewhere. Always look for the facts *in the passage* first.

11 **A** Ask yourself why the author wrote this article. The title is a good clue: *How Laws are Made*. Use POE to dump all the other choices. The passage contradicts *B*, since both the Senate and the House are involved in introducing and voting on bills. *C* describes a detail—but certainly not the main purpose of the whole article (The role of a lot of other people beside the President gets mentioned.) Can *D* for the same reason. The passage describes how a bill can get hung up—but A is a stronger answer because *every sentence in the article* supports the explanation of how a bill becomes law.

12 **B** The purpose of the article is to impart information about how laws are made. It is not primarily to vividly illustrate (*descriptive—A*), argue (*persuasive—C*), or analyze a subject (*essay writing—D*).

Summary

In this chapter, we've given you tools for describing what you've read, so let's update your toolbox for the MCAS exam. You should now be able to approach multiple-choice questions with combinations of the following:

- POE to get rid of misleading and wrong answer choices

- Aggressive Guessing to get you to the right answer choice quickly

- Word parts to define words

- Derivations to identify how words are related

- Context clues to locate main ideas and supporting details

- Seven-step process for tackling multiple-choice questions

- Purpose and structure to comprehend what you're reading

- Mood and tone to identify the character of a text

- Standard and nonstandard English styles

Chapter 5

The Literature Part of the English Language and Literature Exam

When you open your ELA Grade 10 MCAS exam, you'll see a real hodgepodge of reading selections. The exam is a grab bag of literature goodies, in the same way that you don't know what specific loot you'll lug home on Halloween night. If we knew the specific excerpts on your exam, we'd just cover those materials. But since the MCAS exam people are very hush-hush, this chapter will help you cover your bases with *any* passage that might appear on your MCAS exam.

By the time you're finished with this chapter, you'll understand the basics of nonfiction, fiction, poetry, and drama. You'll be in a powerful position to tackle any goody that appears in your exam grab bag. We'll turn those tricks into treats.

Genre

In the previous chapter we mentioned that you will receive about eight literature passages on your ELA Grade 10 MCAS exam. The MCAS exam writers want a balance of different types of reading—just like you might come home on Halloween night with all different sorts of things; candy corn, Snickers bars, Hershey Minis, and Mounds. In short, you'll be looking at a selection of different genres. *Genres* are simply different kinds of texts, such as nonfiction and fiction.

Nonfiction

If you were to note all the reading you've done this year, you might end up with a list that looks something like this: cereal boxes, history textbooks, science articles, newspaper stories, instructions to *Quake II*, announcements, journal articles, and a few novels for English class. Except for the last item, this list elucidates (makes clear) the genre we call *nonfiction*, or writing that is based on the truth. Pretty big category, huh? Nonfiction includes biographies, autobiographies, manuals, essays, articles, science writings, self-help books, and historical accounts.

Literary criticism

Nonfiction also encompasses a specialized kind of writing about literature and fiction, called *literary criticism.* In books and essays on literary criticism, authors analyze and evaluate individual works and usually develop an argument about the worthiness or an interpretation of a novel or poem. (Literary criticism is often *persuasive* writing, because the author's main idea is an argument.) As you already know, there is no shortage of opinions in the world. Think of how different your opinion is from your English teacher's. Likewise, critics differ considerably in their opinions, and they have different criteria for evaluating the worth of a piece of literature, which they call theories.

Myths

Nonfiction also includes very old tales that were once considered true. Have you come across a reference to Zeus (or Jupiter), the mighty God who hurled thunderbolts across the sky when he got really mad? The ancient Greeks told each other this myth to entertain and to explain thunderstorms. Different cultures create different myths, but in all these different locations, *myths* share the similarity of describing and explaining natural phenomena—such as how the earth was made or why we have seasons. Originally, these stories were considered true accounts by the people who told them, usually long ago. Some people might classify myths as a type of fiction, because they are stories, but because they were once thought "true," we felt they could be listed as nonfiction. These ancient stories were shared orally, passed down through the repeated telling of the story, and hence, they take place in a much earlier time.

So far, no mythology or literary criticism reading has been selected as a sample passage on the MCAS exam—but we want you to be aware that you might get one. Instead, the 1998 and 1999 ELA Grade 10 MCAS chose the more conventional kinds of nonfiction that you're already familiar with—an excerpt from a history book about Ulysses S. Grant and Robert E. Lee, an interview with Bill Moyers, informational manuals, and a selection from Richard Rodriguez's autobiography. Let's hope they keep up the good work!

You should definitely review chapter 4 and make sure you can identify *main ideas* and *supporting details,* as well as recognize how the *organization* and *purpose* affect writing. These principles are very important to comprehending nonfiction reading.

Nonfiction practice

We predict, based on previous exams, that you will get around three passages of nonfiction when you take your edition of the ELA Grade 10 MCAS exam. Those passages will reflect a range of styles, structures, purposes, and topics. Maybe you'll get something historical, a reading on nature or science, and an essay about some issue of contemporary importance. We want you to be well-versed in nonfiction, so you can handle any questions on any material deftly.

Check out the following article, excerpted from "21 Easy Steps to Personal Environmental Health Now," and answer the questions that follow it.

21 Easy Steps to Personal Environmental Health Now
by National Institute of Environmental Health Sciences

(Courtesy of the National Institute of Environmental Health Sciences, National Institutes of Health)

1 We call it environmental health, but it's your scene, teen. Your environment *is* your health. For example: Purifying city water supplies is a major reason that you probably are going to live twice as long as someone born a century ago.

2 You've got a personal environment, too.

3 To keep yourself fit and healthy, as well as live longer, you've got to take care of that personal environment as well as the rain forests, whales, and ozone layer. So some of us at the National Institute of Environmental Health Sciences have put together a checklist of things you can do.

4 1. Read the label, Mabel:

5 Compare it with the labels on other products to see if you are buying the safest product for what you want to get done. Is it for inside use or out? Should you use the product with rubber gloves, respirators or goggles—and do you have them? If a label says, "Open windows and ventilate," hey, there's a reason. (Maybe you won't go brain-dead. Maybe the company won't get sued.)

6 2. Turn it down then, Townshend:

7 This may hit where you live, but even your favorite rock, or Bach, if too loud, can leave you asking Wha'? Noise can make hearing decline and produce ringing, buzzing, or roaring in the ears or head, forever. That's a long time to be asking people to repeat things.

8 3. Leo, check for CO:

9 Carbon monoxide from space heaters and other home heating sources can kill. You need smoke alarms, of course, but they won't alert you to CO. For that, you need to buy a carbon monoxide alarm.

10 4. Grow some plants, Vance:

11 There's evidence that plants, inside the house as well as out, clean the air.

12 5. Put drugs high, Vi:

13 Iron-containing vitamins or drugs like aspirin can kill a kid brother or sister who thinks they're candy. Lock them up (we don't mean your baby brother), or put them out of reach. Same with paint thinners, drain openers, and other chemicals. Post the number of your nearest poison control center.

14 6. Know the dangers of your job, Rob:

15 Even writers get paper cuts. You can fall off a ladder or be exposed to risks from petroleum products and solvents. Computer use and other repetitive tasks can lead to carpal tunnel syndrome. Take care.

16 7. Your cold may be your cat, Matt:

17 You could be allergic to dust mites, your cat, the pollen from trees, or cockroaches. A-a-a-choo! And wheeze! Plastic mattress and pillow covers and the elimination of dust-holders like curtains and rugs in your bedroom may help. Or, if it's trees and pollen that get to you, air conditioning and filters may provide relief.

Let's do the first question together:

1.   In what paragraph does the checklist of ways to stay safe begin?

    A. paragraph 1

    B. paragraph 2

    C. paragraph 3

    D. paragraph 4

Here's how to crack it:

1 **D** Put your finger on the point where the checklist begins. The answer is right in the text. A checklist is just what it sounds like—a list of items to check off as you do each one. Checklists—like this one put together by the National Institute of Environmental Health Sciences—are often numbered. Just go back and find #1—"Read the label, Mabel." It's in the fourth paragraph down, so *D* is your answer.

Try these questions on your own and check yourself against the answers that follow.

2.   What does the word *ventilate* mean in paragraph five?

    A. expose to air

    B. breathe deeply

    C. freshen up

    D. read carefully

3.   What does the writer use to make the information in the checklist more catchy and memorable?

    A. quotes from famous people

    B. humorous rhymes

    C. well-known slogans

    D. popular song lyrics

4. How is this article structured?

   A. as a narrative

   B. as an outline

   C. as a sequential series of steps

   D. as a checklist

5. What is the best inference we can make from paragraphs 14 and 15 (point 6) about what the writer is suggesting?

   A. Do not take a job that requires you to climb ladders.

   B. Do not complain about petty problems like paper cuts.

   C. Computer users suffer more physical problems than other employees.

   D. If you are aware of dangers in your job, you can keep yourself safer.

6. Which paragraph states the purpose of this piece of writing?

   A. paragraph 1

   B. paragraph 2

   C. paragraph 3

   D. paragraph 4

7. In paragraphs 12 and 13, the author

   A. offers advice on how to avoid harm to kids from legal drugs and chemicals.

   B. explains how legal drugs can be as dangerous as illegal ones.

   C. summarizes the major poisons that harm children every year.

   D. contrasts the dangers of prescription and illegal drugs.

8. Which of the following would you LEAST expect to find later in this article?

   A. advice on what to do if you have a family history of baldness

   B. suggestions about how to avoid heat stroke

   C. information about the importance of wearing seat belts

   D. directions about how to test for dangerous levels of radon in your home

Answer Key

2   **A**   Look carefully at paragraph five. *Ventilate* happens with open windows and will somehow prevent brain-dead-ness. You might guess the correct answer choice is *A* at this point, or eliminate wrong answer choices. *C* and *D* make absolutely no sense here, so knock off those two. This leaves you with a choice between *A* and *B*. Of these two, you may suspect that *A* is a better choice because *going brain-dead* is something that would happen if you breathed deeply (choice *B*)—rather than something that prevents brain-death. Exposing yourself to more air makes sense—definitely *A*.

3   **B**   Those rhymes may be hokey, but they catch your eye, right? Even if you don't zero in on *B* right away, you can arrive at it by POE. *A, C,* and *D* all go out the window because there aren't any of these in the excerpt—no quotes, no famous slogans, and no song lyrics.

4   **D**   This information is not a narrative—to tell a story—so cross off *A*. There's no outline provided, so eliminate *B*. *C* isn't quite right because although the safety points are numbered, they're not meant to be steps you take in order (sequential). This structure is a numbered checklist, which you are told directly in paragraph three.

5   **D**   Return to paragraphs 14 and 15 and put it in your own words. The author says *take care*. Just because choices *A* and *C* include some words from the original paragraph doesn't make them right—in fact the author doesn't agree or say any of these things. The paper cuts refer to a very specific detail, not to the broader point of the paragraph.

6   **C**   The purpose is often near the beginning of a piece of informational writing. Sure enough, right there in paragraph three, the writer tells you why she or he put together the checklist: to help you take care of your personal environment and stay healthy.

7   **A**   You have to go back to paragraphs 12 and 13 and ask yourself what the author is saying. Before you even glance at your choices, you know you want something like "Keep dangerous stuff like medicines and cleaners out of kids' reach." Choice A is the closest match. The paragraph doesn't explain, summarize, or contrast these substances.

8   **A**   This question requires you make a prediction, so it's not an answer directly in the text. Ask yourself what all the advice has in common and what the purpose of the article is. It's about making your surroundings safer, right? *B, C,* and *D* all have to do with that—but not *A*. Your family history—what's in your genes—is something inside you, not a factor in your personal environment.

Fiction

A couple of the passages that you will read and analyze on the MCAS exam will likely be *fiction*, or a genre of writing about people and events that aren't real. The fiction that you're probably most familiar with is the *novel*, a book-length narrative account. You might also be familiar with historical fiction—fiction that uses imaginary characters, but is set in realistic historical times. In *Across Five Aprils,* Irene Hunt describes a fictitious family (the Creightons) that lives during the Civil War. The book is a work of fiction, but the Civil War really happened, so the book is a historical fiction. Science fiction, fantasy, suspense, romance, and mystery are other examples of fiction genres.

Fiction is usually structured as narrative and is heavily influenced by mood (the atmosphere of a piece) and tone (the attitude conveyed by the language). If you need to review what we're talking about when we say narrative, mood, and tone, flip back to page 68.

Fiction terms

People who study literature employ a lot of fancy words to describe what happens in fictional works. Your MCAS examiners may use these fancy words, without explaining these terms to you, so you'll need to be fluent with this vocabulary before you take the exam. In addition to helping you understand multiple-choice questions on the ELA exam, you can use this vocabulary in your open-response answers and in your composition—so these terms will help you get a higher score in many areas.

Characterization: What the characters are like

Authors usually show us *characterization* through description of character's appearance, comments, actions, thoughts, and what others say about them. In an excerpt like *The Winnipeg Wolf* that appeared in chapter 3, the narrator's observations of the wolf give us a characterization of the wolf's personality.

Conflict: The struggle that drives the plot

This kind of conflict has similarities to the *conflicts* you have with your parents—it's about the main character overcoming adversity. Common challenges that characters have to surmount are:

> Internal struggle, such as the tension between a character's feelings and beliefs in *Hamlet,* when the main character grapples with avenging his father's death.

Struggle between two people, such as the clashing factions in Shakespeare's *King Lear* or Harry Potter's efforts to triumph over evil adversaries.

Conflict between a person and the forces of nature, such as Jack London's short story "To Build a Fire," in which a man labors against cold to save his life.

Dialogue: Conversations between characters

Dialogues sometimes use *dialect* (see page 73) in order to create authenticity.

Plot: The story line or what happens in the fictional narrative

Plot lines usually follow this rough outline of development.

Exposition: When the background, setting, and characters are introduced.

Rising action: When a problem (or problems) arises and the *conflict* begins to unfold.

Climax: When the conflict reaches its height of tension and excitement. The *climax* can also be called the *turning point*, because it's usually a critical moment in the plot.

Falling action: When the action of the plot starts to slow down right after turning point.

Resolution: When part or all of the problem is resolved and the story ends. Sometimes the resolution is called a *denouement*, especially when the outcome is very dramatic and emotional. Some books have more than one plot, or they have a main plot (the most important story that's happening) with a few smaller *subplots*. Shakespeare liked subplots because he liked giving the audience a break from a tense drama or a racking tragedy with a comical buffoon or a light-hearted scene. For example, in *Henry IV, Part I,* the more dramatic plot—Hal's conspiracy to assert his authority over the crown—is balanced with a little levity by a humorous subplot—Falstaff's shenanigans at the pub.

Point of view: The vantage point from which the story is told.

> The most typical perspectives are:

> First-person: When the narrator is telling the story directly and uses the word "I." In *The Heart of Darkness,* Marlowe tells his story directly to you the reader. First-person accounts usually create intimacy.

> Omniscient third person: When the narrator knows all and refers to characters as "he" or "she." In Edith Wharton's novel, *The Age of Innocence,* the omniscient third-person narrator has the freedom to comment on characters and their choices.

> Limited third person: When the narrator knows only what any observer might know. Often this limited information sets up the reader, as Henry James did in *Turn of the Screw.*

Protagonist: Main character.

> Famous protagonists are Huck Finn and Celie in *The Color Purple* and, soon, we predict that Harry Potter will be the most famous main character of all.

Fiction drill

This drill doesn't present information in the 'official' exam format—but it's a quick test to see how well you've grasped the fiction jargon.

Check off the one true definition as opposed to the two fake definitions for each of the following.

I.   A protagonist is

   _____ the main character of a novel, play, or story

   _____ a secondary character who supports the main character, or protagonist

   _____ a character from a novel, play or story who represents moral purity

II. A denouement is

   _____ the intellectual, spiritual, or emotional development of a literary character

   _____ the resolution of conflict or plot after the climax of a story

   _____ a poem in which point of view changes from beginning to end

III. The climax is

_____ the point where the conflict is resolved

_____ when the narrator introduces the setting and characters

_____ the moment of greatest tension in the plot

IV. Atmosphere is

_____ the physical setting for a novel, story, or play

_____ the overall feeling of a work, related to tone and mood

_____ the literary period in which a novel, story, play, or poem is written

V. Satire is

_____ a work that makes fun of something or someone

_____ a play written to evoke sympathy from the audience

_____ a humorous story told in rhyme

VI. Subplot is

_____ action taken by a secondary character to undermine the main character

_____ a line of action secondary to the main action

_____ a line of action that has taken place before the novel, story, or play begins

VII. A first-person account is told by

_____ the narrator in first person

_____ an observer, who knows all

_____ an observer, who possesses limited knowledge

Answer key

I. A protagonist is *the main character of a novel, play, or story.*

II. A denouement is *the resolution of conflict or plot after the climax of a story.*

III. The climax is *the moment of greatest tension in the plot.*

IV. Atmosphere is *the overall feeling of a work, related to tone and mood.*

V. Satire is *a work that makes fun of something or someone.*

VI. Subplot is *a line of action secondary to the main action.*

VII. A first-person account is told by *the narrator in first person.*

Poetry

If we gave you these lines, what genre would you say "The Old Apple Tree" bleongs to?

The Old Apple Tree

by Paul Laurence Dunbar

> There's a memory keeps a-runnin'
> Through my weary head to-night,
> An' I see a picture dancin'
> In the fire-flames' ruddy-light;
> 'Tis the picture of an orchard
> Wrapped in autumn's purple haze,
> With the tender light about it
> That I loved in other days.

Yep, we're turning our attention to *poetry*!

Poetry is easy to identify, because unlike fiction—which is written in full sentences—poetry is written in *verse*. Does this mean a poet can do anything she wants? Nope. Poets have a lot more flexibility than novelists, but they have rules that they must follow, too. These rules relate to meter (how many syllables the poem has) and rhyme scheme (how the lines repeat sounds).

On the 1999 ELA Grade 10 exam, students were asked questions about two poems. Because the people who create the exam like to provide a mix of genres, chances are good you'll see at least one poem on your exam.

Rhyme schemes

Have you read any of Shakespeare's sonnets? Or maybe you recall the limericks that taught you the words *mendacious* (cowardly) and *dolorous* (sad) in chapter 3. Every sonnet—by Shakespeare or not—is fourteen lines long. The limericks each contain five lines. Both of these are poems that follow prescribed rules about how many lines they contain and specific patterns of rhyming words.

Here are the first eight lines from a Shakespearean sonnet about love; notice how the final words rhyme. This rhyme heightens the melody of the words and gently emphasizes Shakespeare's point about the "ever-fixed" constancy of true love.

> Let me not to the marriage of true minds
> Admit impediments. Love is not love
> Which alters when it alteration finds,
> Or bends with the remover to remove:
> Oh, no! it is an ever-fixéd mark,
> That looks on tempests and is never shaken;
> It is the star to every wandering bark,
> Whose worth's unknown, although his height be taken.

If there is a poem on your MCAS exam, you will almost certainly be asked to identify the patterns of rhyme within a poem, known as its *rhyme scheme*. So let's practice charting a rhyme scheme together, using the partial sonnet above as an example.

To find the rhyme scheme, designate the first line with the letter A. Any subsequent line that rhymes with "minds" will be also get an A. But look at the ending for the second line: "Love" doesn't rhyme with "minds." It's a new sound, so it receives a new letter—B. Any line that rhymes with "love" will get the letter B. How does the third line end? Does it rhyme with either line one or two? Yes, "minds" and "finds" rhyme perfectly; we indicate this by matching line three with line one, giving both an A. What about the fourth line? Hey, wait a minute! This is a little sneaky: remove doesn't *really* rhyme with *love*, but in the case of rhyme scheme, because the words are deliberate attempts to rhyme, we do give line four the same letter as line two. This charting continues until the end of a stanza (a group of lines designated by a break in the poetry, much like a paragraph in prose). What rhyme scheme did you end up with?

Let me not to the marriage of true minds	A
Admit impediments. Love is not love	B
Which alters when it alteration finds,	A
Or bends with the remover to remove:	B
Oh, no! it is an ever-fixéd mark,	C
That looks on tempests and is never shaken;	D
It is the star to every wandering bark,	C
Whose worth's unknown, although his height be taken.	D

Poetry terms

As we mentioned above, some types of poetry are defined by specific rhyme schemes, such as the limerick, which always has an AABBA rhyme scheme. Other kinds of poetry are described by the number of syllables used in each line. And still other kinds of poems are classified by subject matter and mood. Here are some specific kinds of poems that you may need to know for your MCAS exam.

Ballad: A poem of several stanzas like "Barbara Allen" and "The Rime of the Ancient Mariner," that were often originally meant to be sung.

Elegy: A melancholy or sad poem, often in remembrance of someone who has died.

Epic poetry: Poetry like *The Odyssey* or *The Iliad* that tells at length about a hero's achievements.

Free verse: A poem with little or no rhyme.

Haiku: A three-line Japanese poem that often tries to capture the essence of a moment. Haikus have five syllables in the first line, seven in the second line, and five in the last line.

Lyrical poetry: Songlike outpourings of the poet's thoughts and feelings.

Narrative poetry: Poems that tell a story.

Sonnet: This is a fourteen-line poem, often about love.

Stanza: A division in a poem, usually marking a cycle of rhyme or meter.

Poetry drill

For each of the following, match the term to its definition.

I.	Epic	a.	a section of poetry, a poem "paragraph"
II.	Elegy	b.	long poem about the adventures of a hero
III.	Lyric	c.	poetry that expresses the poet's emotions
IV.	Stanza	d.	a poem mourning the dead
V.	Meter	e.	patterns of stressed and unstressed syllables in a poem

Answer key

I. B.

II. D.

III. C.

IV. A.

V. E.

Poetry practice

Try a few questions based on the following poem from Children of the Night, *and then check out your answers on page 97.*

Richard Cory

by Edwin Arlington Robinson

Whenever Richard Cory went down town,
We people on the pavement looked at him:
He was a gentleman from sole to crown,
Clean favored and imperially slim.

And he was always quietly arrayed,   **5**
And he was always human when he talked;
But still he fluttered pulses when he said,
"Good morning," and he glittered when he walked.

And he was rich, —yes, richer than a king, —
And admirably schooled in every grace: **10**
In fine, we thought that he was everything
To make us wish that we were in his place.

So on we worked and waited for the light,
And went without the meat, and cursed the bread;
And Richard Cory, one calm summer night,   **15**
Went home and put a bullet through his head.

9. What is the rhyme scheme of the first stanza of "Richard Cory"?

   A. ABAB

   B. ABCD

   C. ABCA

   D. ABCB

10. In lines 10-14, the speaker is saying that

    A. everyone knew that Richard Cory only pretended to be wealthy.

    B. Richard Cory thought he was better than everyone else.

    C. Richard Cory went to great lengths to make people jealous.

    D. everyone envied the wealthy, elegant Richard Cory.

11. In the final stanza, the poet emphasizes the meaning through

    A. nature.

    B. logical ideas.

    C. a surprise ending.

    D. a dream.

Answer key

Here's how you crack these questions:

9 **A** This one's simple. Remember how you figure out the rhyme scheme? Look at the final word in each of the four lines in the stanza: *town, him, crown, slim*. Assign each word a letter (starting with A and working your way through the alphabet). Use the same letter for words that rhyme.

Town = A

Him = B

Crown = A (since it rhymes with town)

Slim = B (since it rhymes with him)

Your aggressive guess about the answer is ABAB.

10 **D** Go back to lines 10-14 and put them in your own words. Your paraphrase might have said: Richard Cory was one rich guy, and we all wanted to be in his shoes. Use POE to eliminate choices *A, B*, and *C* make Cory sound negative; you're looking for a choice that builds him up as someone rich and desirable. Answer choice *D*, the only one you haven't crossed off, is a good fit with your guess.

11 C This is one of those questions that requires you to gather clues in the text. Go to the last stanza and think about how it made you feel the first time you read it. Surprised, right? The last thing you expect this guy with the perfect life to do is kill himself! The poet is stressing his meaning—about how money doesn't necessarily make you happy, and people aren't always what they seem—by surprising you. *C* seems to be the best match to your aggressive guess.

You can also use POE to eliminate the incorrect choices. There is no description of nature in the last stanza. This is all about people—the hardworking guys scraping by and the suicidal Richard Cory—so cross off *A*. Richard Cory's suicide seems to make no sense. It is *not* logical, so get rid of *B*. There's no evidence that this is a dream, so eliminate *D*. *C* is the correct answer choice.

Drama

Drama, as you probably already know, is a genre written with the intention that it will be performed and spoken aloud. Plays are usually written in prose (although Shakespeare wrote his plays in verse), and they use a lot of characters and dialogues to help the audience understand what's going on.

Dramatic terms

In the last two years, the ELA Grade 10 MCAS exam has given one reading passage from a play. So don't be surprised if you see one when you take your exam. Like fiction and poetry, there are a few terms that exam preparers will assume you're already familiar with. Consequently, if they do give you an excerpt from a play, you will need to know these few words below, in order to field the questions effectively.

> Comedy: A play that depicts humorous incidents in which a protagonist faces moderate difficulties, but overcomes them and the play ends happily. Nearly all of Neil Simon's plays and a few of Shakespeare's (such as *All's Well That Ends Well*) dramas are comedies.

> Monologue: A speech given by one person. A specific type of monologue is the *soliloquy,* in which a character speaks his or her internal thoughts aloud—thereby giving you an expression of the mood and motivations of a character—but the words are an aside. They are not addressed to another character; it's as if the character is thinking out loud.

Prose is just a fancy way of saying *not poetry*. In other words, it's just regular English.

Tragedy: A drama in which a protagonist's situation and mood changes from happiness to suffering. This resolution might be the result of the protagonists' actions (as *Othello* ends or as *The Iceman Cometh* concludes) or the result of the inescapable limits of the human condition (as *The Cherry Orchard* ends).

Dramatic drill

Put each word in the pair in its appropriate blank.

I.   The narrative point of view is also called _____.

An author's attitude toward his or her subject is _____.

tone/voice

II. A long speech by one character in a play or story is _____.

A long speech by one person not meant to be heard by other characters is _____.

monologue/soliloquy

III. The force that gives rise to the plot is _____.

The point at which the story reaches its emotional peak is _____.

conflict/climax

IV. To say how two things are the same is to _____ them.

To say how two things are different is to _____ them.

contrast/compare

V.   A play in which the protagonist overcomes difficulty is a _____.

A play in which the protagonist is unable to overcome difficulty, either because of his or her actions or because of human nature is a _____.

comedy/tragedy

VI. Language that does not mean exactly what it says is _____.

Language that means exactly what it says is _____.

literal/figurative

Answer key

I.   The narrative point of view is also called *voice*.

       An author's attitude toward his or her subject is *tone*.

II.   A long speech by one character in a play or story is a *monologue*.

       A long speech by one person not meant to be heard by other characters is a *soliloquy*.

III.   The force that gives rise to the plot is *conflict*.

       The point at which the story reaches its emotional peak is *climax*.

IV.   To say how two things are the same is to *compare* them.

       To say how two things are different is to *contrast* them.

V.   A play in which the protagonist overcomes difficulty is a *comedy*.

       A play in which the protagonist is unable to overcome difficulty, either because of his or her actions or because of human nature is a *tragedy*.

VI.   Language that does not mean exactly what it says is *figurative*.

       Language that means exactly what it says is *literal*.

Literary Devices

All these genres—nonfiction, fiction, poetry, and drama—each use a variety of tools to create emotional mood, an attitude, a setting, and characterization. One of the most effective implements that an author possesses, to help them draw a mood more artfully or to help them persuade more eloquently, is the literary device.

Have you read anything by Stephen King? He is a master of casting a mood in his books because he is a master at using *literary devices* (or little tricks to make writing more juicy or evocative) to create a desired tone. When Stephen King introduces Carrie White in his suspense novel *Carrie*, he employs a *metaphor* and tells us that she is a "frog among swans." When Carrie's gym teacher prods her to get going, startling the girl so she blurts "ohuh?", King extends his metaphor by saying "it was a strangely froggy sound, grotesquely apt." If King didn't use a metaphor, how would he convey his point? He might write something like: Carrie White's classmates saw her as a subhuman. Bor-ing! Could he sell millions of copies of a book that sounds like this? Literary devices are more powerful than straightforward language to describe how Carrie is a disgusting creature. Plus, King gets to set a mood with this metaphor. This scene is set in the humid girls locker room, so the setting feels uncomfortable. There's an ominous mood he's establishing, possibly that of a swamp or the feeling in the air before a thunderstorm.

Literary devices can also make writing sound pleasing to our ear—a task that is especially important with poetry, but also with plays and dialogue in fiction. The musical *Cats* set a collection of T.S. Eliot's poetry to music. Eliot's poetry was easily adapted to song, because Eliot used rhyme schemes and literary devices that make his poetry euphonious (pleasing to our ears).

Here's an example of what we mean: One of Eliot's poems describes Bustopher Jones, a sophisticated cat who saunters through town. "And just before noon's not a moment too soon/ To drop in for a drink at the Drones." He also describes the cat strolling in a black coat, wearing "well-cut trousers," and shod with spats. Did you catch the *alliteration* in the line "drop in for a drink at the Drones"—don't these words roll of your tongue? And what about Bustopher's wardrobe? We might say that Eliot engages in *personification;* he's making the cat seem as if it's a well-dressed English gentleman.

Terms

The MCAS examiners may not select anything by Stephen King or T.S. Eliot, but they'll definitely want you to prove that you can spot the following literary devices and that you understand how the author is using them in a given piece of writing. Yoo-hoo! Are you listening? Literary devices are *definitely* on your exam. We provide you with a drill and two sections to practice on. All this attention reflects our belief that literary devices can be sneaky to spot, but can make a big difference on your ELA Grade 10 final exam score!

Alliteration

The reoccurrence of initial consonant sounds is *alliteration*. For example, "if well done, alliteration is a sweetly satisfying sound" like Eliot's line, "drop in for a drink at the Drones."

Allusion

An *allusion* is a reference to a well-known person, myth, historical event, biblical story, etc.

Antithesis

Antithesis occurs when two contrasts are presented close together, often using similar language, such as H.L. Mencken's pithy quote, "Those who know—do. Those who don't— teach," and Neil Armstrong's famous words, "That's one small step for man, one giant leap for mankind."

Figurative language

Language that is not meant literally, such as a metaphor or simile, is *figurative language*.

Flashback

The *flashback* is a literary device that serves as an interruption in the action to show a scene that took place earlier.

Foreshadowing

Foreshadowing is a sort of hint of things to come—usually a very unpleasant event. If you've read further in *Carrie* you know that many of the things that happen early in the book to Carrie foreshadow things that happen later in the book—but to the other girls.

Hyperbole

A wild exaggeration would be to say "her actions dropped away into nothingness," otherwise known as a *hyperbole*.

Irony

A situation that is the opposite of what you'd expect—or a comment that means something very different from what the speaker is literally saying—is *irony*.

Metaphor

Metaphors are comparisons between two unlike things that do not use the word *like* nor *as*. Examples: "I am a Rock," "Carrie is a frog among swans," and a line from the Sonnet above, Love "is the star to every wandering bark."

Onomatopoeia

The use of words that sound like what they mean, such as "gulp" and "hiss," is *onomatopoeia*.

Oxymoron

An *oxymoron* is a self-contradictory expression, like "absolutely unsure," "pretty ugly," or "rolling stop"

Did the words *figurative speech* and *metaphor* sound familiar? D'oh! We went over these in chapter 3, when we explained that authors may compare two unlike things in either a *metaphor* or a *simile* (further down on the list). The 1999 MCAS exam stressed these two literary devices—so check out page 48 if you need to refresh your memory further.

Personification

Speaking of an inanimate object as human is *personification*. Example: "The ship began to creak and protest as it struggled against the rising sea," and Bustopher Jones being described as if he were a human.

Rhetorical question

A *rhetorical question* is an unnecessary question—made unnecessary because the speaker goes on to answer his or her own query. What is the point of a rhetorical question? Well, a rhetorical question might be used to emphasize an important fact or development.

Simile

A comparison between two things using the word *like* or *as* is a *simile.* Example: "my love is like a red, red rose."

Understatement

The opposite of hyperbole, an *understatement* downplays the extremity or severity of a situation.

Literary devices drill

Determine which literary device best describes the following sentences.

I ate a jumbo shrimp.   _____

His eye was a camera.   _____

The car's engine sputtered angrily.   _____

Lucy lingered longingly.   _____

It was the best concert ever!   _____

She's as weak as a kitten.   _____

The bee buzzed in my ear.   _____

Overkill on literary devices? No way. On the 1999 ELA Grade 10 MCAS exam, there were about ten—*ten!*—questions on literary devices. We're repeating this material because we believe that the exam will ask you repeatedly about this material—and we want you to get the answer right repeatedly.

Answer key

I ate a jumbo shrimp. is an example of *oxymoron.*

His eye was a camera. is an example of *metaphor.*

The car's engine sputtered angrily. is an example of *personification.*

Lucy lingered longingly. is an example of *alliteration.*

I saw the greatest show on earth! is an example of *hyperbole.*

She's as weak as a kitten. is an example of *simile.*

The bee buzzed in my ear. is an example of *onomatopoeia.*

Literary devices practice

Let's see how well you can identify and remember these devices by reading the passage below and answering questions on it.

The Cobweb

by Saki (as modified by Gloria Levine)

(Courtesy of Project Gutenberg)

1 The farmhouse kitchen probably stood where it did as a matter of accident or haphazard choice; yet its situation might have been planned by a master-strategist in farmhouse architecture. Dairy and poultry-yard, and herb garden, and all the busy places of the farm seemed to lead by easy access into its wide flagged haven, where there was room for everything and where muddy boots left traces that were easily swept away. And yet, for all that it stood so well in the center of human bustle, its long, latticed window, with the wide window-seat, built into an embrasure beyond the huge fireplace, looked out on a wild spreading view of hill and heather and wooded comb. The window nook made almost a little room in itself, quite the pleasantest room in the farm as far as situation and capabilities went. Young Mrs. Ladbruk, whose husband had just come into the farm by way of inheritance, cast covetous eyes on this snug corner, and her fingers itched to make it bright and cozy with chintz curtains and bowls of flowers, and a shelf or two of old china. The musty farm parlour, looking out on to a prim, cheerless garden imprisoned within high, blank walls, was not a room that lent itself readily either to comfort or decoration.

2 "When we are more settled I shall work wonders in the way of making the kitchen habitable," said the young woman to her occasional visitors. There was an unspoken wish in those words, a wish which was unconfessed as well as unspoken. Emma Ladbruk was the mistress of the farm; jointly with her husband she might have her say, and to a certain extent her way, in ordering its affairs. But she was not mistress of the kitchen.

3 The yellow, wrinkled old dame who hobbled and muttered about the kitchen, looking like a dead autumn leaf which the winter winds still pushed hither and thither, had once been Martha Crale; for seventy odd years she had been Martha Mountjoy. For longer than anyone could remember she had pattered to and fro between oven and wash-house and dairy, and out to chicken-run and garden, grumbling and muttering and scolding, but working unceasingly. Emma Ladbruk, of whose coming she took as little notice as she would of a bee wandering in at a window on a summer's day, used at first to watch her with a kind of frightened curiosity. She was so old and so much a part of the place, it was difficult to think of her exactly as a living thing. Old Shep, the white-nozzled, stiff-limbed collie, waiting for his time to die, seemed almost more human than the withered,

dried-up old woman. He had been a riotous, roystering puppy, mad with the joy of life, when she was already a tottering, hobbling dame; now he was just a blind, breathing carcass, nothing more, and she still worked with frail energy, still swept and baked and washed, fetched and carried. If there were something in these wise old dogs that did not perish utterly with death, Emma used to think to herself, what generations of ghost-dogs there must be out on those hills, that Martha had reared and fed and tended and spoken a last goodbye word to in that old kitchen.

When the half-frightened curiosity had somewhat faded away, Emma Ladbruk was uncomfortably conscious of another feeling towards the old woman. She was a quaint old tradition, lingering about the place, she was part and parcel of the farm itself, she was something at once pathetic and picturesque—but she was dreadfully in the way. Emma had come to the farm full of plans for little reforms and improvements, in part the result of training in the newest ways and methods, in part the outcome of her own ideas and fancies. Reforms in the kitchen region, if those deaf old ears could have been induced to give them even a hearing, would have met **4** with short shrift and scornful rejection. Emma, with the latest science of dead-poultry dressing at her finger-tips, sat by, an unheeded watcher, while old Martha trussed the chickens for the market-stall as she had trussed them for nearly four-score years—all leg and no breast. Above all, the coveted window corner, that was to be a dainty, cheerful oasis in the gaunt old kitchen, stood now choked and lumbered with a litter of odds and ends that Emma, for all her nominal authority, would not have dared or cared to displace; over them seemed to be spun the protection of something that was like a human cobweb. Decidedly Martha was in the way. It would have been an unworthy meanness to have wished to see the span of that brave old life shortened by a few paltry months, but as the days sped by Emma was conscious that the wish was there, disowned though it might be, lurking at the back of her mind.

She felt the meanness of the wish come over her with a qualm of self-reproach one day when she came into the kitchen and found an unaccustomed state of things in that usually busy quarter. Old Martha was not **5** working. A basket of corn was on the floor by her side, and out in the yard the poultry were beginning to clamor a protest of overdue feeding-time. But Martha sat huddled in a shrunken bunch on the window seat, looking out with her dim old eyes as though she saw something stranger than the autumn landscape.

6 "Is anything the matter, Martha?" asked the young woman.

"'Tis death, 'tis death a-coming," answered the quavering voice; "I knew 'twere coming. I knew it. 'Tweren't for nothing that old Shep's been howling all morning. An' last night I heard the screech-owl give the death-**7** cry, and there were something white as run across the yard yesterday; 'tweren't a cat nor a stoat, 'twere something. The fowls knew 'twere something; they all drew off to one side. Ay, there's been warnings. I knew it were a-coming."

The young woman's eyes clouded with pity. The old thing sitting there so white and shrunken had once been a merry, noisy child, playing about in lanes and hay-lofts and farmhouse garrets; that had been eighty odd years ago, and now she was just a frail old body cowering under the approaching chill of the death that was coming at last to take her. It was not probable that much could be done for her, but Emma hastened away to get assistance and counsel. Her husband, she knew, was down at a tree-felling some little distance off, but she **8** might find some other intelligent soul who knew the old woman better than she did. The poultry followed her in interested fashion, and swine grunted interrogations at her from behind the bars of their styes, but barnyard and rickyard, orchard and stables and dairy, gave no reward to her search. Then, as she retraced her steps towards the kitchen, she came suddenly on her cousin, young Mr. Jim, as every one called him, who divided his time between amateur horse-dealing, rabbit-shooting, and flirting with the farm maids.

9 "I'm afraid old Martha is dying," said Emma. Jim was not the sort of person to whom one had to break news gently.

10 A grin spread over his good-natured features.

11 "It don't look like it," he said, nodding towards the yard. Emma turned to catch the meaning of his remark. Old Martha stood in the middle of a mob of poultry scattering handfuls of grain around her. But she threw the grain deftly amid the wilderness of beaks, and her quavering voice carried as far as the two people who were watching her. She was still harping on the theme of death coming to the farm.

12 "I knew 'twere a-coming. There's been signs an' warnings."

13 "Who's dead, then, old Mother?" called out the young man."

14 'Tis young Mister Ladbruk," she shrilled back; "they've just a-carried his body in. Run out of the way of a tree that was coming down an' ran hisself on to an iron post. Dead when they picked un up. Aye, I knew 'twere coming."

15 And she turned to fling a handful of barley at a belated group of guinea-fowl that came racing toward her.

* * * *

16 On a cold grey morning Emma Ladbruk stood waiting, with her boxes already stowed in the farm cart, till the last of the market produce should be ready, for the train she was to catch was of less importance than the chickens and butter and eggs that were to be offered for sale. From where she stood she could see an angle of the long latticed window that was to have been cosy with curtains and gay with bowls of flowers. Into her mind came the thought that for months, perhaps for years, long after she had been utterly forgotten, a white, unheeding face would be seen peering out through those latticed panes, and a weak muttering voice would be heard quavering up and down those flagged passages. She made her way to a narrow barred casement that opened into the farm larder. Old Martha was standing at a table trussing a pair of chickens for the market stall as she had trussed them for nearly four-score years.

12. What does the "cobweb" in the title symbolize?

   A. the power of Nature

   B. Emma's sense of being trapped

   C. Martha's predatory ways

   D. Shep's unavoidable death

13. What kind of literary device is the author utilizing in the title, "The Cobweb"?

   A. alliteration

   B. flashback

   C. metaphor

   D. oxymoron

14. In paragraph 1, Saki writes ...*its long latticed window, with the wide window-seat.* This is a good example of what literary device?

   A. simile

   B. irony

   C. metaphor

   D. alliteration

15. In paragraph 3, Saki says that *The yellow, wrinkled old dame who hobbled and muttered about the kitchen, looking like a dead autumn leaf which the winter winds still pushed hither and thither.* What literary device is this an example of?

   A. antithesis

   B. hyperbole

   C. simile

   D. oxymoron

16. The excerpt at the end of paragraph 3 *...Emma used to think to herself, what generations of ghost-dogs there must be out on those hills, that Martha had reared and fed and tended and spoken a last goodbye to in that old kitchen* uses what device?

   A. metaphor

   B. flashback

   C. personification

   D. irony

17. In paragraph 7, Martha's words "*'Tis death, 'tis death a-coming,*" are a great example of:

   A. flashback.

   B. foreshadowing.

   C. irony.

   D. alliteration.

18. In paragraph 8, *The poultry followed her in interested fashion, and swine grunted interrogations at her from behind the bars of their styes* employs which of the following?

   A. metaphor

   B. personification

   C. irony

   D. flashback

Answers

12 **B** Use POE to get rid of *C* and *D* right off the bat. Martha isn't very friendly, but she's not predatory, like a fox or a vulture. The title usually refers to an important idea in the story. Shep, the dog, plays a very minor part in the story and doesn't die. Nature isn't really important in this story—it's really about the conflict between Emma and Martha, so *A* seems weak.

Scan the story for the word *cobweb*, and you'll find it mentioned after a description of the "litter of odds and ends" Martha leaves in the kitchen that Martha doesn't dare move: "...over them seemed to be spun the protection of something that was like a human cobweb." Choice *B* fits because here and throughout the story the narrator emphasizes how powerless Emma feels in Martha's presence—almost like a bug caught in a spider's web.

13 **C** Emma compares her situation to that of being trapped in a cobweb, but she doesn't draw that comparison by using the words *like* or *as*. The cobweb's a *metaphor* for her life with Martha on the farm.

14 **D** Maybe you noticed the repetition of consonants and went right for *D*. You can also get the same result by crossing off incorrect answer choices. This description has no figurative speech, so *A* and *C* are wrong. Irony is a situation opposite of what you'd expect, which hardly describes this window, so nix *B*.

15 **C** Find the sentence in the text. Examine it closely. Is the word *like* leaping at you? Yes, this is a simile.

16 **B** A flashback takes us back to a previous time from the rest of the text. This is a typical example because the rest of the narrative takes place while Martha is an old woman.

17 **B** Remember that foreshadowing is a hint of things to come and sure enough, Mr. Ladbruk dies. Notice how you think the old lady is predicting her own death when, in fact, she's foreshadowing Emma's husband's death. Just so you know, the ending is ironic; a situation that is the opposite of what you're expecting.

18 **B** The pigs and hens here are being treated as if they are people, interrogating Emma and following her, so this is an example of personification.

More Literary Devices Practice

Try your hand with literary devices with a second passage. This reading is an excerpt from a play by Oscar Wilde, and see how well you answer questions about the play.

The Importance of Being Earnest

by Oscar Wilde

1 **Lady Bracknell** [Pencil and notebook in hand]: I feel bound to tell you that you are not down on my list of eligible young men, although I have the same list as the dear Duchess of Bolton has. We work together, in fact. However, I am quite ready to enter your name, should your answers be what a really affectionate mother requires. Do you smoke?

2 **Jack:** Well yes, I must admit I smoke.

3 **Lady Bracknell:** I am glad to hear it. A man should always have an occupation of some kind. There are far too many idle men in London as it is. How old are you?

4 **Jack:** Twenty-nine.

5 **Lady Bracknell:** A very good age to be married at. I have always been of the opinion that a man who desires to get married should know either everything or nothing. Which do you know?

6 **Jack** [after some hesitation]: I know nothing, Lady Bracknell.

7 **Lady Bracknell:** I am pleased to hear it. I do not approve of anything that tampers with natural ignorance. Ignorance is like a delicate exotic fruit; touch it and the bloom is gone. The whole theory of modern education is radically unsound. Fortunately in England, at any rate, education produces no effect whatsoever. If it did, it would prove a serious danger to the upper classes, and probably lead to acts of violence in Grosvenor Square.

19. Upon learning that Jack smokes, Lady Bracknell says: "I am glad to hear it. A man should always have an occupation of some kind." Her response is an example of

    A. irony.

    B. soliloquy.

    C. symbolism.

    D. stage directions.

20. Lady Bracknell says that "ignorance is like an exotic fruit." This phrase uses a(n)

    A. oxymoron.

    B. soliloquy.

    C. irony.

    D. simile.

21. Lady Bracknell's comment that "education produces no effect whatsoever" is an example of a

    A. flashback.

    B. simile.

    C. hyperbole.

    D. metaphor.

22. What tone characterizes Wilde's writing?

    A. cynical

    B. sunny

    C. objective

    D. exotic

Read another scene, which occurs a little later in the play, and answer the questions that follow it.

1 **Jack:** Oh, Gwendolen is as right as a trivet. As far as she is concerned, we are engaged. Her mother is perfectly unbearable. Never met such a gorgon. I don't really know what a gorgon is like, but I am quite sure that Lady Bracknell is one. In any case, she's a monster, without being a myth, which is rather unfair... I beg your pardon, Algy, I supposed I shouldn't talk about your own aunt in that way before you.

2 **Algernon:** My dear boy, I love hearing my relations abused. It is the only thing that makes me put up with them at all. Relations are simply a tedious pack of people who haven't got the remotest knowledge of how to live, nor the smallest instinct about when to die.

3 **Jack:** Oh, that is nonsense!

4 **Algernon:** It isn't!

5 **Jack:** Well, I won't argue about the matter. You always want to argue about things.

6 **Algernon:** That is exactly what things were originally made for.

7 **Jack:** Upon my word, if I thought that, I'd shoot myself...(A pause.) You don't think there is any chance of Gwendolen becoming like her mother in about a hundred and fifty years, do you Algy?

8 **Algernon:** All women become like their mothers. That is their tragedy. No man does. That's his.

9 **Jack:** Is that clever?

10 **Algernon:** It is perfectly phrased! And quite as true as any observation in civilized life should be.

11 **Jack:** I am sick to death of cleverness. Everybody is clever nowadays. You can't go anywhere without meeting clever people. The thing has become an absolute public nuisance. I wish to goodness we had a few fools left.

23. When Jack compares Gwendolyn's mother to a gorgon, he is making a(n)

    A. oxymoron.

    B. allusion.

    C. soliloquy.

    D. hyperbole.

24. In paragraph 2, what is it that Algernon is saying about Lady Bracknell?

    A. She's worthy of defending.

    B. She admires him immensely.

    C. She is annoying because she's ignorant and outliving her welcome.

    D. She is a gorgon.

25. Algernon is using which literary device when he says that relatives haven't *the remotest knowledge of how to live, nor the smallest instinct about when to die*?

    A. alliteration

    B. foreshadowing

    C. antithesis

    D. rhyme scheme

26. When Jack responds to Algernon in paragraph 7 by saying *...any chance of Gwendolen becoming like her mother in about one hundred and fifty years*, he is using a(n)

    A. oxymoron.

    B. allusion.

    C. soliloquy.

    D. hyperbole.

27. What does Jack mean when he says *Is that clever?*

    A. Is that correct?

    B. Is that clear?

    C. Is that foolish?

    D. Is that a tragedy?

Answer key

Check your answer choices against the correct answers.

19 **A** As you may recall, irony indicates a situation that is the opposite of what you'd expect. If you told the parents of someone you dated that you smoked, what would be their reaction? It might not bear much resemblance to Lady Bracknell's words! Would most of us describe smoking as an occupation? She's interviewing Jack in order to get her daughter married, after all! You can also eliminate the incorrect answer choices here: Lady Bracknell is not speaking to herself (*B*); she isn't conveying some other, deeper meaning (*C*); nor is she giving actors directions about where to move and how to gesture, so cross off *D*.

20 D The word *like* indicates that Lady Bracknell's comparison is a simile. You can also rule out the incorrect answer choices here: Her statement isn't a contradiction (an oxymoron). Her words aren't a speech to herself (a soliloquy). And they certainly don't contrast with what she really means (an irony), as no one is exactly sure what she means. You can rule out *A, B,* and *C.*

21 C Before you even look at your choices, you can guess that *hyperbole* is the answer. It's a big exaggeration to say that education doesn't have any effect at all. Terms like "absolutely never" and "none whatsoever" often signal exaggeration or hyperbole. Use POE to zap those other choices. A is clearly wrong, because Lady Bracknell is not recalling something earlier. Toss out *B* and *D* since both are types of comparisons and Lady Bracknell isn't making a comparison.

22 A Put the question in your own words—*what attitude characterizes this play?* Read the passage carefully, keeping this question in mind. Words like sunny (*B*) and objective (*C*) are blatantly wrong. There's no *Rebecca of Sunnybrook Farm* cheerfulness and equally absent is the impartial tone of journalism and science writing. Look at the text carefully—smoking is an occupation, "there are far too many idle men in London as it is," and "I do not approve of anything that tampers with natural ignorance." Even if you don't know that cynical means distrustful of human motives, you would certainly nix D, exotic. That leaves *A*, cynical, and indeed Wilde is scathingly distrustful of people—especially Lady Bracknell.

23 B An allusion is a reference to some other piece of literature or myth. A gorgon is a mythical monster, so Jack's comparison is an allusion to Greek mythology. POE crosses off *A*, a contradiction, and *C*, a speech to himself. You might describe comparing Lady Bracknell to a mythical beast an exaggeration, but look closer. Jack isn't sure that she is (he waffles). *D* is a much weaker answer choice than *B* (which hits the nail on the head).

24 C Look at the text. First, we know that Algernon is describing his aunt, Lady Bracknell. *B* is obviously wrong (because he describes her, not the other way around). Look very closely at the text. Algernon is saying he loves "hearing my relations abused." The correct answer choice is something critical (abuse), so eliminate *A.* Both *C* and *D* fit the abuse category, so again, read Algernon's words carefully. Definitely *C.* You might also notice that Jack—not Algernon—calls Lady Bracknell a gorgon, so you'd have to eliminate *D.*

25 C Can this possibly be alliteration, the repetition on consonants? No. Can this possibly be foreshadowing? Nothing even vaguely similar to this sentence transpires in the excerpt, so no. Are you looking at an example of antithesis—the juxtaposition of two similar clauses. Well, yes! "Remotest" contrasts with "smallest" and "live" sets off "die." Check *D*, just to be positive. No rhyme, no rhyme scheme; cross off *D*. *C* is the correct answer choice.

26 D Here Algernon is exaggerating grossly—speaking in hyperbole—because he doesn't actually believe that Lady Bracknell is 150 years old, nor does he think his beloved Gwendolen will live to be 150 years old. He's just exaggerating for effect—to underscore how *old* Lady Bracknell seems to him. You might aggressively guess. POE gets rid of the incorrect answer choices because Algernon isn't speaking in contradictions (*A*); he isn't alluding to a biblical story or a myth (*B*); and he certainly isn't speaking to himself (he's speaking with Jack), *C*.

27 A *Clever* in this context appears to mean something different than the way we typically use the word. Algernon goes on to say "it is perfectly phrased!", indicating that clever refers to something perfect, something good. Use POE and scratch off *C*, *foolish*, and *D*, *tragedy*, since neither is positive. To decide between *A* and *B*, read the text closely—would Jack be able to say "I am sick to death of clarity"? Probably not. Clever in this context has a definition closest to answer choice *A*.

Session Practice

Wow! We have dragged you to all four corners of the English language. Take a break, and come back to this section after you've reviewed chapters 4 and 5 again (if you feel that you need to). Next we're going to see if you can put all this cumulative information together.

This section is a mix of the previous material, and is designed to look like a real session of the Grade 10 ELA MCAS exam.

> We don't think you should worry about time right now, but note what time you're starting (just write it in the margin here), so you have an idea of how much time you spend on this section.

The following selection is an excerpt from an essay by Andrew Lang about Nathaniel Hawthorne's novel, The Scarlet Letter. *Read the excerpt and then answer the questions that follow.*

Adventures Among Books

by Andrew Lang

(Courtesy of Project Gutenberg)

Hawthorne did not set himself to "compete with life." He did not make the effort—the proverbially tedious effort—to say everything. To his mind, fiction was not a mirror of commonplace persons, and he was not the analyst of the minutest among their ordinary emotions. Nor did he make a moral, or social, or political purpose the end and aim of his art. Moral as many of his pieces naturally are, we cannot call them didactic. He did not expect, nor intend, to better people by them. He drew the Rev. Arthur Dimmesdale without hoping that his Awful Example would persuade readers to "make a clean breast" of their iniquities and their secrets. It was the moral situation that interested him, not the edifying effect of his picture of that situation upon the minds of novel-readers. He set himself to write Romance, with a definite idea of what Romance-writing should be; "to dream strange things, and make them look like truth."

Session 1, Multiple-choice Questions

1. According to Lang, Hawthorne's primary purpose in creating the character of the Rev. Dimmesdale was to

    A. point out a weakness in the social class system of his day.

    B. write a good story that brings an imaginary situation to life.

    C. psychoanalyze a regular person's commonly Freudian motivation.

    D. teach readers a moral lesson and thereby improve them.

2. In the second sentence, when Lang says "fiction was not a mirror of commonplace persons," what literary device is he using?

    A. personification

    B. alliteration

    C. metaphor

    D. hyperbole

3. Which word best defines the word *didactic*?

    A. immoral

    B. twofold

    C. analytical

    D. instructive

4. What is Lang's purpose in writing this essay?

    A. to describe Hawthorne's life

    B. to tell us why Hawthorne wrote about moral subjects

    C. to challenge Hawthorne's ideas of Romance

    D. to confirm Hawthorne's importance

The following selection consists of two poems, "The Tryst" by Christopher Morley, and "Trees" by Joyce Kilmer. Read the two poems and answer the questions that follow.

The Tryst

by Christopher Morley

According to tradition
The place where sweethearts meet
Is meadowland and hillside
And not the city street.
Love lingers when you say it
By lake and moonlight glow;
The poets all o.k. it—
It may be better so!
And yet I keep my trysting
In the department stores
I always wait for Emma
At the revolving doors.
It might dismay the poets,
And yet it's wholly true-
My heart leaps when I know it's
My Emma pushing through!
It may be more romantic
By brook or waterfall
Yet better meet on pavements
Than never meet at all;
I want no moon beguiling
No dark and bouldered shore,
When I see Emma smiling
And twirling through the door!

Trees

by Joyce Kilmer

I think that I shall never see
A poem lovely as a tree.
A tree whose hungry mouth is prest
Against the earth's sweet flowing breast;
A tree that looks at God all day,
And lifts her leafy arms to pray;
A tree that may in Summer wear
A nest of robins in her hair;
Upon whose bosom snow has lain;
Who intimately lives with rain.
Poems are made by fools like me,
But only God can make a tree.

5. What is the rhyme scheme of the first stanza of "The Tryst"

    A. ABAB

    B. ABCB

    C. CDCD

    D. BCDC

6. When Christopher Morley describes *my heart leaps when…*, he's employing which literary device?

    A. onomatopoeia

    B. antithesis

    C. alliteration

    D. personification

7. In line 21 of "The Tryst," what does the word *beguiling* mean?

    A. enchanting

    B. shining

    C. leaping

    D. meeting

8. In line 22 of "The Tryst," what part of speech is *bouldered*?

    A. adjective

    B. noun

    C. verb

    D. pronoun

9. In lines 1-2 of "Trees," the poet means

    A. poetry would not be possible without nature as inspiration.

    B. a great poem is finer than any scene from nature could ever be.

    C. nature is more beautiful than any poem crafted by a human being.

    D. scenes from nature are beautiful but fleeting, while poems last.

10. In "Trees," line 2 uses which literary device?

   A. metaphor

   B. simile

   C. hyperbole

   D. understatement

11. "And lifts her leafy arms to pray" is an example of

   A. alliteration.

   B. assonance.

   C. foreshadowing.

   D. hyperbole.

12. How are the themes of these two poems alike?

   A. Both poems glorify nature.

   B. Both poems are about how wonderful it is to be in love.

   C. Both poets emphasize that poets understand what others cannot.

   D. Both poets point out that poetry isn't everything.

The Cherokee and Chippewa are two tribes of Native Americans. Read the Cherokee and Chippewa creation myths below and answer the questions that follow.

Cherokee Creation Myth

(Courtesy of PJ Criss, from the *Book of Gods, Goddesses, Heroes, and Characters of Mythology* at www.cybercomm.net/~grandpa/gdsindex from an oral account paraphrased in "Through Indian Eyes" by The Reader's Digest Association)

Long, long ago, a great island drifted in a vast ocean. This island hung from four thick ropes suspended from the sky, which was solid rock. At first there were some plants and animals on the island, but no people. It was always dark and, consequently, none of the plants or animals could see anything.

The plants and the animals wanted to see more—they wanted to see the island hanging from the sky, the sky made of stone, the way each other looked. They begged the sun to help them and the sun created a path that took it across the island from east to west each day. When he saw what had been done, the Great Spirit commanded the animals and plants to stay awake for seven days and seven nights. They tried to keep the heavy-lids of their eyes from dropping, but many of the animals and most of the plants could not keep their eyes open, and let the heavy weight of their eye lids drop, and fell into a deep sleep. Those plants that did stay awake, such as the pine and cedar, the Great Spirit allowed to remain green all year, in reward. All the rest, on the other hand, were forced to lose their leaves each winter. Those animals that managed to fight the weight of their eyelids, such as the sharp owl and the strong mountain lion, were rewarded with the ability to see easily in the dark. Then the people appeared. That is another story.

Chippewa Creation Myth

In the beginning there were no people or animals. At that time, woman lived alone in a cave, subsisting on roots and berries. One night, a magical dog crept into her cave and lay on the bed beside her.

As the hours passed, the dog began to change. His body became smooth, his limbs grew straight, and his nose shrank, changing his features into those of a handsome warrior's.

As you may have already guessed, nine months later the woman gave birth to a baby boy. That child was the first Chippewa male and his progeny are the Chippewa people.

13. The Cherokee myth makes use of what device to describe the trees?

    A. personification

    B. alliteration

    C. metaphor

    D. simile

14. According to the Cherokee creation myth, some trees lose their leaves because they

    A. caught the sun and took it across the island.

    B. did not keep the animals all awake.

    C. stayed awake for seven days and seven nights.

    D. failed to follow the Great Spirit's instructions.

15. According to the Cherokee myth, why can owls and mountain lions see in the dark?

    A. because they stayed awake

    B. because they fell asleep

    C. because they have better vision

    D. because they live on an island.

16. In the Chippewa myth, the word *subsisting* means

    A. leaning.

    B. surviving.

    C. weakening.

    D. ceasing.

17. In the Chippewa myth, the word *limbs* means

    A. arms and legs.

    B. parts of a tree.

    C. hair and nails.

    D. eyes and ears.

18. In the Chippewa myth, the word *progeny* means

   A. cousins.

   B. ancestors.

   C. crops.

   D. descendants.

19. In the Cherokee myth, we find that the dog-man's "body became smooth." What part of speech is the word *smooth*?

   A. adverb

   B. verb

   C. adjective

   D. noun

Answer key

Find out how long it took you to complete this section by checking what time you noted on page 113, when you began the session. Are you around 45 minutes—or a little over? On the exam you'll have 45 minutes, and then you can ask for a reasonable extension, possibly another five to 20 minutes. We want you to have a general idea of whether you can slow down or whether you might need to answer questions a little more quickly on the sample exams ahead.

1 **B** Scan the article for the character name, Rev. Dimmesdale, and you find your answer in the final four lines. Hawthorne mainly wanted to write a good story—specifically a good romance. By POE, you can knock off *A*, there's no discussion of the social class system in Hawthorne's day. Eliminate *D*, because the passage tells us that the story is *not* mainly didactic (written to instruct or preach to the reader). You can get rid of *C*, because the passage says nothing about psychoanalysis—and it states that Hawthorne was *not* interested in looking at common, regular people in detail.

2 **C** Find the sentence: *To his mind, fiction was not a mirror of commonplace persons...* Use POE and cross off any answer choices that you know are wrong such as *A, personification*. *B, alliteration*, is also wrong (it simply wasn't used). But *C, metaphor*, seems possible, so leave it alone. Look at *D, hyperbole*. Is this sentence a dramatic overstatement? Hardly. Cross off *D*. This leaves you with *C*, a *metaphor*, which makes perfect sense since Lang implies a comparison between fiction and mirrors.

3 **D** You may know what the word *didactic* means, in which case you aggressively guessed after reading the questions and the passage carefully. But let's say you have no clue what *didactic* means. Find the word in the text and use POE to knock out the wrong answer choices. *A* is obviously wrong, because the sentence begins "Moral as many of his pieces are, we cannot call them *didactic*." *B* is likewise farfetched. So what else can you do? Read the text closely to discern any clues about what *didactic* means (remember Clover?). Sure enough, the very next sentence says that Hawthorne did not intend to "better people" with his stories. Didactic has something to do with bettering—what about guessing *D, instructive*. Didactic refers to *something written to instruct*.

4 **B** Start with POE and get rid of choices that are plainly wrong. Cross off *A*, as Lang does not discuss Hawthorne's biography, and eliminate *D*, because Hawthorne's importance is likewise not the subject of the essay. Why did Lang write this essay? Look at the text closely. *It was the moral situation that interested him*. Morality is a main theme here. Look at the

two remaining answer choices. Answer choice *C* says the author is challenging Hawthorne. Does the writing seem to attack Hawthorne? No, it appears to be trying to clarify or explain something about Hawthorne. Cross off *D* and go with *C*.

Reading Selection #2

5 **B** Review page 94 if you can't recall how to map rhyme schemes. This is a typical poetry question, and it's easy to get right; know how to map rhyme schemes.

6 **D** Would you say that "my heart leaps" is an example of a word that makes a sound? Nope, so get rid of A. Is this phrase an example of antithesis, two phrases that parallel one another? No, send *B* packing. There are no repeating sounds, so you can cross off C. This leaves you *D, personification*, something you might have aggressively guessed as well.

7 **A** Look closely at the context. *Beguiling* is something that describes a romantic moon. That eliminates *C, leaping*, and *D, meeting*, right away. But how do you choose between *A* and *B*? If you have to guess, you have a 50 percent chance. But maybe you've heard the expression guileless referring to a naïve person. This means that guile is the opposite of innocent; it's cunning and deceitful. Something *beguiling* is something enchanting; the correct answer choice is *A*.

8 **A** Examine the text, *no dark and bouldered shore*. Both dark and bouldered describe the shoreline, which makes this word an adjective.

9 **C** Go back to lines 1-2 of "Trees" and say them in your own words. Trees are lovelier than poems—so eliminate *B*, which states the opposite. The poem isn't about inspiration or duration, so get rid of *A* and *D*, too. That leaves you with *C*, exactly what the poem says.

10 **B** Read line two closely. Did the word *as* jump out at you? This is a simile.

11 **A** Using POE, you should have crossed everything out but *alliteration*. If the *lifts* and *leafy* jumped out at you right away, you might have aggressively guessed and then double-checked your answer.

12 **D** You probably can't guess aggressively on this one. Just knock down your choices, one by one. *A* is no good, because it doesn't describe Morley's poem, and *B* is no good because it doesn't describe Kilmer's. *D* is much stronger than *C* because both speakers admit that poets are flawed. In the first poem, the speaker says somewhat ironically that "The poets all o.k. it" (portraying love in a natural setting), but not him. In the second poem, the speaker says poets can't create anything as beautiful as a tree.

Reading Selection #3

13 **A** You might have guessed aggressively on this one because plants don't sleep, awaken, or accept rewards. But POE can get you to the same place: The trees are not alliterative. They are not a metaphor because they aren't representing something else. There are no similes in this story.

14 **D** Find the answer and put your finger on it. At the end of the story you learn that, "The animals and plants were told by the Great Spirit to stay awake for seven days and seven nights, but most could not and slept. Those plants that did stay awake, such as the pine and cedar were *rewarded by being allowed to remain green all year*. Eliminate choice *C*, because it is completely wrong. Cross off *A* and *B*, because they are also false—although they do borrow words from the story.

15 **A** Cross off anything that's wrong, a common ploy to distract you. *B* is definitely wrong. The story says nothing about their vision nor makes a point of the island, so *C* and *D* are also wrong. That leaves *A*.

16 **B** Sniff around the word "subsisting" and you find "nuts and berries." You might think to yourself: The woman seems to be doing fine, getting along by eating nuts and berries. The closest match is *B*. The other three don't make sense in the sentence, so don't fall for them.

17 **A** Avoid traps by staying focused on the context. The dog is changing into a man. Keep that mental picture in mind as you try to figure out what "limbs" means in this context. It makes sense that the man-dog's arms and legs are straightening, right?

18 **D** Make an aggressive guess. This child was the first Chippewa boy, so how would the Chippewa people that came later be related to him? They'd be his kids and grandkids and great-grandkids and... You get the idea. The best match with your guess would be "descendants."

19 **C** Smooth describes the body. What's that term for a word that describes a noun? Right—an adjective. Any time you have a word that tells how something feels, looks, smells, tastes, or sounds, you have an adjective.

Spot any weaknesses

Questions 1, 4, 9, 12, 14, and 15 all relate to chapter 4, the material on main ideas, supporting details, purposes, and organization. Review chapter 4 if you realize that you're having a hard time with reading comprehension.

Questions 2, 5, 6, 10, 11, and 13 all tested you on the content we covered in chapter 5, genres and literary devices. Make sure you know your literary devices. If you got several of these questions wrong, definitely go back to page 100. Maybe try your hand at some of the drills in this area.

Questions 3, 7, 16, 17, and 18 review vocabulary. Review chapter 3 if you want to refresh your memory about how to define words you don't know.

Questions 8 and 19 question your grammar knowledge, so you could turn to page 83, in chapter 3, or to page 148, in chapter 6, if you need to brush up on parts of speech.

Summary

Believe it or not, you have covered the majority of the material on the Grade 10 ELA MCAS exam. You've also given yourself a huge boost on the writing part of the exam (covered in chapter 6), because you now know so much about English language and literature.

So, let's go over all the tools that you now have at your disposal:

- POE

- Aggressive guessing

- Context clues

- Word parts (prefixes, roots and suffixes)

- Derivations

- Seven-step process

- Grammar rules

- Main ideas and supporting details

- Structures and purposes of writing

- Literary devices such as similes, metaphors, hyperbole, and irony

- Mood and tone

- Genres such as fiction, plays, myths, and nonfiction

- Rhyme schemes in poetry

Chapter 6

Cracking the Open-Response and Composition Sections

In addition to the multiple-choice questions on the English Language Arts Grade 10 MCAS exam, there are several open-response questions and a composition section that both involve some writing. In both cases, you'll be given a writing "prompt" (a topic or theme that you will write about) that will test you on some aspect of literature. This isn't as frightening as you might think. The prompts relate to all the material we covered in chapters 4 and 5, such as the author's purpose and the mood or tone of a piece of writing. Because you already have an inside track with this material, you're especially well positioned to tackle the open-response and composition prompts.

Still, there are some special tips and techniques that can help you write especially strong answers. This chapter will improve your understanding (and therefore your score) on both these parts of the ELA exam.

Grading system

Before we go into the details of how to ace the composition and open-response questions on the Grade 10 ELA exam, we're going to let you know how it's scored. You can't expect to get a perfect grade if you don't understand where the points come from. So, how *are* they scored? Well, it's rather simple, actually.

The Composition

Your composition is scored in two primary areas: *topic development* and *English conventions*. Topic development means how well you developed and supported your ideas with details, and it's worth 12 of the total 20 points on your composition. English conventions means your use of language, including sentence structure and vocabulary, and it's worth the other eight points on the composition.

You'll end up with a performance level that is ranked as either advanced, proficient, needs improvement, or failing. To achieve the advanced level on your Composition you will need to:

Write a well-organized, developed composition

Express yourself clearly

Support your writing with extensive details from the readings

Sustain the reader's interest through effective language, sentence structure, and vocabulary

Create compositions that indicate knowledge of grammar, spelling, and punctuation.

Don't worry—we'll cover these items carefully, so you'll be able to get an advanced score on your ELA exam.

Open-Response Problem

The scorers have an easier method for scoring the shorter, open-responses—they just assign the answer a score from one to four. The scorers will not be looking for one "correct" response to the prompt. On the other hand, they don't just pull your score out of a hat. They will be looking for an answer that is stated clearly, supported with ample examples from the text, well organized, and grammatically as well as mechanically correct. We'll devote a whole section of this chapter on how to give them what they want.

> The open-response questions are scattered among the regular multiple-choice questions on three sessions of the ELA exam. The composition section of the exam is given on one day (over two sessions) a couple of weeks prior to the rest of the ELA exam.

> Your composition is scored by two graders who each assign you between one and six points for your topic development and between one and four points for your use of English. So your final composition score can range from between four and 20 points.

What Exactly Do They Want?

When the MCAS scorers read your composition and open-response answers, they want to see that you expressed your topic clearly, stuck to it, and supported it well. They'll also be keen to see signs that you understand how to revise your writing.

Make absolutely sure that you have read the question carefully, so you can properly answer the question the MCAS folks are asking. Double-check your answer against the question. In other words, make sure that *your* topic is *their* topic!

The key to a high score is looking back over your writing and making edits that take your answer up another notch. You should be able to improve your writing from the original draft—either by deleting, adding, or reshuffling what you have written into a more logical order. Show that you're able to polish your writing by eliminating any errors in grammar, usage, punctuation, capitalization, and spelling. We reviewed some of these basics in chapter 3, and, as we promised then, we'll go over more of the mechanics in this chapter.

But before we get into all the specifics of what these test examiners want in your answers, let's talk about presentation and some really easy things you can do to get a high-scoring answer. These aren't things that are *supposed* to affect your grade, but they are things that might unintentionally influence the grade you get on your open-response answers and composition. Let's go over these things so you'll be able to get the most points on these sections of the exam.

Length

Let's start with something simple—what the graders see (literally) when they look at your paper: how much you've written.

You will receive a separate English Language Arts Long Composition booklet for writing your Composition. The word long here is pretty vague—but your essay should fill about two handwritten pages, and contain at least five well-organized paragraphs. Each paragraph should have between three to six sentences. That means each paragraph makes a point and then elaborates with supporting details that show you've understood and thought about the literature. If you've got more support for your argument, don't worry about writing more sentences or another paragraph.

For an open-response question, five to seven sentences should do the trick. Writing less than this makes it look like you really don't have anything substantive to say, so definitely try to reach these suggested lengths. We'll be showing you how easy it is to do this, later in the chapter.

Penmanship

You are given time to write a first draft of a composition and then to write your revised, edited version. Be as messy as you want on the first draft. However, when it comes time to write your final draft on the lined pages in the answer booklet, write neatly. Clear cursive is fine, and so is neat printing.

The graders don't really like messy handwriting or fancy loopy lettering that's hard to read. You could be a future Pulitzer-Prize winner, but the scorer needs to understand your brilliant ideas or you won't get much credit for your insights.

EXAMPLE OF BAD HANDWRITING

> Hawthorne's story has a gloomy atmosphere. He creates the gloomy feeling when he describes the dark woods and bad thoughts of his main character.

EXAMPLE OF GOOD HANDWRITING

> Hawthorne surrounds his story in a gloomy atmosphere. He creates a sense of dreariness through his descriptions of both external and internal worlds. The descriptions of the dark, desolate woodland setting and the examination of the character's dark, anxious thoughts work together to produce a feeling of impending doom.

Pretend that you are a Composition scorer. Which one looks like it was written by a student, rushing to finish the exam? Which one looks like it was written by a student who thought more about what he or she wanted to say? Which one will get a higher score? You guessed it—the neat one.

Margins

Another thing you should do is pay attention to the margins around your answer. There are clear margins—the borders of a box—where your answer should be. Try not to run over these. Also, be sure to line up where you begin each line, so that the visual effect will look clear and organized.

Again, this stuff is not supposed to hurt your score, but it can easily influence the graders.

EXAMPLE OF RAGGED MARGINS

> *Goodman Brown is nervous in the beginning.*
> *He calls himself as a "wretch" for*
> *   leaving his wife behind. He seems guilty*
> *and his wife seems innocent and it seems*
> *   as if something bad is about to happen.*

EXAMPLE OF STRAIGHT MARGINS

> *For some unknown reason, Goodman Brown is*
> *agitated when we get our first view of him. He*
> *berates himself as a "wretch" for leaving his wife*
> *("Faith") and goes off to do whatever it is he*
> *plans to do. The contrast between the seemingly*
> *virtuous person he leaves behind and whatever*
> *he is about to face implies something sinister.*

Which composition looks like it was written by someone with an organizational plan? Which one looks like it was written by someone who didn't take the time to put things in any logical order—and who probably hasn't cleaned up his or her room since the last millennium? Now, these assumptions may very well be wrong. Ms. Neat may not really have much of an organizational strategy. Mr. Messy may have written a brilliantly developed and organized response. The grader may or may not detect this. Do you want to risk it? Not for something as easy to correct as legible handwriting and neat margins! It's also not a good idea to stick additions or changes in the margins, either. The grader may not read them.

Obvious Paragraphs

So you've used neat handwriting and kept inside the margins. There's one final thing that you can do to make this composition reader-friendly: Indent new paragraphs. The whole point of a paragraph is to make things easier for the reader. You indent at the beginning of a paragraph to signal, "Yo, reader! We're shifting gears!" The ideas in one paragraph should be about the same thing, and each paragraph should be a little different from the paragraph before and after it.

The indent—a nice big space of at least half an inch—also makes things easier on the reader's eyes. Instead of one big blob of words, offer your reader nice manageable bites of three to five sentences each.

To summarize, we want you to get the most credit for your answers for your written material on the MCAS exam. So make sure that you've:

> Written plenty of sentences
>
> Used readable handwriting
>
> Stayed within the margins
>
> Indented your paragraphs

So, let's stop talking about how your answer will look and start focusing on what you're going to say. Let's get the meat of the matter—the ideas in your written answers.

We'll first tell you about open-response answers and then we'll go over the composition.

Open-Response Answers

Woven throughout the multiple-choice section of the exam are several questions that require you to give short written responses. These questions often ask you to analyze a provided passage. In chapter 3, we showed you how you can analyze words by breaking them down into parts. Likewise, you can analyze a piece of literature by looking at its parts—such as word choice, literary devices, mood, tone, and supporting details —and how each of these relate to the whole. You have to think about how and why the authors put the pieces together the way they did.

We'll show you a handful of sample open-response questions now, just to familiarize you with the format of the problems. We'll show you how to crack the responses a bit later.

1. In this account of the Chicago fire, the author has used vivid language. Find two examples of such language in the description and describe how each has helped the author accomplish her purpose.

2. Using information from the interview you just read, explain the author's attitude toward writing plays. Include evidence from the interview to back up your answer.

3. In what ways does the travel writer show an appreciation for music? Cite at least two examples from the travel diary entry you have just read to support your answer.

Here's an open-response question along with a sample scoring guide (they call it a scoring rubric) for assigning points

4. Read the excerpt from David Smith's book, *The Playful Professor*. How do the ways Irv treats Becky and Fred demonstrate that he is a good father to them? Support your answer with examples from the excerpt.

Score	Description
4	The student came to a perceptive conclusion about the character's behavior and used plenty of strong support from the excerpt.
3	The student drew a basic conclusion about the character's behavior and used an adequate number of examples from the excerpt. However, there could have been more supporting details.
2	The student came to one very basic conclusion about the character's behavior and used some limited support from the excerpt—but not enough.
1	The student made some vague generalization(s) about the character's behavior and may have made some false statements. There are no details to support the student's answer—or the details used are not appropriate.
0	The student's answer is wrong or does not answer the question.
Blank	The student did not write a response.

So what overall trends did you notice in the rubric or scoring guide? Two things, right? You noticed that they wanted the answer to make some kind of point (a "conclusion") and they wanted your answer to have lots of "support" or specific details from the text that relate to the conclusion. Let's talk about a structure that will get you *both* of these—in other words, a solid four-point answer plan.

Structure

Most of the open-response questions can be answered in one or two well-organized paragraphs, coming to a total of five to seven sentences. Here's a one-paragraph framework that will work with nearly all of the open-response items that you'll encounter.

Sentence 1: The topic sentence

Introduce the main idea of your answer. Say what you plan to say by restating the idea in the question. For example, if the prompt asks you why the author considers history an important area of study, your topic sentence might look like this:

> The author considers history an important area of study for three main reasons...

Sentences 2, 3, 4: The body of the paragraph

These supporting sentences will win you the bulk of your score in an open-response answer. These sentences need to make it vividly clear that you have *read the selection carefully* and thought about it. It is here that you need to pull out at least three pieces of evidence from the text to support your answer. If you find more support for your topic sentence, you can put more sentences into the body of the paragraph.

You should definitely quote from the text if you find valuable information in it. However, it's very important that you use your own words to show that you know what that quote means and why it is important.

Final Sentence: The conclusion

There doesn't have to be anything brilliant in the open-response conclusion—a simple sentence that ties things up will do. Summarize what you've said, but say it a little differently from the way you said it in the first sentence.

> The author feels strongly that history is a vital part of our lives.

Variations on the framework

Depending on the question, you might vary the framework of your response. For example, you might be asked to compare or contrast two poems or two excerpts. Here's what students were asked to do on an actual MCAS:

> Compare the themes of the two poems you have just read.

Compare means to discuss the similarities. There are several different ways you might organize the body of your answer. Here is one structure for answering a comparison question:

1. One way both themes are alike

    a. first poem

    b. second poem

2. A second way both themes are alike

    a. first poem

    b. second poem

3. A third way both themes are alike

    a. first poem

    b. second poem

Suppose you were asked both to compare and contrast the themes. *Contrast* means talk about the differences. You might just expand the framework above by adding to it.

4. One way both themes are different

    a. first poem

    b. second poem

5. Another way both themes are different

    a. first poem

    b. second poem

Or, here's an alternative structure for a comparison question:

1. One way both themes are alike

    a. first poem

    b. second poem

2. One way both themes are different

    a. first poem

    b. second poem

And if you have more ideas:

3. Another way both themes are alike or different

    a.   first poem

    b.   second poem

Finally, you might choose to compare and contrast the themes in a third organization:

1. One aspect of theme—such as how the poems treat love

    a.   how both poems are alike

    b.   how the poems are different

2. A second aspect of theme—like how the poems treat loss

    a.   how both poems are alike

    b.   how the poems are different

3. A third aspect of theme—like what each poet is saying about human nature

    a.   how both poems are alike

    b.   how the poems are different

Example

Does this stuff seem a little fuzzy to you still? Let's stop talking in general, and start talking about a specific example. We'll try an open-response question together, so you can see exactly what we're talking about:

The following selection consists of two poems, "I Shall Not Care" by Sara Teasdale and "Grey Rocks and Greyer Sea" by Charles Roberts. Read the two poems and answer the question that follows.

I Shall Not Care

by Sara Teasdale

When I am dead and over me bright April
Shakes out her rain-drenched hair,
Though you should lean above me broken-
    hearted,
5 I shall not care.
I shall have peace as leafy trees are
    peaceful,
When rain bends down the bough
And I shall be more silent and cold-hearted
Than you are now.

Grey Rocks, and Greyer Sea

by Charles G. D. Roberts

Grey rocks, and greyer sea
And surf along the shore
And in my heart a name
My lips shall speak no more.
5 The high and lonely hills
Endure the darkening year—
And in my heart endure
A memory and a tear.
Across the tide a sail
10 That tosses, and is gone—
And in my heart the kiss
That longing dreams upon.
Grey rocks, and greyer sea,
And surf along the shore—
15 And in my heart the face
That I shall see no more.

5. How is the theme of "I Shall Not Care" different from the theme of "Grey Rocks and Greyer Sea"? Use specific evidence from both poems to support your answer.

Here's how you crack it:

First read both poems carefully and ask yourself what they're about.

The speaker in "I Shall Not Care" seems to be a bitter woman who is telling her lover that he'll be sorry when she's gone, right? He'll be out there broken-hearted in the rain, and she'll be at peace.

The speaker in the other poem, "Grey Rocks and Greyer Sea," is a lover, too—but he seems to be missing his love terribly as he looks out at the sea.

So you've come up with two ways that the poems are alike and two ways that they are different. The first framework we gave you above, then, would be useful in jotting down and organizing your ideas:

1. Alike

   a. Both speakers—lost their loves

   b. Both—talking about nature

2. Different

   a. Teasdale's speaker's been rejected, thinking about her own death.

   b. Roberts' speaker's lost his love, thinking about how she's dead and gone.

Now take your jottings and make them into sentences. Remember what we said earlier about the structure of your open answer? Sentence 1 is the topic sentence. It introduces the main idea. The body of the response follows, with details from the text to support the main idea. Finally, the conclusion is used to tie it together. Let's try it.

Great response

Here is one really stellar, or above average, response to the prompt:

The poems "I Shall Not Care" and "Grey Rocks, Greyer Sea" make an appropriate pairing because they both talk about lost love, but from very different viewpoints. In both poems, the speakers discuss the loss of a lover and describe their natural surroundings. Teasdale's speaker looks ahead to April and spring, when the "leafy trees are peaceful," and the rains come ("when rain bends down the bough.") Roberts' speaker sadly reflects on missing his love— he uses the word "lonely" and says he'll have to "Endure the darkening year."

The speaker's attitudes are quite different, though. Teasdale's speaker has apparently been rejected by her callous, "silent and cold hearted" lover, and she comforts herself with the thought that someday things will be different. He will be "broken hearted." On the other hand, Roberts' speaker is really mourning his loved one, who is dead and gone. He seems to hold her image "in my heart." In conclusion, Teasdale's and Roberts' speakers have both lost their lovers, but the former is bitter about being tossed aside by her beau, while the latter is grief-stricken after the death of his beloved.

We'd score this answer at the "advanced" level. The response to the question shows a thorough understanding of both poetic themes and the explanation provides strong support from both poems.

Good response

You don't have to hit your answer out of the park, though! You can score a single and do just peachy on the ELA Grade 10 Test.

So here's a really solid answer:

The theme of "I Shall Not Care" and "Grey Rocks" differs because of the tone of the poems. In the first poem, the emphasis is on <u>not</u> caring. Teasdale says she pictures her lover mournful of her death while she "shall not care," and comments that she will eventually be the "more silent and cold-hearted" of the two. In the second poem, Roberts cares a lot his love is gone. He's mourning her and saying he's missing her.

Poor response

In contrast, here's an answer that would have failed. Pretend you're the grader. Why might you reject this answer?

there are not many similarities or differences to the two poems. They are writen by two different people after all. If you compare and contrast the two poems, the first one is about someone who thinks she is going to die. The second one is about the see and how much someone misses someone else's face.

Why would you fail this second response? Maybe because it's way too short. There should be at least five sentences. If you're scoring this exam, you're looking for an understanding that shows good comprehension, thoughtful insight, and plenty of support. You can't do all these things in a skimpy answer!

You might also give this response low marks because there are glaring errors in capitalization and paragraphing. (The first word should be capitalized and indented.) Then there are the errors in spelling ("writen" instead of "written" and "see" instead of "sea." Keep in mind, the spelling of "sea" is given by the second poem!) The scoring guide doesn't tell scorers specifically to mark you down for these kinds of errors—but they *are* looking for solid, clear explanations—and these silly kinds of mistakes make an explanation hard to follow.

But the biggie, the most important mistake in the second answer, is that the response does not indicate that the student read the poems. Students were asked to read both poems carefully and point out specific similarities and differences. This writer made two vague stabs at retelling the story behind each poem, but without one specific supporting detail from the poems themselves. This student could be talking about two poems read several years ago! If you were grading this response, you'd be skeptical that the student even bothered to look at the poems.

Practice

Now try a couple of open-response questions on your own, based on an excerpt you read in chapter 3 from *The Winnipeg Wolf* by Ernest Seton (on page 44).

6. In *The Winnipeg Wolf*, how does the author convey his attitude toward the wolf? Support your answer with evidence from this excerpt.

7. Consider the opening description of the setting in this passage. Analyze how the author's use of language and imagery helps the reader imagine the storm.

Sample answers

Check out these answers, sample responses that would be given "Advanced Level" scores.

6. In *The Winnipeg Wolf*, Ernest Seton's word choice, imagery, and direct commentary combine to convey a sense of admiration for the legendary wolf. He uses awed words to describe the "great, grim wolf" that "looked like a lion," or a noble beast. He also uses imagery, such as showing us a picture of the wolf as a "lonely warrior" defending himself with a "curl on his lips [that] looked like scorn." These images suggest that the wolf resembles a fearless human hero. Finally, Seton's respect for the wolf is evident in the commentary that he provides. He chooses to describe his final view of the animal, "statuesque as before, untamed, unmaimed, and contemptuous of them all."

7. Ernest Seton is a master of description who makes the winter storm seem real and immediate. He helps the reader not only "see" but "feel" the storm through personification, vivid word choice, repetition, and ample sensory detail. By attributing the origination of this "heavy-laden eastern blast" to a Storm King, the author conveys the impression that this immense storm is being driven by some greater presence. By repeating the word "snow" and piling up adjectives in the third line ("snow, snow, snow—whirling, biting, stinging, drifting snow"), the author suggests just how all-encompassing and unrelenting the blizzard was.

Composition

Have you ever seen a house that looks like it's about to fall apart? The roof has huge holes in it, or the pillars that hold up walls or the roof are tilted, incapable of supporting the house. Contrast this picture with a sturdy house, one that has everything in its place, doing its job. Where would you choose to live?

Building an essay is not unlike building a house. Instead of lumber for supporting beams, you use a main idea to set up the structure of your house. You hang a roof and walls on that organization, or specific supporting ideas about your main idea. The people who score your exam feel most comfortable when your writing is structurally sound and meets their basic specifications. Imagine the scorers as building inspectors. They'll look at the walls and the roof to see that everything is sturdy, but they don't care what color paint you use.

For your composition, you will need to build an essay that is structurally sound; in other words, well organized. Here's a writing framework that you can use on any long composition prompt that will help you build a sturdy essay, sort of a master building plan that you can use and change to fit your needs.

Structure

You should plan your composition to be about five paragraphs in length. Each separate paragraph should have between three and six sentences in it. Of course this format isn't set in stone, but it's a good general framework to follow.

Paragraph 1: The introductory paragraph

Use the first paragraph to explain what you're going to write about. Tell them what the main idea —or the thesis—of your composition is. Be a word thief, and take some words from the prompt. If the question asks you to describe the main character in "The Open Door" by Saki, your introduction should specifically say that you're making a point about the main character. It might start out something like this:

> The first sentence in a paragraph is always the most important. All the other thoughts in a paragraph should follow it.

> In "The Open Door," by Saki, the main character...

Mention the general point or points that you plan to expand in each of the next paragraphs. For example, you could mention that the main character is *ambitious, hardworking, and somewhat cruel*, then you have the rest of your composition to back up your statements.

Paragraph 2: The first paragraph of the body

Expand on your first point. (In the composition that we're creating here, that would be that the main character is ambitious.) As you explain what you mean, use plenty of details in the story for support. The details you use in your composition are like using nails in your walls; they make it stronger.

Paragraph 3: The second paragraph of the body

Flesh out your second point. (In our composition, our second point is that the character is hardworking.) Remember to draw examples right from the story (specific instances where the character appears hard-working). If you use quotes, always include your own comment on what the quotes mean or show. It's good to use quotes, but you want to show that you actually understand them.

Paragraph 4: The third paragraph of the body

Develop your third point. (In our composition, we're discussing that the character is cruel.) Like paragraphs one and two, this should have at least three sentences. This won't be hard, because you need to demonstrate the main character's cruelty and you'll be giving specifics from the text about how cruel the protagonist is.

Are you noticing a common theme in our paragraphs? We can't stress enough how important it is to *elaborate* your ideas on the writing portions of your ELA MCAS exam. Don't include a reason unless you can back it up. Give plenty of details from the literature you have been handed (or the piece you have chosen) to support your reasoning. Show the MCAS exam scorers that you *really read the piece of literature* and that you have support from the text that show you know what you're talking about!

Keep in mind: Your composition might have more than three points, of course, and then it should probably have more than three body paragraphs. The whole point of paragraphs is to make it your writing reader-friendly. You want to help your reader follow your ideas, literally making it easier to read your composition. To those ends, you should break up your ideas at least every half-page or so. And *every* idea in a paragraph should somehow build on the main idea of that paragraph.

Paragraph 5: Conclusion

Sum up everything that you've said. (In this hypothetical scenario, you might think about the character's nature and conclude by saying *I think the main character is driven, focused, and mean because Saki wants us to…*) Go one step further and end the composition with an interesting thought about all the previous paragraphs. For example, what was your personal response to the character? Did you think the character's traits make him or her more—or less—likable and believable? Adding your opinion to the conclusion shows that you really understand what you're writing about.

Seven Steps for Success

I bet you're now wondering exactly how you're going to take this framework and use it to build ideas for compositions on the MCAS exam. The answer is really easy. There are seven straightforward steps that can help you tackle any composition on your ELA exam. Here they are:

1. Understand the topic

First, you have to read the topic listed in the question very closely. Put it in your own words. This is your road map to the composition. If you read it wrong, you'll write about the wrong thing—what a waste! You have to be absolutely positive that your answer responds to the question that the examiners asked. You can underline, or tag, the key words in the prompt. For example, words like *compare* or *explain* are key words, telling you what the answer needs to do.

2. Brainstorm ideas

Once you understand the prompt, jot down your ideas down quickly—as many as you can, just keep them flowing. Don't worry about complete sentences or spelling at this point. You need to develop your main idea (your conclusion) first, as this is essential to constructing your essay.

3. Organize your ideas

Okay, now you have a main idea that answers the question given to you. List at least three main points that you want to make. These big ideas will be mentioned in the introductory paragraph, then each one will be developed in its own paragraph. Some people find it useful to start with one of those traditional outlines that you've probably used in the past. Here's a standard example:

    I.   One main point

    II.   A second main point

    III. A third main point

4. Organize supporting details

Under each idea, place related reasons, examples, explanations, or illustrations that come from the text. If you're using a traditional outline to organize these, they are lettered like this, remember?

I. First Point

    A. Supporting detail

    B. Another supporting detail

    C. A third supporting detail

II. Second Point

    A. Example in the text

    B. Another example in the text

    C. A third example in the text

III. Third Point

    A. Specific detail from the reading

    B. Another specific detail from the reading

    C. A third specific detail in the reading

5. Plan your conclusion

Decide on an ending thought for your composition that will clarify your whole essay. An adequate ending summarizes what you've said and also answers: "Why does all of this matter?" Remember, it's okay to use your personal opinions in the conclusion. You might connect the beginning of your composition to its end in some way. You may might put some imagination into your writing here with a prediction. There's no place like the conclusion for showing your flair for language or a unique perspective.

6. Put your plan into action

Using the ideas you have jotted down and organized, write the first draft of your composition on your scratch paper. Translate your listed details into complete sentences. You should end up with an introductory paragraph, at least three more paragraphs, and a concluding paragraph. Each of these paragraphs should be roughly three to six sentences long (a topic sentence and some sentences with specific details).

7. Revise your writing

When you come back to the second session of the composition, you'll be able to revise and review your essay. This is a great opportunity to make sure that your essay is as good as possible, because you'll be seeing it with fresh eyes and you can devote yourself to thinking about the spelling, the grammar, and the punctuation (things you probably couldn't focus on while you were busy brainstorming and organizing your essay).

Focus on Revisions

There will be a break between step six, when you've taken your outline and fleshed it out into sentences, and step seven, when you'll revise and review your composition.

This is a wonderful thing, because it means you'll come back to your 'rough draft' with a slightly new perspective. In this section, we want to show you three specific techniques that can maximize your second composition session. When you revise your essay, you should look for three specific things in your first draft: your vocabulary, any misspellings; and your grammar.

Vocabulary

The first thing you should do in the second composition session is look at your word choices in the rough draft. One of the signs of polished writing is a varied and effective *vocabulary*. To help you get the most points possible, you want to show that you have excellent control of the language and that you don't need to resort to using the same words over and over.

When you're rereading your open responses and composition, look closely at the words you've chosen. Don't be satisfied with the first words you thought of; reach for more precise words that convey *exactly* what you mean in a more colorful tone.

If you used:	Try substituting:
going	traveling, journeying, searching, racing
says	hollers, whispers, mentions, hints, emphasizes
guy	the person's occupation (such as painter, journalist, or blacksmith) or a word that describes a characteristic (such as sage, mastermind, or newcomer)
nice	delicious, delightful, coveted, thoughtful, sweet
looked	examined, peered, glared, glanced, scowled

You can also make your language pack more punch by using details. Instead of saying: Here's a picture of Dee Dee when she was younger. You could say: Here's a picture of Dee Dee when she was younger, with dark brown curly hair, sporting a sleeveless top that reveals smooth caramel-colored arms.

The idea is to examine your first draft's vocabulary and to take the words up a notch, where you can, in order to get more points.

Spelling

Are you wondering what else you can do to make the composition even better? The second thing you can do as you revise your rough draft is to ensure that you don't make any silly spelling mistakes.

> Remember: More precise wording *doesn't* necessarily mean longer. One really good specific word is preferable to a lot of boring words.

We can't tell you how to spell every word in the English language, but we are going to provide a short list of some of the most commonly misused and misspelled words. (If you want a comprehensive list of every word, we recommend a much thicker and heavier book—the dictionary.)

Misused Words

accept/except	I will *accept* late papers *except* when you have a reason why they are overdue.
alot	You will hear this in *a lot* of conversation, but never join the words as one.
alright	Never, never use this. It is not *all right* to use this because it is not a word.
your/you're	Where's *your* hat? *You're* going to have cold ears.
its/it's	The armadillo turned *its* head. *It's* unusual to see one wearing sunglasses.
their/they're/there	*They're* over *there* in *their* tent. [Note: this is reverse alphabetical order.]
Here/hear	Stand right *here* and you can *hear* someone whisper from way over there.
affect/effect	I don't know how this news will *affect* you, but it has had a big *effect* on me.
principal/principle	The high school *principal* believes in the *principle* that if something can go wrong, it will.
who's/whose	*Who's* the one *whose* smelly socks fell out of his gym bag?
presents/presence	You can get me *presents* if you want, but your *presence* at my party is more than enough.

| where/wear | *Where* will you ever *wear* that orange shag blazer? |
| were/we're | While they were at the mall yesterday, we're going to the mall today. |

Special Spellings

f*ie*ld, y*ie*ld, bel*ie*ve, n*ie*ce, p*ie*ce **but** rec*ei*ve, n*ei*ther, dec*ei*ve, *ei*ght, w*ei*ght, h*ei*ght, r*ei*gn

natur*al*, referr*al*, miner*al* **but** pick*le*, hand*le*, and doub*le*

dist*ance*, inst*ance*, resist*ance* **but** differ*ence*, rever*ence*, def*ense*, and nons*ense*

refrigerat*or*, fact*or*, predat*or*, direct*or* **but** work*er*, butt*er*, litt*er*, ev*er*

There are also a few basic spelling rules you might want to review.

Drop the silent *e* before adding *ing* or *ed*
use using used

paste pasting pasted

examine examining examined

excite exciting excited

Adding *ed* to verbs that end "vowel + consonant"
(Remember: a, e, i, o, and u are vowels. All other letters are consonants.)

Double the final consonant before adding *ed* or *ing*

clap clapped

kid kidded

plop plopped

cup cupped

refer referred

win winning

tap tapped

offer offered

layer layered

lather lathered

mention mentioning

Warning: You emphasize or stress the second part of refer. You say reFER. Therefore you double the *r*. R-E-F-F-E-R-R-E-D. If the end of a word is *not stressed,* forget the doubling.

Adding endings to words that end in *y*

For words that end "consonant +y, " change the *y* to *i* before adding *es* or *er* or *ed* or *ly*

family families

responsibility responsibilities

ceremony ceremonies

early earlier

party partied

happy happily

(but *not* if the word ends "vowel + y: monkey—monkeys, chimney—chimneys)

Use *ly* to turn adjectives into adverbs (*usually*).

Exceptions include words that end in "y" like that trio of cheerful words:

happy-happily/ merry-merrily/ gay-gaily

slow slowly

complete completely

careful carefully

final finally

Grammar

Finally, in your second session with your composition, you want to be sure that you're catching any silly punctuation mistakes. Let's go over the obvious things that you'll want to be sure you catch and fix before you copy your composition into the final book.

Tip: Have you ever heard someone say "any old" when they mean "any *one*, meaning not any *particular* one"? Give me any old pen. I don't care which one. That's not just any old shoe. It's a Superfly 400 shoe. Test whether a word is a specific name by seeing if you can put "any old" in front of it. If you can, it's not, and the word shouldn't be capitalized.

Capitalization

There are three main rules of capitalization that you need to remember.

1. Capitalize proper nouns—names of *specific* people, places, and things: Grandma Jessie, Connecticut River, Washington High School, Erin Bryant, February, General Equivalency Diploma, Rosetta Stone, Smithsonian Institution, Japanese, Antarctica, Hudson Avenue, Bear Mountain, Mississippi River. **But:** a grandmother, a high school, a junior, a month, a diploma.

2. Begin the first word of every sentence with a capital. This rule isn't tested often on the multiple-choice section of your MCAS exam, but be sure you remember it when you write your Composition!

Wrong: George cannot tell a lie. he ate some cherry pie.

Correct: George cannot tell a lie. He ate some cherry pie.

3. Capitalize the first word of a quote.

"Oh, no!" Melvin exclaimed.

Marsha asked, "Why not?!"

"I hope my parents aren't waiting up," Tabitha said.

Mrs. Haltiwanger looked at the clock. "It's past midnight."

Commas

There are several specific instances when you should use a comma (,):

To separate items in a series.

Example: The refrigerator is filled with old bottles, bowls, and cartons.

She whined, stomped, cried, hiccuped, and sighed.

To separate two complete ideas in a sentence that are separated by *and, or,* or *but.*

A complete idea is one that could stand on its own as a sentence because it expresses a whole idea. It has both a subject and a verb.

Example: I saw that I had a good chance to score, and the defender knew that she'd better act quickly.

The swelling on my ankle is better now, but it will be hard to get my soccer cleat back on.

I could try cramming it in with all of my might, or I could just put on a sock and go shoeless.

Note: You do *not* use a comma to separate phrases joined by *and* or *or* if they are *not* complete ideas.

Incorrect: He ate all the ice cream, and returned the box in the freezer.

The words "returned the box in the freezer" can't stand alone as a complete idea, can they? No! The subject—the "who"—is missing, so you wouldn't add a comma.

Correct: He ate all the ice cream and returned the box to the freezer.

To interrupt a thought

As a writer you may use a few nonessential words that separate subject and verb in a sentence. They are interrupters—but you can restrain them by fencing them off with commas—one before and one after.

Example: Uncle Jerry, *whose hair was thinning*, disliked being compared to a bald eagle.

The words *whose hair was thinning* are not really essential to the sentence about Uncle Jerry because the sentence would still make sense without them.

An interrupter can be lifted out of the sentences without changing the meaning. If you take out the words *whose hair is thinning*, do you still have a complete sentence with the same meaning? Yes.

Example: Boomerang, my crazy cat, sits on my keyboard.

Sometimes the interrupter is one word or phrase that follows another and both refer to the same thing. That nonessential word or phrase is called an *appositive* and is set off from the rest of the sentence by commas. "Boomerang" and "my crazy cat" are interchangeable; they refer to the same thing.

In direct address.

If you speak directly to someone, you use a comma to show that your statement doesn't apply to the whole world.

> Example: Nathaniel, why are you still in front of the TV?
>
> Cat, get off my keyboard!

Other cases

Commas are used in a series of other instances, such as dates and letters and mailing addresses.

> Examples: March 3, 2000
>
> Dear Buddy,
>
> Sincerely,
>
> Middletown, MA 06543.

Here are some common comma mistakes:

Do not use a comma *after* a word like *but*. Only use the comma *before* a word like *but*—and only when the word separates two *complete* ideas that could each stand alone as a sentence. Remember?

Incorrect: Mike brushes his teeth every night but, Saturday and Sunday.

Correct: Mike brushes his teeth every night but Saturday and Sunday.

Incorrect: I want to go to the prom but, I don't want to spend money on a limo.

Correct: I want to go to the prom, but I don't want to spend money on a limo.

Tip: It's important not to overuse commas. When in doubt, leave it out! When there's a rule that covers it, put it in!

Periods

Use a period at the end of a sentence. We knew you knew that, but the trickier part is figuring out whether you *have* a sentence.

> Incorrect: Making tamales with family members. (There is no subject, therefore no sentence. Who is making tamales? Watch out for "sentences" on the MCAS that begin with *ing* words.)

> Correct: Berthe Rivera is making tamales with family members.

> Incorrect: Although this morning practice time may seem early. Most swimmers on the varsity team were able to get up before dawn and into the water by 5:00 a.m.

> Correct: Although this morning practice time may seem early, most swimmers on the varsity team were able to get up before dawn and into the water by 5:00.

> Incorrect: Some scientists regard termites not as simple pests. But as intriguing subjects insects for research.

You usually don't start a complete idea with a word like *but,* do you? Then don't set the idea off from the rest of the sentence with a period.

> Correct: Some scientists regard termites not as simple pests but as intriguing subjects for research.

Abbreviations

Use a period after abbreviations. An abbreviation is a shortened form of a word: Mt., U.S., St., or Rd. are examples. When you use an abbreviation, you need to stick in a little period (.) to show that you've left out some letters.

Examples:

United States	U.S.
Mount McKinley	Mt. McKinley
Green Street	Green St.

Quotation marks and commas

Use a comma to separate a quote from the speaker.

> "I have a report to do," Curtis said.

> "You're no help," Curtis complained.

Curtis yelled, "I thought you were going to help me!"

Curtis asked, "Where are you?"

Note: It's exception time. You *don't* use a comma to separate the quote from the speaker when the speaker is named *after* his exclamation or question. Exclamation points and question marks are unfriendly and they don't like commas beside them.

"I thought you were going to help me!" Curtis yelled.

"Where are you?" Curtis asked.

The rest of punctuation marks

Colons

Use a colon (:) to introduce a list. The colon can often be translated "as follows" or "as a result" or "this list."

Reuben went to the convenience store for the *following*: chips, salsa, soda, popcorn, pretzels, and antacid.

She had only one request: money

Use the colon after the salutation of a business letter.

Dear Members of the Board of Education:

Dear Editor:

To Whom It May Concern:

Be careful not to use a colon instead of a semicolon, or vice versa. When you see a semicolon, check to make sure that there is a complete idea on either side.

Incorrect: Highlights of the show will include; a speech by the President, appearances by several celebrities, and a fireworks display near the Washington Monument.

Correct: Highlights of the show will include: a speech by the President, appearances by several celebrities, and a fireworks display near the Washington Monument.

Correct: I flunked algebra last year; however, I took it over in summer school and got an A.

> When you see a colon, check to make sure that you can translate it, "as follows."

Question marks

The tricky part isn't knowing when to use a question mark, but when *not* to use it.

Use a question mark to indicate a direct question.

Questions usually start out: Who? What? When? Where? Why? or How?

Do not use a question mark after a statement *about* a question.

"How do I look?" Arnold wondered how he looked.

"Are there any jobs?" Hermione inquired whether there were any jobs.

"What's the matter, Nelson?" Nelson's father asked him what was bothering him.

Exclamation points

Use these punctuation marks to show strong feeling—especially excitement or anger: Nonsense!

Don't you dare touch me!

Oh, my!

Go away!

You probably won't need to use them at all in your open responses or long composition. Exclamation points usually signal more informal pieces, such as a friendly letter or a piece of conversation written in dialogue form.

Apostrophes

Apostrophes (') are squiggles that show up in two situations—when you want to show possession or contraction.

Use an apostrophe to show possession or belonging: the bridge's shelter, the man's bald head, Henry's doughnuts, the plan's benefit, Thomas's locker, three countries' borders

Note: When showing ownership with a word that already ends in s:

if the word is singular, add apostrophe + s (Thomas's)

if the word is plural, add the apostrophe alone (countries')

Sorry, but we can't have any rules that don't have exceptions. (Hey, we're only the messengers here.) Some possessive words do not contain apostrophes:

The ticket is *mine*.

The popcorn is *yours*.

The cat used *its* paw.

The mascara is *hers*.

Whose wallet is this?

The fault is *theirs*.

The championship title is *ours*.

All these words indicate possession (the ticket belongs to me; the popcorn to you).

Incorrect: The contest featured cheerleaders' from several schools.

Correct: The cheerleaders' uniforms are different this year.

You can also use an apostrophe to indicate the missing letters in a contraction:

I'll (I will)

couldn't (could not)

would've (would have)

Notice that the apostrophe replaces the missing letters in the words above.

Here are some more contractions you should know:

Contractions of *am* and *are*

I'm   you're   we're   they're

Contractions of *is*

he's   she's   it's   who's   what's   there's   where's

Contractions of *will*

I'll   you'll   she'll   he'll   we'll   they'll

Contractions of *would*

I'd   you'd   he'd   she'd   we'd   they'd

Contractions of *have*

I've   you've   we've   they've

Contractions of *not*

    isn't   aren't   wasn't   hasn't   doesn't   shouldn't   couldn't   can't   won't

"Quotation Marks," <u>Underlining</u>, and *Italics*

Use quotation marks for separating dialogue from nondialogue. We guarantee that at least one of the passages on the writing exam will contain dialogue. It helps if you understand which words count as dialogue.

Enclose quoted words—either spoken or written—between quotation marks. Make sure that you haven't included other words from the sentence. Put anything besides exact words outside the quotes. That includes question marks—unless the quote, itself, is a question.

Incorrect: He took one look at her and, "Asked how are you feeling?"

Correct: He took one look at her and asked, "How are you feeling?"

Don't use quotation marks for *indirect* quotations. Quotations are only used when the words in between are someone's *exact* words.

Incorrect: She said that "she felt much better after eating something."

Correct: He asked how she was feeling.

Correct: She said, "I feel much better now that I've eaten something."

Start a new paragraph every time a new speaker speaks and remember to indent all paragraphs.

Igor shouted, "You're up, Thor!"

Thor cried out, "I can't find my lucky bat. You know I can't play with any other bat! It's the one I always use."

Igor said , "You call that your *lucky* bat?" Igor then turned and walked away.

Put quotes around *short* works like the names of poems, chapters, magazine or newspaper articles, particular episodes of TV shows and short plays.

"Why Can't You Behave?" (song)

"Breaking the Code" (chapter of book)

"Recycling Girl Scout Cookies" (magazine article)

"Capitals Rally to Tie Hurricanes" (newspaper article)

"Joey's Big Break" (episode of TV program—*Friends*)

"The Raven" (poem)

"The Tell-Tale Heart" (short story)

When you are writing your composition out by hand, use underlining to indicate the names of *whole* books, magazines, newspapers, *long* plays. Italics—*slanted print like this*—are often used instead of underlining to show that something is the name of a long piece. But since you can't *write in italics*, when you write something out by hand—such as when you do your composition—you need to know when to underline.

To Kill a Mockingbird (book)

Time (magazine)

Hamlet (full-length play)

Composition Sample

Okay, so we've given you an outline (our building master plan that you can adapt as necessary for building the perfect composition), a seven-step process for creating a solid composition, and three specific ways you'll improve your composition during the second session (word choice, spelling, and punctuation). Let's put all three of these components into action and we'll walk through creating a composition *together*.

Bart, a high school sophomore in the Boston suburb of Newton, received this prompt on his ELA exam:

8. In literature, as in real life, people often pursue a particular goal. Choose and name a piece of literature that you have read in class or on your own in which someone pursues a goal. Describe the goal and explain whether the character is successful in attaining it.

Getting Started

Using our seven steps above, let's help Bart get started:

1. Understand the topic

Read the prompt carefully. You are supposed to identify a piece of literature in which a character is aiming at something. Tag words like *goal* and *character* and *explain*. Describe that goal and explain whether the character reaches it in the end. In Bart's case, he picked *The Great Gatsby*. The character Jay Gatsby in *The Great Gatsby* had a goal. The next step is to think more specifically about what it was (You could choose any piece of literature you're familiar with—*Pride and Prejudice, Great Expectations,* or *Beloved,* for example.)

2. Brainstorm ideas

Now is the time to let those creative juices flow. Brainstorm. Toss out as many reasons as you can think of. Don't stop to decide which ideas are good and which aren't at this point. You definitely should not worry about full sentences, spelling errors, or specifics like word choice. Just develop a main point (a thesis) about Gatsby's fascination with the American dream—maybe that he failed in achieving his dream—and as many supporting details about this thesis that come to your mind.

3. Organize the ideas

You've got a lot of stuff down about Gatsby's dream—his poor roots, his illegal activities to make money, his fascination with Daisy. Group them into clusters—what are some specific areas that Gatsby failed in? Here are Bart's main points (specific areas where Gatsby strove to attain the American Dream):

    I.   Wealth

    II. Power

    III. Love

4. Organize your supporting details

Take the examples you've got down from stage two and put them under the categories they belong. Gatsby's fascination with Daisy belongs to part III, love, right? Now, go through each category and think of more examples to support each point. Think to yourself *What are some specific ways that Gatsby failed in his attempt to make money? …specific ways that Gatsby failed to gain power?* Bart is going to use this outline to create his essay— each of these main ideas can be expanded into a topic sentence for a separate paragraph in the body of his letter. Each of his specific examples and details can become supporting sentences within those paragraphs of his composition. Now Bart has:

    I.   Wealth

        A.   poor family

        B.   penniless in the military

        C.   gets rich through bootlegging, bond schemes

II. Power

    A. befriends millionaire with a yacht

    B. makes Mafia ties

    C. buys big house and invites important (powerful) people

III. Love

    A. as a soldier, falls in love with Daisy

    B. loses Daisy first time to marriage

    C. reunites with Daisy, but loses her again

If you have more reasons, you may have more body paragraphs. That's great!

5. Plan your conclusion

Bart decides that Gatsby's failure is related to Fitzgerald's ideas about materialism and the ways that Gatsby confused material success with happiness. Bart could also choose to say why Gatsby's failure matters. Or, he could summarize his ideas on how Gatsby pursued his dream and failed by explaining how Gatsby's loss personally affected him as a reader.

6. Put your plan into action

Bart has two steps to go. Now, he takes his organized ideas and expands the phrases into complete sentences. On this first draft—written on scratch paper—he makes as many erasures and cross-outs as he wants.

Bart's first draft

This version of Bart's answer would earn a "Proficient" score because it uses some really good evidence from the novel.

In The Great Gatsby, *by F. Scott Fitzgerald, the central character, Jay Gatsby pursued the American dream. He primarily pursued this dream in three areas—wealth, power, and love. To understand Gatsby's dream you must first define the American dream because his dream surely stems from it. The American dream is that any man—no matter what his origins are—could reach his goal through hard work (whether the goal was to become rich, famous, or powerful). In other words, no matter who you are, if one sets your sights on a goal and work hard, you reach your goal. The actuality was that the fulfillment of the American dream implies elbow your way to the top, sometimes* displacing others along the way. In the end, the American dream was often equated to material success.

Jay Gatsby really believed in the American dream because he was raised real poor on a farm. He is humiliated and drops out of college after two weeks because he can't stand working as a janitor. Fitzgerald use a lot of green imagery. This green symbolizes undying hope, Gatsby's "romantic readiness." The dream of the settlers for a promising future in the land of opportunity and Gatsby's unwavering dream that one day Daisy would become his. The color green is mentioned when Gatsby decadent home is being built and trees are chopped down. Gatsby also believed that power would lead to his dream. He has relentlessly pursued the accumulation of powerful friends, who appear at his weekly parties.

Gatsby was a romantic. He loved Daisy mostly because of her aesthetic appeal. loved to be in love because it was beautiful. Gatsby's greatest quality according to Nick was his gift for hope." The capacity for wonder of the settlers paralleled Gatsby's undying hope. Even with the reality that Daisy was married and had a child, Gatsby refused to believe anything other than that he would reach his goal and obtain Daisy. It was the city that fought Gatsby's dream: a land without morals, where people pursued happiness without fear of the consequences. It was impossible for Gatsby's dream to succeed. His dream was a thing of the past. And just as one cannot relive the past (although some would disagree), one cannot pluck a dream from a time already behind them. Gatsby believed that if you work hard, you can reach the American dream. But the dream was never reached. Instead, one fine morning you wake up to the horrible realization that society will not allow anyone to obtain in its entirety, the American dream. At the end, the narrator talks about how we beat on into the past, like boats against the current. People will toil endlessly in an effort to achieve the American dream, but it is in vain. It is as useless as paddling against the current. In conclusion, Gatsby attained the American dream, but did not win any happiness (or his true love) from his pursuit of money, power, or love. I think Fitzgerald is trying to tell us that money is a mirage, and that happiness does not come with or from money.

Revise

After session one, Bart returns to this draft and performs the final step, revising. In this step, with Bart, you'll reread your composition to make it as good as possible before copying it into the final booklet. That means proofread your first draft, be careful to:

Check if there are places where you can add more specific details that support your general ideas. When Bart returns to his rough draft after session one and reads through it, he realizes that some things might need to be better explained, such as why Gatsby desired Daisy so obsessively.

Add any descriptive details or examples that will help readers "see" precisely what you mean. Bart realizes that you could give more information about how Gatsby rose from penniless origins and went about acquiring money and power.

Replace boring, ho-hum words with more effective, words and expressions. Bart realizes that he used the word "dream" many, many times. He needs to eliminate this repetition and think of some more specific and interesting words.

Check that all the paragraphs are about the same length. Bart's last paragraph is really long—he needs to examine this and see if there's more than one idea in this paragraph, so he can break his text into more paragraphs.

Proofread the composition for grammar, spelling, or punctuation errors. Bart finds a few sentence fragments and checks that he didn't make any spelling, grammar, and punctuation mistakes (because he was too busy to think about this stuff when he was creating his draft).

Now that these changes are made, Bart copies his final version into his exam booklet and makes sure that the booklet has his identification information correct.

Remember that the final copy of your composition is written on the lined pages you are given at the beginning of the exam session. The booklet with the lined pages is the important one. Make sure your name and information are correctly filled out on the final booklet!

Final Draft

Compare this second essay with the first version. This one will surely get even more points, because it's more clearly organized, uses a more varied vocabulary, and has been proofread.

In The Great Gatsby by F. Scott Fitzgerald, the central character, Jay Gatsby, pursued the American dream. He primarily pursued this fantasy in three areas—wealth, power, and love. Unfortunately for Gatsby, his attempt to achieve his goals were dismal and he never truly realized his aspirations. In other words, Gatsby discovered that the American dream (that any man—no matter what his origins are—could reach his goal through hard work) is hollow.

Jay Gatsby really yearned for wealth because he was raised in poverty on a farm in North Dakota. He finds being poor humiliating and drops out of college after two weeks because he can't stand working as a janitor. Fitzgerald focuses on the importance of money to Gatsby through his use of green imagery. The color green is mentioned when Gatsby decadent home is being built and trees are chopped down; and it's mentioned several other times in the story. This green symbolizes his undying hope, which is first introduced to us when we oversee Gatsby stretching his arms toward a green light over the sea.

Gatsby also believed that power would lead to his fulfillment of his hopes. He has relentlessly pursued the accumulation of powerful friends, who appear at his weekly parties. There are hints he made his money through illegal means—such as a reference to the corrupt 1919 World Series and hints of bootlegging. Indeed, we later find out that Gatsby's entire fortune comes from illegal activities.

Finally, Gatsby's ambition is focused on attaining love, his unwavering aspiration that one day Daisy would become his. This was Gatsby's ultimate desire: to obtain Daisy and live happily ever after, even though she was already married with a child. Gatsby never doubted the fulfillment of his deepest yearning. He had become consumed with this mirage—as it turns out, the green light in the sea is a light sitting on the dock of Daisy's yard. His dream went unfulfilled when Daisy refused to marry him. Thus, it had become his all consuming passion to make Daisy his, which he believes can only happen if he gains great material wealth. Material goods were only a tool in obtaining Daisy.

But Gatsby's aspirations, while in many ways fulfilled, prove to be unsatisfying for him. Even with the reality that Daisy was married and had a child, Gatsby refused to believe anything other than that he would reach his goal and obtain Daisy. It was impossible for Gatsby's ideals to come true. His dream was a thing of the past. Gatsby believed if you worked hard, you will reach the ultimate goal—the American dream. But he never found this to be true. Despite showing Daisy his beautiful English clothes, his fancy house, and his lavish parties, she still rejects him. Gatsby's last act, drowning himself in his pool, seems to represent Gatsby's drowning in his excesses.

In conclusion, Gatsby attained the American dream, but did not win any happiness (or his true love) from his pursuit of money, power, or love. I think Fitzgerald is trying to tell us that money is a mirage, and that happiness does not come with or from money.

Can you see how this answer is much stronger? It not only employs good solid evidence (references to the novel), and its paragraphs are more clearly organized around a main idea. Bart has varied the word *dream*, with more interesting and precise words such as *mirage*, *aspiration*, and *yearning*.

Practice

Respond to the prompt (about a character's pursuit of a goal) with your own choice of literature. Here's the prompt again:

8. In literature, as in real life, people often pursue a particular goal. Choose and name a piece of literature that you have read in class or on your own in which someone pursues a goal. Describe the goal and explain whether the character is successful in attaining it.

Try to brainstorm a main idea, supporting details, and evidence. Then flesh your outline into sentences.

Yes, do this *right now*. Even though this is difficult, the truth is that you create and support opinions all the time—when you see a movie you like, or when you fight with your parents over clothing. A composition may be a new way of expressing these opinions, however, and we want you to get familiar with this format so you'll feel like a pro when you have to take the composition part of the exam.

_____

_____

_____

_____

_____

_____

_____

_____

_____

_____

_____

Got your composition written? Look at your draft against this checklist.

Did you:

____ state your topic clearly in the introduction?

____ give plenty of specific supporting evidence for the central idea?

____ put in only ideas that support that main idea?

____ ensure that your sentences and paragraphs follow a logical order?

____ offer a conclusion that wraps up your ideas?

Now, pretend you've come back to your composition and it's the second session. Proofread your essay to make sure the grammar, punctuation, and spelling are correct. Make sure that you're using the most vivid vocabulary words you can. Here's a second checklist of things to pay attention to during the second reading.

Have you made sure that:

____your words are varied?

____you've used the most specific and interesting words you can think of?

____ the grammar is correct?

____ the capitalization is correct?

____ any fragments and run-ons are eliminated?

____your spelling is error-free?

____the punctuation (commas, quotation marks, semicolons, etc.) is accurate?

Now write out your final composition on the following two lined pages.

_____

_____

_____

_____

_____

_____

_____

_____

_____

_____

_____

_____

_____

_____

_____

_____

_____

_____

_____

_____

So try self-grading yourself on this final version. How do you think you did on topic development and grammar conventions?

Topic Development _____/6points

Standard English Conventions _____/4 points

TOTAL: _____/10 points

2 Scorers: TOTAL X 2 = _____/20 points

Bravo!

More Prompts

The more writing you do between now and the MCAS composition, the better. You might have to write about a piece of literature on the exam, and we can't predict what that might be. On the other hand, you might be given a general topic and be asked to write on a work of literature that you choose. Here are some composition topics for writing practice. Who knows? One might even end up on the exam you take!

Identify a work of literature that you have studied in class or read on your own which develops one of the following ideas. Select one scene from the work and explain in an essay how that idea is developed.

___What doesn't kill you makes you stronger

___Evil will triumph over good

___Love conquers all

___Beauty is in the eye of the beholder

___Technology has destructive potential

> We're listing a handful of potential writing prompts, just so you can familiarize yourself with the types of composition topics you might see and so you can practice if you want to.

In literature, as in real life, characters sometimes seek revenge. Identify a work in which a character seeks revenge. Explain in an essay what the situation is and whether the character's efforts are successful.

Sometimes a character in one story resembles a character in another. Identify two characters from two separate short stories, novels, or plays. Explain how the characters are alike, and how they differ.

The setting plays an important role in some stories. Choose a novel you have read, and write an essay in which you describe the setting and explain its significance to the story.

In many stories, characters have tragic ends. Choose a novel or play you have read and write an essay explaining how the character was propelled to destruction.

Most stories contain conflict. Choose a novel or play that you have read and write an essay in which you explain two types of conflict that occur in the story.

Many books have been made into movies. Compare and contrast a book you have read with the movie version you have seen. Explain in your essay what changes were made in the movie version—and tell which version you found more effective.

Choose a character from a novel or play you have read. Explain in an essay why you would or would not want to be that character and how that character is or is not like you.

Many fictional heroes display courage. Choose a novel or play you have read and write an essay defining courage and explaining how the hero displays it.

In fiction as in life, characters often undergo personal struggles. Choose a novel or play you have read and compare and contrast the personal struggles of two characters in the story.

Identify two novels and write an essay comparing and contrasting what each has to say about one of the following: death, prejudice, poverty, injustice, cowardice.

Many pieces of literature are about journeys. Choose a novel or play and write an essay about the journey taken—and its outcome. Be sure to describe the physical journey taken and the personal growth the character experienced along the way.

Stories from different cultures often teach us something about those cultures. Identify a work of literature that describes a particular custom. Select an episode in which that custom is described and explain in an essay what the practice is and what it teaches you about the culture from which it comes.

Young fictional characters in different stories often share common concerns. Identify two young characters in two separate stories, novels, or plays and explain in an essay how they go face similar problems.

Appearance and reality are often two very different things in real life, and this is a common theme in literature as well. Choose a piece of literature and write an essay about how appearance and reality are at odds in one episode from that story.

And finally...

GOOD LUCK! You won't need it, though, because you have something even better—you've got all the skill and preparation it takes to be a winner!

Part III

The Practice Tests

Chapter 7
MCAS ELA Practice Test 1

The following selection is an excerpt from a novel by Mark Twain, The Tragedy of Pudd'nhead Wilson. *As you read the excerpt, try to "hear" the voices of the townspeople as they discuss their newest resident. When you have finished reading, answer the questions that follow.*

The Tragedy of Pudd'nhead Wilson

by Mark Twain

1 ...In that same month of February, Dawson's Landing gained a new citizen. This was Mr. David Wilson, a young fellow of Scotch parentage. He had wandered to this remote region from his birthplace in the interior of the State of New York, to seek his fortune. He was twenty-five years old, college bred, and had finished a post-college course in an Eastern law school a couple of years before.

2 He was a homely, freckled, sandy-haired young fellow, with an intelligent blue eye that had frankness and comradeship in it and a covert twinkle of a pleasant sort. But for an unfortunate remark of his, he would no doubt have entered at once upon a successful career at Dawson's Landing. But he made his fatal remark the first day he spent in the village, and it "gaged" him. He had just made the acquaintance of a group of citizens when an invisible dog began to yelp and snarl and howl and make himself very comprehensively disagreeable, whereupon young Wilson said, much as one who is thinking aloud:

3 "I wish I owned half of that dog."

4 "Why?" somebody asked.

5 "Because I would kill my half."

6 The group searched his face with curiosity, with anxiety even, but found no light there, no expression that they could read. They fell away from him as from something uncanny, and went into privacy to discuss him. One said:

7 "'Pears to be a fool."

8 "'Pears?' said another. "'*Is*' I reckon you better say."

9 "Said he wished he owned *half* of the dog, the idiot," said a third. "What did he reckon would become of the other half if he killed his half? Do you reckon he thought it would live?"

10 "Why, he must have thought it, unless he IS the downrightest fool in the world; because if he hadn't thought it, he would have wanted to own the whole dog, knowing that if he killed his half and the other half died, he would be responsible for that half just the same as if he had killed that half instead of his own. Don't it look that way to you, gents?"

11 "Yes, it does. If he owned one half of the general dog, it would be so; if he owned one end of the dog and another person owned the other end, it would be so, just the same; particularly in the first case, because if you kill one half of a general dog, there ain't any man that can tell whose half it was; but if he owned one end of the dog, maybe he could kill his end of it and—"

12 "No, he couldn't either; he couldn't and not be responsible if the other end died, which it would. In my opinion that man ain't in his right mind."

13 "In my opinion he hain't *got* any mind."

14 No. 3 said: "Well, he's a lummox, anyway."

15 "That's what he is;" said No. 4. "He's a labrick— just a Simon-pure labrick, if there was one."

16 "Yes, sir, he's a fool. That's the way I put him up," said No. 5. "Anybody can think different that wants to, but those are my sentiments."

17 "I'm with you, gentlemen," said No. 6. "Perfect jackass—yes, and it ain't going too far to say he is a pudd'nhead. If he ain't a pudd'nhead, I ain't no judge, that's all."

18 Mr. Wilson stood elected. The incident was told all over the town, and gravely discussed by everybody. Within a week he had lost his first name; Pudd'nhead took its place. In time he came to be liked, and well liked too; but by that time the nickname had got well stuck on, and it stayed. That first day's verdict made him a fool, and he was not able to get it set aside, or even modified. The nickname soon ceased to carry any harsh or unfriendly feeling with it, but it held its place, and was to continue to hold its place for twenty long years.

1. What is the setting of this excerpt?

   A. Scotland

   B. an Eastern law school

   C. New York

   D. Dawson's Landing

2. The first two sentences of paragraph 6 say, "The group searched his face with curiosity, with anxiety even, but found no light there, no expression that they could read. They fell away from him as from something uncanny, and went into privacy to discuss him." What does this show about the group's reaction to the newcomer?

   A. They are awed by this mysterious man, with his enigmatic manner.

   B. They are worshipful of this man, who seems omnipotent.

   C. They are afraid of this man, who seems threatening.

   D. They are disturbed by this man, whom they do not understand.

3. In paragraph 13, what does the word *lummox* mean?

   A. newcomer

   B. a clumsy person

   C. obvious

   D. offensive

   ver•dict (vur' dikt) 1. In law, the finding of a jury given in court 2. a judgment; decision [ME<verdit AF<L *verum dictum*, true word]

4. According to the dictionary entry above, in which language did the word *verdict* originate?

   A. Latin

   B. Greek

   C. Swahili

   D. German

5. This excerpt can best be described as

   A. informational writing.

   B. persuasive writing.

   C. humorous writing.

   D. nature writing.

6. David Wilson is characterized by the narrator as

   A. candid and forthright.

   B. handsome and affected.

   C. tactless and rude.

   D. ignorant and cruel.

7. What is the significance of the title of Twain's novel, "The Tragedy of Pudd'nhead Wilson"? What does it indicate about the central theme of the story? Support your answer with evidence from this excerpt.

In this excerpt from Narrative of the Life of Frederick Douglass, An American Slave, *Douglass describes his escape from slavery. When you have finished reading, answer the questions that follow.*

Narrative of the Life of Frederick Douglass

by Frederick Douglass

1   I now come to that part of my life during which I planned, and finally succeeded in making, my escape from slavery. But before narrating any of the peculiar circumstances, I deem it proper to make known my intention not to state all the facts connected with the transaction. My reasons for pursuing this course may be understood from the following: First, were I to give a minute statement of all the facts, it is not only possible, but quite probable, that others would thereby be involved in the most embarrassing difficulties. Secondly, such a statement would most undoubtedly induce greater vigilance on the part of slaveholders than has existed heretofore among them; which would, of course, be the means of guarding a door whereby some dear brother bondman might escape his galling chains. I deeply regret the necessity that impels me to suppress any thing of importance connected with my experience in slavery. It would afford me great pleasure indeed, as well as materially add to the interest of my narrative, were I at liberty to gratify a curiosity, which I know exists in the minds of many, by an accurate statement of all the facts pertaining to my most fortunate escape. But I must deprive myself of this pleasure, and the curious of the gratification which such a statement would afford...

2   My object in working steadily [for my master] was to remove any suspicion he might entertain of my intent to run away; and in this I succeeded admirably. I suppose he thought I was never better satisfied with my condition than at the very time during which I was planning my escape. The second week passed, and again I carried him my full wages; and so well pleased was he, that he gave me twenty-five cents (quite a large sum for a slaveholder to give a slave), and bade me to make a good use of it. I told him I would.

3   Things went on without very smoothly indeed, but within there was trouble. It is impossible for me to describe my feelings as the time of my contemplated start drew near. I had a number of warm-hearted friends in Baltimore—friends that I loved almost as I did my life—and the thought of being separated from them forever was painful beyond expression. It is my opinion that thousands would escape from slavery, who now remain, but for the strong cords of affection that bind them to their friends. The thought of leaving my friends was decidedly the most painful thought with which I had to contend. The love of them was my tender point, and shook my decision more than all things else. Besides the pain of separation, the dread and apprehension of a failure exceeded what I had experienced at my first attempt. The appalling defeat I then sustained returned to torment me. I felt assured that, if I failed in this attempt, my case would be a hopeless one—it would seal my fate as a slave forever. I could not hope to get off with any thing less than the severest punishment, and being placed beyond the means of escape. It required no very vivid imagination to depict the most frightful scenes through which I should have to pass, in case I failed. The wretchedness of slavery, and the blessedness of freedom, were perpetually before me. It was life and death with me. But I remained firm, and, according to my resolution, on the third day of September, 1838, I left my chains, and succeeded in reaching New York without the slightest interruption of any kind. How I did so—what means I adopted, what direction I traveled, and by what mode of conveyance—I must leave unexplained, for the reasons before mentioned.

4   I have been frequently asked how I felt when I found myself in a free State. I have never been able to answer the question with any satisfaction to myself. It was a moment of the highest excitement I ever experienced. I suppose I felt as one may imagine the unarmed mariner to feel when he is rescued by a friendly man-of-war from the pursuit of a pirate. In writing to a dear friend, immediately after my arrival at New York, I said I felt like one who had escaped a den of hungry lions. This state of mind, however, very soon subsided; and I was

again seized with a feeling of great insecurity and loneliness. I was yet liable to be taken back, and subjected to all the tortures of slavery. This in itself was enough to damp the ardor of my enthusiasm. . . . I was afraid to speak to any one for fear of speaking to the wrong one, and thereby falling into the hands of money-loving kidnappers, whose business it was to lie in wait for the panting fugitive, as the ferocious beasts of the forest lie in wait for their prey. . .

5 It was a most painful situation; and, to understand it, one must needs experience it, or imagine himself in similar circumstances. Let him be a fugitive slave in a strange land—a land given up to be the hunting-ground for slaveholders—whose inhabitants are legalized kidnappers—where he is every moment subjected to the terrible liability of being seized upon by his fellowmen, as the hideous crocodile seizes upon his prey!—I say, let him place himself in my situation—without home or friends—without money or credit—wanting shelter, and no one to give it—wanting bread, and no money to buy it,—and at the same time let him feel that he is pursued by merciless men-hunters, and in total darkness as to what to do, where to go, or where to stay— perfectly helpless both as to the means of defense and means of escape—in the midst of plenty, yet suffering the terrible gnawings of hunger—in the midst of houses, yet having no home . . . I say, let him be placed in this most trying situation—the situation in which I was placed—then, and not till then, will he fully appreciate the hardships of, and know how to sympathize with, the toil-worn and whip-scarred fugitive slave.

8. Which word is closest to the meaning of *vigilance* in paragraph 1?

   A. carelessness

   B. cruel

   C. greed

   D. watchfulness

9. The author mentions his friends in Baltimore, because

   A. they made life miserable for Douglass.

   B. they assisted Douglass in making his escape plans.

   C. Douglass wants to thank them.

   D. Douglass wants readers to know how conflicted he felt about escape.

10. In paragraph 4, what does the word *mariner* mean?

    A. fisherman

    B. sailor

    C. hostage

    D. slave

11. This excerpt is an example of a(n)

    A. biography.

    B. autobiography.

    C. satire.

    D. persuasion.

12. What does the author want the reader to remember most from this excerpt?

    A. The wretchedness of slavery and the hardship of his escape.

    B. The assistance the author received after his escape from slavery.

    C. The utter release and joy experienced after his escape from slavery.

    D. The importance of helping people who are alone in a strange city.

13. The author's tone could be characterized as

    A. woeful.

    B. angry.

    C. concerned.

    D. objective.

14. Why was the decision about whether or not to attempt escape a difficult one for Douglass? What were the pros and cons he considered, and how did he make his decision? Use specific information from the excerpt to support your answer.

These lines are excerpted from "Song of Myself," the first of 12 poems in Leaves of Grass, by Walt Whitman. Read the excerpt and then answer the questions that follow.

"Song of Myself"

by Walt Whitman

I CELEBRATE myself,
 And what I assume you shall assume,
For every atom belonging to me, as good belongs
 to you.
I loafe and invite my Soul,
5 I lean and loafe at my ease, observing a spear of
summer grass...

Houses and rooms are full of perfumes-the
shelves are crowded with perfumes,
I breathe the fragrance myself, and know it and
10 like it,
The distillation would intoxicate me also, but I
shall not let it.
The atmosphere is not a perfume, it has no taste
of the distillation, it is odorless,...

15 My respiration and inspiration, the beating of my heart, the passing of
blood and air through my lungs,
The sniff of green leaves and dry leaves, and of
the shore, and dark-colored sea-rocks, and of
hay in the barn,
20 The sound of the belched words of my voice,
words loosed to the eddies of the wind,
A few light kisses, a few embraces, a reaching
 around of arms,
The play of shine and shade on the trees as the
25 supple boughs wag,
The delight alone, or in the rush of the streets, or
along the fields and hill-sides,
The feeling of health, the full-noon trill, the song
of me rising from bed and meeting the sun.

15. Which is a motif of this poem?

    A. inequality among human beings

    B. the meaninglessness of existence

    C. the corruption of the human spirit

    D. the inseparableness of body and soul

16. The word "loafe" is best defined as meaning

    A. idle.

    B. exultant.

    C. dance.

    D. race.

17. What is the best word to describe the tone throughout this poem?

    A. self-congratulatory

    B. exultant

    C. cautionary

    D. disapproving

18. The word *supple* most means

    A. playful.

    B. shady.

    C. flexible.

    D. heavy.

19. This poem is an example of

    A. metered poetry.

    B. a sonnet.

    C. blank verse.

    D. free verse.

20. In line 24, "the play of shine and shade on the trees..."what part of speech are the words "shine" and "shade"?

A. noun

B. verb

C. adjective

D. adverb

Writing Prompt, Sessions 2A and 2B Composition

21. BACKGROUND FOR WRITING

The following paragraphs are from the opening of a short story by Nathaniel Hawthorne. It is sunset and a young man has just given his new wife a parting kiss. When you have finished reading the excerpt, complete the writing assignment that follows.

So they parted; and the young man pursued his way until, being about to turn the corner by the meeting-house, he looked back and saw the head of Faith still peeping after him with a melancholy air, in spite of her pink ribbons.

"Poor little Faith!" thought he, for his heart smote him. "What a wretch am I to leave her on such an errand! She talks of dreams, too. Methought as she spoke there was trouble in her face, as if a dream had warned her what work was to be done tonight. But no, no; 't would kill her to think it. Well, she's a blessed angel on earth; and after this one night I'll cling to her skirts and follow her to heaven."

With this excellent resolve for the future, Goodman Brown felt himself justified in making more haste on his present evil purpose. He had taken a dreary road, darkened by all the gloomiest trees of the forest, which barely stood aside to let the narrow path creep through, and closed immediately behind. It was all as lonely as could be; and there is this peculiarity in such a solitude, that the traveler knows not who may be concealed by the innumerable trunks and the thick boughs overhead; so that with lonely footsteps he may yet be passing through an unseen multitude.

WRITING ASSIGNMENT

Consider the atmosphere in the passage above. Write an essay that describes the atmosphere and analyzes how Hawthorne conveys it. In developing your essay, you might want to consider such elements as imagery, diction, setting, and characterization.

The following selection contains instructions for following the Freedom Trail in Boston. Read the instructions carefully and then answer the questions that follow.

Freedom Trail

1   Most of the Boston National Historical Park sites are connected by the Freedom Trail. Recognized as a National Recreation Trail, the 3-mile trail is a walking tour of 16 sites and structures of historic importance in downtown Boston and Charlestown.

2   Ninety-minute tours begin at the Visitor Center at 15 State Street and cover the heart of the Freedom Trail from the Old South Meeting House to the Old North Church. Tours leave at regular intervals in the spring, summer, and fall, weather permitting. Call (617) 242-5642 for daily schedule or (617) 242-5689 for group reservations.

3   Begin your tour of the Freedom Trail at Boston Common, land purchased in 1634 as a militia "trayning field" and for the "feeding of Cattell." During the battle of Bunker Hill the British embarked for Charlestown from the Common. Artist Gilbert Stuart is buried in the Central Burying Ground.

4   The gold-domed Massachusetts State House sits at the crest of Beacon Hill, overlooking Boston Common. Designed by Charles Bullfinch and completed in 1798, the "new" State House is still the home of the Massachusetts legislature.

5   Located opposite the State House is the monument to Robert Gould Shaw and the 54th Massachusetts Regiment, the starting point for the Black Heritage Trail.

6   Hours: 9:00 a.m. - 5:00 p.m., Monday through Friday. Thirty-minute guided tours of the State House are available 10:00 a.m. - 4:00 p.m., Monday through Friday, except holidays. Call (617) 727-3676 for more information.

7   Admission: Free

8   Park Street Church

9   Built in 1809, Park Street Church stands on "Brimstone Corner" — a name that refers to the sermons that were delivered here and to the gunpowder that was stored in the church's basement during the War of 1812. William Lloyd Garrison gave his first antislavery speech in Park Street Church.

10   Granary Burying Ground

11   Adjacent to Park Street Church is the Granary Burying Ground, where many notable Americans are interred including Declaration of Independence signers John Hancock, Robert Treat Paine, and Samuel Adams. Also buried here are the victims of the Boston Massacre.

22. The main purpose of this article is to

    A. convince readers that walking the Freedom Trail is an educational experience.

    B. provide clear directions about how to get from one point to the next.

    C. inform walkers about the historic significance of each site.

    D. prove that Boston contains the most important sites in our nation's history.

23. What style of English characterizes the quotes in the first sentence in paragraph 3: "Begin your tour of the Freedom Trail at Boston Common, land purchased in 1634 as a militia 'trayning field' and for the 'feeding of Cattell'?"

    A. archaic

    B. dialect

    C. slang

    D. informal

24. When would it be possible to take a tour of the State House?

    A. Memorial Day

    B. Monday at 8:00 a.m.

    C. Saturday at 9:00 a.m.

    D. Friday afternoon

25. Which of the following is true of Park Street Church?

    A. Tranquil anti-war sermons were often delivered there.

    B. Gunpowder was stored there during the Civil War.

    C. A famous abolitionist gave his first speech there.

    D. It was rebuilt after being blown up during the War of 1812.

26. In paragraph 8, what does the word *interred* mean?

    A. buried

    B. listed

    C. remembered

    D. shown

27. Which type of information is NOT found in this trail guide?

    A. The guide suggests a sequence for making stops along the trail.

    B. The guide details when various sites along the trail are open and what they cost.

    C. The guide details when the trail was designed and by whom.

    D. The guide describes each site found along the trail.

28. Suppose someone dropped you off at the Granary Burying Ground. You decided to backtrack along the Freedom Trail to where it begins. Describe in a paragraph where you would go and what you would see.

This excerpt is from Act 3 Scene 1 of Much Ado about Nothing *by William Shakespeare. Read the excerpt and then answer the questions that follow.*

Much Ado About Nothing

by William Shakespeare

HERO: Now, Ursula, when Beatrice doth come,

As we do trace this alley up and down,

Our talk must only be of Benedick:

When I do name him, let it be thy part

5　To praise him more than ever man did merit.

My talk to thee must be how Benedick

Is sick in love with Beatrice: of this matter

Is little Cupid's crafty arrow made,

That only wounds by hearsay.

10　[Enter BEATRICE, behind.]

Now begin;

For look where Beatrice, like a lapwing, runs

Close by the ground, to hear our conference.

URSULA: The pleasant'st angling is to see the fish

15　Cut with her golden oars the silver stream,

And greedily devour the treacherous bait:

So angle we for Beatrice; who even now

Is couched in the woodbine coverture.

Fear you not my part of the dialogue.

HERO: Then go we near her, that her ear lose

20　nothing

Of the false sweet bait that we lay for it. . .

[They advance to the bower.]

URSULA: But are you sure

That Benedick loves Beatrice so entirely?

HERO: So says the prince, and my new-trothed

25　lord.

O god of love! I know he doth deserve

As much as may be yielded to a man;

But nature never fram'd a woman's heart

Of prouder stuff than that of Beatrice;

30　Disdain and scorn ride sparkling in her eyes,

Misprising what they look on, and her wit

Values itself so highly, that to her

All matter else seems weak. She cannot love,

Nor take no shape nor project of affection,

35　She is so self-endear'd.

URSULA: Sure I think so; And therefore certainly it were not good

She knew his love, lest she make sport at it.

HERO: No; rather I will go to Benedick,

And counsel him to fight against his passion.

40　And, truly, I'll devise some honest slanders

To stain my cousin with. One doth not know

How much an ill word may empoison liking.

URSULA: O! do not do your cousin such a wrong.

She cannot be so much without true judgment,—

45　Having so swift and excellent a wit

As she is priz'd to have,—as to refuse

So rare a gentleman as Signior Benedick.

29. This excerpt describes a conversation

    A. between Hero, Ursula, and Beatrice.

    B. that Hero and Ursula want Beatrice to overhear.

    C. from which Hero and Ursula deliberately exclude Beatrice.

    D. that Beatrice and Hero have about Ursula and Benedick.

30. Hero says:

    Our talk must only be of Benedick:
    When I do name him, let it be thy part
    To praise him more than ever man did merit.
    My talk to thee must be how Benedick
    Is sick in love with Beatrice: of this matter
    Is little Cupid's crafty arrow made,
    That only wounds by hearsay.

    Based on these lines, Hero apparently believes which of the following to be true?

    A. You need to protect your girlfriends from making the wrong choices in men.

    B. Men should be warned against loud, complaining woman.

    C. Anyone who is rude enough to eavesdrop deserves to be hurt by what they hear.

    D. There's nothing wrong with a little deception by matchmakers.

31. In lines 13-16, what literary device does Shakespeare use?

    A. metaphor

    B. alliteration

    C. simile

    D. rhyme scheme

32. In line 25, when Hero mentioned "my new-trothed lord," to whom is she referring?

    A. the Lord of the region

    B. her husband

    C. Benedick

    D. Beatrice

33. Here is Ursula's statement:

"She cannot be so much without true judgement
Having so swift and excellent a wit
As she is priz'd to have—as to refuse
So rare a gentleman as Signior Benedick."

Which of the following is the correct rhyme scheme for these lines?

A. ABAB

B. ABCB

C. ABCD

D. ABAA

34. From this passage, you can surmise that *Much Ado About Nothing* is:

A. a comedy

B. a tragedy

C. propaganda

D. a narrative

35. Summarize this scene. Include the physical setting, the positions of the three characters, the nature of the conversation, and its impact on Beatrice. Use specific details from the passage to support your answer.

On January 20, 1997, President Clinton gave his second Inaugural Address. Read the following excerpt from that speech carefully, and then answer the questions that follow it.

Second Inaugural Address

by President William Jefferson Clinton

1 My fellow citizens: At this last presidential inauguration of the 20th century, let us lift our eyes toward the challenges that await us in the next century...

2 The future is up to us. Our founders taught us that the preservation of our liberty and our union depends upon responsible citizenship. And we need a new sense of responsibility for a new century. There is work to do, work that government alone cannot do: teaching children to read; hiring people off welfare rolls; coming out from behind locked doors and shuttered windows to help reclaim our streets from drugs and gangs and crime; taking time out of our own lives to serve others.

3 Each and every one of us, in our own way, must assume personal responsibility—not only for ourselves and our families, but for our neighbors and our nation. Our greatest responsibility is to embrace a new spirit of community for a new century. For any one of us to succeed, we must succeed as one America.

4 ...My fellow Americans, as we look back at this remarkable century, we may ask, can we hope not just to follow, but even to surpass the achievements of the 20th century in America and to avoid the awful bloodshed that stained its legacy? To that question, every American here and every American in our land today must answer a resounding "Yes."

5 This is the heart of our task. With a new vision of government, a new sense of responsibility, a new spirit of community, we will sustain America's journey. The promise we sought in a new land we will find again in a land of new promise.

6 In this new land, education will be every citizen's most prized possession. Our schools will have the highest standards in the world, igniting the spark of possibility in the eyes of every girl and every boy. And the doors of higher education will be open to all. The knowledge and power of the Information Age will be within reach not just of the few, but of every classroom, every library, every child. Parents and children will have time not only to work, but to read and play together. And the plans they make at their kitchen table will be those of a better home, a better job, the certain chance to go to college.

7 Our streets will echo again with the laughter of our children, because no one will try to shoot them or sell them drugs anymore. Everyone who can work, will work, with today's permanent under class part of tomorrow's growing middle class. New miracles of medicine at last will reach not only those who can claim care now, but the children and hardworking families too long denied...

8 Fellow citizens, let us build that America, a nation ever moving forward toward realizing the full potential of all its citizens.

36. According to Clinton, what Americans need above all else for the new, 21st century is

    A. a government that will teach children to read.

    B. a government that will reclaim the streets from criminals.

    C. responsible citizens who will work together.

    D. a nation where environmental protection receives priority over economic growth.

37. The statement that, "Our schools will have the highest standards in the world, igniting the spark of possibility in the eyes of every girl and every boy" is an example of

    A. irony.

    B. alliteration.

    C. metaphor.

    D. personification.

38. What is the tone of this speech?

    A. hopeful and exhortatory

    B. exhilarated and blissful

    C. harsh and cynical

    D. admonishing and cautioning

39. Based on the ideas in this speech, what do you think Clinton would support?

    A. Expanding the Department of Education.

    B. Encouraging students to perform volunteer work.

    C. Reducing government spending on drug abuse prevention.

    D. Eliminating federal programs for monitoring gangs.

40. What does President Clinton believe a good citizen's duty to be? Use specific information from the speech to explain Clinton's ideas about a citizen's duty. Give examples from the passage of how a citizen can fulfill that duty.

The following is an excerpt from the introduction by Neil Parsons to Native Life in South Africa *by Solomon Plaatje. Read the excerpt carefully, keeping the function of introductions in mind, and then answer the questions that follow.*

Introduction to Native Life in South Africa by Solomon Plaatje

by Neil Parsons

1   *Native Life in South Africa* is one of the most remarkable books on Africa, by one of the continent's most remarkable writers. It was written as a work of impassioned political propaganda, exposing the plight of black South Africans under the whites-only government of newly unified South Africa...But *Native Life* succeeds in being much more than a work of propaganda. It is a vital social document which captures the spirit of an age and shows the effects of rural segregation on the everyday life of people.

2   Solomon Tshekeisho Plaatje was born in 1878 in the lands of the Tswana-speaking people, south of Mafeking. His origins were ordinary enough. What was remarkable was the aptitude he showed for education and learning after a few years schooling under the tuition of a remarkable liberal German Lutheran missionary, the Rev. Ludorf.

3   At the age of sixteen Plaatje (using the Dutch nickname of his grandfather as a surname) joined the Post Office as a mail-carrier in Kimberley, the diamond city in the north of Cape Colony. He subsequently passed the highest clerical examination in the colony, beating every white candidate in both Dutch and typing.

4   From Kimberley the young Plaatje went on to Mafeking, where he was one of the key players in the great siege of 1899-1900. As magistrate's interpreter he was the vital link between the British civil authorities and the African majority beleaguered inside the town's military perimeter. Plaatje's diaries from this period, published long after his death, are a remarkable record both of the siege and of his early prose experimentation—mixing languages and idioms, and full of bright humour.

5   After the war Plaatje became a journalist, editor first of one Tswana language newspaper at Mafeking and then of another at Kimberley. ...Plaatje's aggravation with the British government can be seen in an unpublished manuscript of 1908-09 titled "Sekgoma — the Black Dreyfus". In this booklet he castigated the British for denying legal rights (specifically habeas corpus) to their African subjects outside the Cape Colony.

6   Plaatje became politically active in the "native congress" movement which represented the interests of educated and propertied Africans all over South Africa. He was the first secretary-general of the "South African Native National Congress", founded in 1912 (which renamed itself as the African National Congress or ANC ten years later)...

7   Its national executive sent a delegation to England, including Plaatje, who set sail in mid-1914... The delegation received short shrift from the government in London which was, after all, more than preoccupied with the coming of the Great War—in which it feared for the loyalty of the recently defeated Afrikaners and wished in no way to offend them. But, rather than return empty-handed like the rest of the SANNC delegation, Plaatje decided to stay in England to carry on the fight. He was determined to recruit, through writing and lecturing, the liberal and humanitarian establishment to his side—so that it in turn might pressure the British government.

8 Thus it was that Plaatje resumed work on a manuscript he had begun on the ship to England, *Native Life in South Africa*. The book was published in 1916 by P. S. King in London.... While in England, Plaatje pursued his interests in language and linguistics by collaborating with Professor Daniel Jones of the University of London —inventor of the International Phonetic Alphabet (IPA) and prototype for Professor Higgins in Shaw's *Pygmalion*, and thus the musical *My Fair Lady*.

9 In the same year as *Native Life* was published, 1916, Plaatje published two other shorter books which brought together the European languages (English, Dutch and German) he loved with the Tswana language...Disillusioned with the flabby friendship of British liberals, Plaatje was increasingly drawn to the pan-Africanism of W. E. B. DuBois, president of the NAACP in the United States. In 1921 Plaatje sailed for the United States on a lecture tour that took him through half the country...In the following year, after Plaatje had left, this new edition of *Native Life in South Africa* was published, by the NAACP newspaper *The Crisis*, edited by DuBois.

10 ...He turned from politics and devoted the rest of his life to literature. His passion for Shakespeare resulted in mellifluous Tswana translations of five plays from *Comedy of Errors* to *Merchant of Venice* and *Julius Caesar*. His passion for the history of his people, and of his family in particular, resulted in a historical novel, *Mhudi (An Epic of South African Native Life a Hundred Years Ago)*, dedicated to his daughter Olive who had died in the influenza epidemic while Plaatje was overseas—described in the dedication as "one of the many victims of a settled system..." It has since been republished in more pristine form and is today considered not just the first but one of the very best novels published by a black South African writer in English.

11 Plaatje lived an extraordinary life but died a largely disappointed man. His feats of political journalism had been largely forgotten and his creative talents had hardly yet been recognised— except in the confined world of Tswana language readership. But today Plaatje is regarded as a South African literary pioneer, as a not insignificant political actor in his time, and as a cogent commentator on his times. He was an explorer in a fascinating world of cultural and linguistic interaction, who was in retrospect truly a "renaissance man".

41. Before going to Mafeking, Plaatje

    A. wrote *Sekgoma*.

    B. translated Shakespeare's plays.

    C. collaborated with Professor Jones on IPA.

    D. carried mail in Kimberley.

42. According to Neil Parsons, when did Plaatje begin work on *Native Life in South Africa?*

    A. When he was en route to America

    B. While he was in England

    C. When he visited Nairobi in Kenya

    D. While on board a ship to England.

43. In paragraph 6, why does the author mention the musical *My Fair Lady*?

    A. He wants to illustrate Plaatje's interest in the theater.

    B. He wants to support the idea that Plaatje was interested in linguistics.

    C. He wants to defend the argument that IPA is more logical than other alphabets.

    D. He wants to imply that Plaatje and Professor Higgins both considered dialect a determinant of social status.

44. In paragraph 7, what is the main clause of the opening sentence?

    A. "In the same year as *Native Life* was published"

    B. "Plaatje published two other shorter books"

    C. "which brought together the European languages (English, Dutch and German)"

    D. "he loved with the Tswana language."

45. *Mellifluous* is best defined as meaning

    A. harsh.

    B. gutteral.

    C. pleasing to the ear.

    D. pleasing to the palate.

46. Which of the following is not offered in the selection as a reason why *Native Life in South Africa* is a remarkable book?

A. It exposed the plight of black South Africans under the whites-only government.

B. It captures the spirit of an age.

C. It shows the effects of rural segregation on the everyday life of people.

D. It is one of the most beautifully written novels in the English language.

47. Using information from the excerpt, explain why Plaatje is considered a pioneer in both literature and politics.

This excerpt is from Episode Six, lines 1110-1185, of Oedipus Rex *by Sophocles. In this famous tragedy, Oedipus (son of Laius and Jocasta) learns that he has unwittingly killed his father and married his mother. Read the excerpt and then answer the questions that follow.*

Oedipus Rex

by Sophocles

[1110] **Oedipus:** Elders, if it is right for me, who have never met the man,

to guess, I think I see the herdsman we have been looking for a long time. In

his venerable old age he tallies with this stranger's years, and moreover I

recognize those who bring him, I think, as servants of mine.

[1115] But perhaps you have an advantage in knowledge over me, if you have seen the

herdsman before.

Chorus: Yes, I know him, be sure. He was in the service of Laius—trusty as

any shepherd.

[The herdsman is brought in.]

Oedipus: I ask you first, Corinthian stranger, if this is the man you mean.

[1120] **Messenger:** He is, the one you are looking at.

Oedipus: You, old man—look this way and answer all that I ask—were you once

in the service of Laius?

Servant: I was...

[1125] For the better part of my life I tended the flocks.

Oedipus: Are you aware of ever having seen this man in these parts?

Servant: Doing what? What man do you mean?

[1130] **Oedipus:** This man here. Have you ever met him before?

Servant: Not so that I could speak at once from memory.

Messenger: And no wonder, master. But I will bring clear recollection to his

ignorance. I am sure he knows well of the time we dwelled in the region of

[1135] **Cithaeron:** for six month periods...he with two

flocks, and I, his comrade, with one...

[1140] **Oedipus:** Did any of this happen as I tell it, or did it not?

Servant: You speak the truth, though it was long ago.

Messenger: Come, tell me now: do you remember having given me a boy in those

days, to be reared as my own foster-son?

Servant: What now? Why do you ask the question?

[1145] **Messenger:** This man, my friend, is he who then was young.

Servant: Damn you! Be silent once and for all!

Oedipus: Do not rebuke him, old man. Your words need rebuking more than his.

Servant: And in what way, most noble master, do I offend?

[1150] **Oedipus:** In not telling of the boy about whom he asks.

Servant: He speaks without knowledge, but is busy to no purpose.

Oedipus: You will not speak with good grace, but will in pain.

Servant: No, in the name of the gods, do not mistreat an old man.

Oedipus: Someone, quick—tie his hands him this instant!

[1155] **Servant:** Alas, why? What do you want to learn?

Oedipus: Did you give this man the child about whom he asks?

Servant: I did. Would that I had perished that day!...

[1160] **Oedipus:** This man is bent, I think, on more delays.

Servant: No, no! I said before that I gave it to him.

Oedipus: Where did you get it from? From your own house, or from another?

Servant: It was not my own: I received it from another.

Oedipus: From whom of the citizens here? From what home?

[1165] **Servant:** For the love of the gods, master, ask no more!

Oedipus: You are dead if I have to question you again.

Servant: It was a child, then, of the house of Laius.

Alas! I am on the brink of speaking the dreaded words.

Oedipus: [1170] And I of hearing: I must hear nevertheless.

Servant: You must know then, that it was said to be his own child. But your

lady within could say best how these matters lie.

Oedipus: How? Did she give it to you?

Servant: Yes, my lord.

Oedipus: For what purpose?

Servant: That I should do away with it.

[1175] **Oedipus:** Her own child, the wretched woman?

Servant: Yes, from fear of the evil prophecies.

Oedipus: What were they?

Servant: The tale ran that he would slay his father.

Oedipus: Why, then, did you give him to this old man?

Servant: Out of pity, master, thinking that he would carry him to another

land, from where he himself came. But he saved him for the direst woe.

[1180] For if you are what this man says, be certain that you were born

ill-fated.

Oedipus: Oh, oh! All brought to pass, all true. Light, may I now look on you

for the last time—I who have been found to be accursed in birth,

[1185]accursed in wedlock, accursed in the shedding of blood.

[He rushes into the palace.]

48. In line 1152 Oedipus tells the Servant, "You will not speak with good grace, but will in pain." Oedipus is

    A. threatening the servant with physical punishment if he does not tell what he knows.

    B. sympathizing with the servant, who has traveled far on arthritic legs to speak to the king.

    C. berating the servant for tactlessness in saying something hurtful about the messenger.

    D. suggesting that the servant will be rewarded for his pains if he reveals what Oedipus wants to know.

49. The servant exclaims in line 1165, "For the love of gods, master, ask no more!" The function of the commas is to punctuate

    A. a noun in apposition.

    B. a noun in direct address.

    C. an interrupting expression.

    D. an introductory clause.

50. Which of the following terms is derived from this story by Sophocles?

    A. Garden of Eden

    B. sophisticated

    C. Oedipal complex

    D. edition princeps

51. The Servant explains that Jocasta instructed him to kill her son because she was

    A. jealous.

    B. afraid.

    C. insane.

    D. evil.

52. Lines 1182-1185, where Oedipus says, "Light, may I now look on you for the last time—I who have been found to be accursed in birth, accursed in wedlock, accursed in the shedding of blood." contain an example of

    A. a rhetorical question.

    B. an apostrophe.

    C. a hyperbole.

    D. symbolism.

Chapter 8

Answer Key for MCAS ELA Practice Test 1

1 **D** Many times, the trick to answering multiple-choice questions correctly is to avoid being led astray by choices mentioned in the passage but presented out of context or incorrectly in the answers. Always look for the answer in the text first. Sure enough, the first sentence tells you that the story takes place in Dawson's Landing. The newcomer's ancestors were from Scotland, he had lived in New York, and he had gotten to an Eastern law school, but these places are not the ones where the scene with Wilson and the men occurs.

2 **D** The words *curiosity* and *anxiety* tell you that these guys don't know what to make of this newcomer, but he makes them nervous. By POE, you can cross off *A* and *B*; you're not looking for an answer with anything like *admiration* or *awe* in it. *C* seems weaker than *D*, because while the men find the new guy pretty weird, the passage says "there was no expression to be read." They're puzzled, not *fearful*. That leaves *D*, which fits the questions well. They are disturbed by the newcomer because they don't understand him.

3 **B** Chances are, you don't use the word *lummox* often. Turn to the passage and dig out clues about the word. One speaker is saying Mr. Wilson has no mind, the next guy says that Mr. Wilson's *a lummox.* The word you're looking for is a noun, and it's no compliment. You can eliminate *C* and *D*, both adjectives. But how are you going to pick between *A, dimwit,* and *B, a clumsy person*. You might have to guess and know that you improved your odds

two-fold. Are they saying all this dialogue because they think Mr. Wilson's a newcomer? That's not the focus at all. They're insulting him —go with **B**, a choice that makes the most sense in this context.

4 **A** Look in the brackets at the end of a dictionary entry to find the word's origins (see page 38). There you find that our word *verdict* comes from the Latin (L) phrase *verum dictum*, meaning true word. (It later went through Anglo-French and Middle English forms, but the question asks where the word *originated* or began.)

5 **C** Humorous writing is intended to make readers smile (see page 39). Did you find this group of men funny when they misunderstood the newcomer by taking him literally? Use POE. The passage is *not* intended to inform with facts, convince with arguments, or reveal the wonders of nature—so you can get rid of *A, B,* and *D*.

6 **A** The narrator uses the words "frankness," "comradeship," and "pleasant," to describe Wilson. Thus, by POE you can eliminate the negative descriptions in C and D. Look at the text. Wilson is "homely," or plain. "Handsome" doesn't fit here—so eliminate B. That leaves you with A, which also makes perfect sense. Anyone known for "frankness" is candid and forthright.

7   Here are two good 4-point open-responses to this question. They each employ ample, or complete, evidence from Twain's story and they each make a well organized point.

> Sample A: The title of Twain's novel refers to the nickname of one of his central characters. On his first day in Dawson's Landing, David Wilson, a young lawyer, earned that unfortunate nickname by making a remark that was misunderstood. Annoyed by the howling of an unseen dog, Wilson jokingly said that he wished he owned half the dog so that he could kill his half. Taking him literally, a group of men from town decided that he was a fool. After all, both halves would die, so why not wish for the whole dog? After a great deal of serious discussion about the matter, they dubbed him "Puddn'head" for being so stupid. But since it was they who were the fools, the title hints that the story makes a point that Wilson isn't the "Puddn'head" of Dawson's Landing.

> Sample B: The citizens of Dawson's Landing have a scornful attitude toward the newcomer, Wilson, although they come to like him later. The author conveys how the men feel about Wilson both through what they, themselves, say and do and through what the narrator says about them.

The conversation among the citizens contain such comments as "'Pears to be a fool," and "the idiot," and "In my opinion that man ain't in his right mind," and "he's a lummox...labrick...jackass..." and finally "If he ain't a pudd'nhead, I ain't no judge, that's all." These men just cannot fathom why Wilson would express the desire to own half a dog. Such a person, they conclude, must be crazy.

The narrator tells the reader directly that although Wilson "came to be liked," he never lost his nickname. "That first day's verdict made him a fool, and he was not able to get it set aside..." These are judgmental people, set in their ways. After they had made their initial, negative assessment, their scorn may have lost its sting, but it never completely disappeared.

8 **D** Do you see the word *vigil* in *vigilance*? If you know that a vigil is a sleepless watch, you can guess that it is a noun (the *ance* ending) that relates to watching. You might aggressively guess D at this point, which meets both criteria, or use POE. First, eliminate *B—cruel*—which is an adjective. Neither *A* nor *C* relate to watching, nor do they make sense when plugged into the original sentence. That leaves you with *D, watchfulness,* which makes perfect sense (slaveholders would become more watchful if Douglass described his escape).

9 **D** Refer to the text that mentions Douglass's friends in Baltimore. Clearly *A, B,* and *C* are wrong. They're his friends, not his tormentors, they didn't help Douglass escape, and Douglass didn't mention that he wanted to thank them. This leaves *D*, that friends made Douglass's decision to leave Maryland hard.

10 **B** You might know the word *mariner* before reading the passage, in which case, guess aggressively before checking that none of the other choices fit in the original sentence. If you don't know the word *mariner,* you may know its root, *mar,* which appears in words like *marine life* and *submarine.* You will guess the word has to do with the ocean. That points you toward *A* or *B* as your answer. Look back at the text. Douglass feels like an "unarmed mariner" being chased by a pirate. Choice *B, sailor,* fits that context.

11 **B** It's pretty obvious that Douglass's purpose isn't satire (humor used to poke fun at a human or societal weakness) or persuasion (argument). Your main task is distinguishing whether it is biography or autobiography. (You can review author's purpose on page 65.) As soon as you recall that *auto* means self, and autobiography is a person's own story about his life, you can nail this one down. Frederick Douglass is talking about his own life and makes frequent use of the pronoun *I,* a sign that this is an autobiography.

12 **A** You want a main idea—the most important thing Douglass says—not a supporting detail. Eliminate *B, C,* and *D,* because they each describe only one small section of the text. The main idea—the overarching theme of every sentence—is how awful slavery is and how hard it is to escape.

13 **D** The tone refers to the attitude of the author—remember *I don't like your tone of voice?* Cross off *C* right away: There's nothing funny about slavery. Look at the text, see what words point toward Douglass's attitude toward his subject. Does he seem sad (*A*) or irate (*C*)? No, there's nothing to indicate sorrow or anger. Instead, he's trying very hard to give you all the facts. He apologizes that he can't give you a "minute statement of all the facts," because he doesn't want to reveal the logistics of his escape, but he nevertheless wants to present a very balanced account. The tone is *D, objective*.

14 A good open response includes plenty of information from the text. Here's a sample that refers often to the text in answering the question:

> The decision to attempt escape was difficult for Douglass because of the dangers, losses, and hardships he faced. First, he needed to overcome any suspicion about his plans to run away by working hard for his master. Then he needed to come up with the strategy for escape. Finally, he had to leave his friends—"friends that I loved almost as I did my life"—possibly forever, and survive as a fugitive in a place without friends, while being chased by "merciless men-hunters." He decided that the advantages of freedom outweighed all of these negatives—even his terrible memories of what had happened when he once failed in an escape attempt. Douglass arrived at the decision to attempt escape by recognizing that this was a matter of life and death, for him. He would be punished terribly and perhaps killed if he failed, but at least he would have made his best effort at a full life, free of chains.

15 **D** A motif is an idea that appears over and over in a piece of literature. Even if you didn't know that, you could use POE to narrow down the field, here. From the title on down, this poem is pretty upbeat, right? The speaker is "celebrating." You don't find negative ideas about things like inequality (*A*), meaninglessness (*B*), nor corruption (*C*). Eliminate these choices. The motif is quite the opposite! Whitman says, "My respiration and inspiration" and "the song of me rising from bed and meeting the sun." He is saying that you can't separate your body and soul (*D*)—and he wouldn't want to!

16 **A** Look at the text and notice that *loafe* appears twice. Whitman says that he "invites" his soul in while loafing, and that he is "at ease." Dancing (*C*) and racing (*D*) seem completely wrong—way too active for the scenes we're reading. What about spear? This seems too active as well. Idle (*A*) makes the most sense. Whitman is lying around, luxuriating, or enjoying the pleasures of his body and soul.

17 **B** To figure out tone, actually try to "hear" the speaker. Don't misread that first line, "I celebrate myself." He's not stuck on himself (*A*); he's talking about how wonderful the body and soul are in general—and the equality of every being ("And what I assume you shall assume"). He talks about how he enjoys all these sense experiences and describes the "delight" of various sights, smells, feelings, and so forth. His is an upbeat tone, not a negative one of warning (*C*) or disapproval (*D*). All you've got left is *B*, which fits perfectly.

18 **C** Find the context in which the word is used: "The play of shine and shade on the trees as the supple boughs wag." What is the speaker noticing? The way the light and shadow shifts and dances as the tree branches wave in the breeze, right? The branches can "wag" like that because they are flexible (*C*), not heavy (*D*). Don't be fooled by *A* and *B* just because they contain words used near "supple" in the poem—always look at the text first for your answer.

19 **D** There isn't a set pattern of rhythm, or rhyme, or number of lines, is there? That eliminates *A*, *B*, and *C*. This is a famous example of free verse—very experimental for Whitman's time. It is "free" of the rules for beat and rhyme that bound many other poets in his day and, just so you know, the verse choice emphasizes Whitman's exuberant tone.

20 **A** This is a bit of a trick question, since "shine" and "shade" are often used as verbs. Look carefully at the poem—and review parts of speech if you need to (see page 52). What is doing the action? What's playing around? The shine and shade are playing around.

21 A superior composition is well-organized, uses great detail from the text, shows good command of vocabulary, and the ability to revise the essay (for punctuation and grammar.). This essay does a great job at all of these elements and would easily get all 20 points:

> Hawthorne surrounds his story in an atmosphere of gloom. He creates this sense of dreariness through his descriptions of both internal and external worlds. By revealing the character's anxious thoughts and describing the dreary woodland setting, Hawthorne produces a feeling of doom.

For some unknown reason, Goodman Brown is agitated when we get our first view of him. He pictures his wife ("Faith") and goes off to do whatever it is he plans to do. The contrast between the seemingly virtuous person he leaves behind and whatever he is about to face implies something dangerous. He worries that she seemed troubled and imagines that she has had a dream about his getting involved in something bad that night. Why is Goodman Brown feeling guilty about leaving his "blessed angel" and vowing that he will never leave her again "after this one night"? Will his wife's bad dream come true? Why is his present mission "evil"?

In the second paragraph, the description of the gloomy forest setting mirrors the character's internal state. The word choice, sounds, and imagery all intensify the darkening atmosphere of the story. The road is described as "darkened by all the gloomiest trees of the forest." Through personification, the trees are described in threatening terms. They "barely stood aside to let the narrow path creep through, and closed immediately behind." By comparing them to people who move only slightly to allow Goodman Brown to pass—and then immediately close ranks behind him—the author suggests that there is something menacing about these trees (and, consequently, something vulnerable about Young Goodman Brown). The references to the "innumerable" trunks and the "thick boughs overhead" suggests that their potential for trapping, overpowering, cutting off from light.

The omniscient point of view allows the narrator to comment directly on the scene, further emphasizing its loneliness and underlying sense of threat. As the narrator speculates about how many spies there might be hidden in the woods, unknown to Goodman Brown, the situation seems all the more dismal. Numerous devices, including diction, alliteration, imagery, and personification help to draw a bleak atmosphere over this scene.

Here's another very good answer to the prompt. This one might get in the range of 16–18 points, because the readers might feel that the essay did not draw enough specific examples from the text, even though the ideas are very good. Here's a solid, good response:

Hawthorne's atmosphere in this selection is creepy because he's showing us a man starting on a trip with bad intentions. First, Hawthorne makes this story bleak by showing us Mr. Brown's wife. He says he's leaving her for an evil purpose and she's had a bad dream about his journey.

Second, Hawthorne makes this trip seem very dark. The trees are closing in on him. The skies are dark.

Finally, Hawthorne makes us feel exactly how lonely Mr. Brown is. There is no one else on the road with him. Someone might be concealed in the forest, but Mr. Brown can't tell. It makes Mr. Brown's trip seem dangerous, as if something really bad could happen at any time.

22 **C** To determine purpose, look at what the writer told you and ask yourself, "Why did the author write this?" In this case, the guide writer provides a brief entry for each stop on the tour, telling what happened there and when it's open. She or he doesn't spend a lot of time on directions (*B*) and doesn't present an argument of any sort (*A*) and (*D*), so you can eliminate these. She or he does present plenty of evidence about each site's history. Someone *else* might use this evidence to argue that the Trail is educational or that Boston is the most historically important place—but the main purpose of *this* writer is to inform and present facts. The writer takes a neutral tone.

23 **A** The question asks what kind of English is used in the quote. In other words, what kinds of expressions are "trayning field" and "feeding of Cattell"? Regional English is dialect, so cross out *B*. It sure doesn't sound like slang, so eliminate *C*. What about informal English? No, it doesn't sound informal either. (Informal is the style we wrote this book in.) The spellings here are very old-timey and the right answer is *A, archaic*.

24 **D** Read the fine print. First find the section on the State House. See where it says that tours are between 9 and 5, Monday to Friday—except holidays? Using POE, that gets rid of *A, B,* and *C*. The right answer is *D*.

25 **C** Run your finger down the guide until you come to Park Street Church in paragraph seven. There you learn that Garrison gave his first antislavery (abolitionist) speech, and "brimstone" orations were delivered from its pulpit. If you know that brimstone speeches are fiery ones, not tranquil, you will eliminate A. What else can you scratch off? Gunpowder was stored in the basement in 1812, not during the Civil War (during the 1860s), so cross off *B*. There's nothing said about that gunpowder or anything else blowing up the church, so get rid of *D*, also.

26 **A** Break this word into word parts—*terra* means earth, as in *terra firma*. You can figure out from this that *in* and *ter* would mean to put into the earth. Go back to the guide. It makes sense that people would be put into the earth in "the Granary Burial Ground," not just *listed* (*B*), *remembered* (*C*), or *shown* (*D*).

27 **C** POE is an ideal strategy here. Is there a suggested order of stops? Yes, the guide details the tour stops in order. Zap *A*. Are there details about each site, hours, and costs? Yes. Cross off B. What about information on the person who designed the trail? NO! This must be the answer, but check the last choice just to be sure. Is each site described? Yup. D's history.

28   Sample response:

> I would walk around the Granary Burying Ground, first, where I would see the burial sites of such men as John Hancock, Robert Paine, Samuel Adams, and the people who died in the Boston Massacre. Then, I would follow the trail to the Park Street Church, which housed gunpowder during the War of 1812 and where William Lloyd Garrison gave his first speech against slavery. From there, I would take the trail to the State House, designed by Charles Bullfinch, and the current meeting place of Massachusetts' lawmakers. Finally I would end up at the Boston Common, where I would see the site from which the British took off for Charlestown during the battle of Bunker Hill. Nearby I would find the burial place of artist Gilbert Stuart.

29 **B** You can tell that the two people conversing are Hero and Ursula (because of the way dialogue is set up with Hero's and Ursula's names alternating). That eliminates *D*, because Beatrice doesn't speak with Hero or Ursula. Hero directs Ursula to move closer to where Beatrice is hidden so that she can better hear their conversation ("Then go we near her, that her ear lose nothing/ Of the false sweet bait that we lay for it."). Thus, you can cross out *A* and *C*.

30 **D** Paraphrase Hero's speech. Did you get something like this? *Let's talk about Benedick and how great he is and say how much he loves Beatrice. Sometimes Cupid needs a little help and we've got to trick her into falling in love with him.* Hero isn't worried about Beatrice making the wrong choice, she wants to help her make the *right* choice— so eliminate *A*. Even if Beatrice is loud (something we don't know from this passage), Hero's going to a lot of trouble to get her together with Benedick, so get rid of *B*. Hero tries to help Beatrice, not punish her. Cross off *C*.

31 **A** Shakespeare is saying that Ursula and Hero are like fishermen—"angling." "So angle we for Beatrice." The comparison should tell you immediately that this is figurative speech— such as *A*, a metaphor. *B*, *C*, and *D* are not examples of figurative speech, so you can safely pick *A* and discard the other answers.

32 B Ever heard the expression *betrothed?* Yes, you probably read it in another Shakespeare play; it refers to people engaged or married. Hero's *new-trothed lord* is her husband. Does that make sense in the context? Yes. What about Beatrice or Benedick in the context? Hero's statement makes no sense with these answer choices. Has the play mentioned any regional lord or nabob? Nope, no mention. Choose *B*, the answer that makes sense in the context.

33 B The rhyme scheme here is a little tricky because "a wit" rhymes with "Benedick." Make sure you understand how to map rhyme schemes for the exam. You can review this on page 94.

34 A You probably aggressively guessed that *Much Ado About Nothing* is a comedy. But, assuming you couldn't, you could use POE and get rid of any incorrect choices. There's nothing sad about this excerpt, so cross off *B*. There's nothing persuasive here (propaganda's a form of persuasion), so eliminate *C*. Is this a narrative? No, it's a play, not a narrative.

35 This open response is largely about putting Shakespeare's words into your own words. Here's a four-point sample answer:

> In this scene, two women, Ursula and Hero, talk about Beatrice and try to get her to eavesdrop on their conversation. They plan ahead of time what they will say in order to get Beatrice and Benedick together. Having agreed to discuss how madly in love Benedick supposedly is with Beatrice, they carry out their plan. As Beatrice listens in, they portray Benedick in glowing terms. Hero says she plans to keep Beatrice in the dark about Benedick's affection, since she thinks Beatrice will only reject and mock him. But Ursula thinks that Beatrice should know that Benedick is a fine catch and believes Beatrice is too smart to turn away such a prize.

36 C The key words in the question are *above all else*. The right choice will relate to a big theme—maybe the main idea—of the speech. Over and over Clinton points out how important it is that the people work together for betterment. He states, "each and every one of us must assume personal responsibility." He tells us that "every American in our land must answer a resounding 'Yes'" to surpass the achievements of our previous century. Answer choice *A* is a supporting detail of this speech that government (alone) cannot teach children to read. Cross *A* off. Clinton mentions how important it is to reclaim our streets from drugs and gangs and crime, but again, this is a supporting detail. Nix *B*.

Clinton wants to balance economic growth with protection of "the great natural bounty"—so *D* is clearly incorrect. The main point of the passage is *C*, responsible citizens can work together to improve America.

37 C By comparing a sense of hopefulness to a "spark"—without using the words "like" or "as," Clinton creates a metaphor (see page 49). Make sure you know these definitions perfectly when you take your MCAS exam; they'll probably show up more than once.

38 A Even without reading the text, you can guess that a president's inaugural speech will have a positive tone, so eliminate *C* and *D* immediately. Talk of "challenges" and "missions" and what we all "must" do lends an exhortatory (urging) tone while phrases like "we shall overcome" and "cures for our most feared illnesses seem close at hand" convey a sense of hope (*A*)—but not total bliss (*B*). Clinton still believes more changes need to occur.

39 B Clinton emphasizes how individual citizens have to take responsibility for improving our country—so it makes sense that he would support students' doing volunteer work. Answer choice *A* contradicts Clinton's belief that government cannot make people learn; *C* and *D* contradict Clinton's support for getting people out of gangs and off drugs. You're left with only *B*, the correct answer choice.

40 Here's an example of a good answer to this open response question:

> According to Clinton, a good citizen is someone who takes responsibility for improving our country. He suggests some ways that an individual could take such action: involvement in literacy programs, employment of people on welfare, reclaiming unsafe neighborhoods, and volunteering. He emphasizes that a good citizen is concerned not only with his or her own wellbeing and that of his family, but with the safety and prosperity of his or her community, country, and world. This kind of America will allow every American to realize his or her potential.

41 D Find where Plaatje heads to Mafeking, place your finger on it, and check what his life has consisted of beforehand. Cross off *A*, *B*, and *C* (all of which he does after he leaves Mafeking). That leaves *D*, that he was a mail carrier in Kimberley. Double-check the text. Yes, before going to Mafeking, Plaatje was a mail carrier in Kimberley, where he earned the top score on the exam.

42 D Find the reference to Plaatje's work on *Native Life in South Africa*. Read the text closely. It says he's completing a work he started on a boat headed to England, answer choice *D*.

43 **D** The entire paragraph is about Plaatje's interest in linguists. *My Fair Lady* is just one supporting detail—about his association with the linguist depicted in the well-known musical—that reinforces a bigger idea (that Plaatje was a skilled linguist.). *A, C,* and *D* may or may not be true, but they are not stated in the paragraph.

44 **B** The main clause contains the sentence's subject and verb. The other choices contain an introductory phrase (*A*), and phrases that modify the main clause (*C* and *D*).

45 **C** The introduction to a book is usually pretty positive—remarking, in this case, about Plaatje's accomplishments and skills. It's a good bet Neil Parsons wouldn't say that Plaatje's translations were rough sounding, so cross off *A* and *B* (both negatives.) Does it make sense to say that Plaatje's work was *pleasing to the palate*? You may not know this, but palate refers to tongue—were people *licking* these Shakespeare translations? Nix D, go with C, that his translations *sounded good.*

46 **D** Skim the article for key words in each choice. If you find the detail, toss out the choice. Although the author praises the work as one of the finest by a black South African writer, he does not go as far as choice D.

47   Here's a sample open response that would receive full credit:

> Plaatje is considered a pioneer in both politics and literature. In the political arena, he wrote propaganda that exposed the evils of apartheid—the separation of blacks and whites in South Africa. He served as an important diplomat during communications between the British civil authorities and the black Africans during the siege at the turn of the 20th century. As a writer, he was fascinated by linguistics. He translated several Shakespearean plays into Tswana. His book <u>Native Life in South Africa</u> served as an important record of black South Africans under apartheid.

48 **A** To get the sense of what Oedipus is saying, look at what has happened up to this point. Oedipus has started out by commanding the servant to "answer all that I ask," but the servant has angered him with vague words and finally by telling the messenger to hush ("Be silent once and for all!"). Oedipus is fed up, and when he talks about pain, he is threatening the old Servant about what will happen if he doesn't answer the questions. He certainly isn't saying anything nice to the poor guy, so eliminate *B* and *D*, nor is he worried about the messenger's feelings (*C*).

49 **B** The servant addresses Oedipus directly (as "master"), so that noun of direct address is set off by commas. Here's an example more like one you might use if you were, say, addressing your mother:

Jeez, mom, stop nagging me!

50 **C** You've heard about the Oedipal complex, right? The idea that secretly every little boy goes through a time when he wants to kill his father and marry his mother? Well, that's exactly what Oedipus did in this story, so it makes sense that that's where we got the term. Although *A*, *B*, and *D* may also contain words that resemble "Oedipus" or the author "Sophocles," there's no obvious connection between the story you have just read and paradise, being sage, or a first edition text, is there?

51 **B** All of these might be emotions that might drive a mother to have her son killed, but only one fits the story. In lines 1176 and 1178, the Servant explains that the mom was afraid that if the boy lived, he would kill his father—as predicted by the "evil prophecies."

52 **B** In addition to being a little punctuation mark ['], an apostrophe is an address to someone not present or an object being treated as if it were an empathic listener. ("Oh, Grandpa Irving, if you could see me now!" or "You, stony mountain, will witness my tears!")

You may encounter a few questions that you simply don't know the answers to—and you don't have to panic at these curve balls. Just stay cool and remember that POE can help you. In this question, eliminate *A* because there's no question mark in the quoted passage, so it's obviously not a question answered by Oedipus, a rhetorical question. Would you say that Oedipus is overreacting? No, probably not—this is a pretty horrific situation and exaggeration is not being used here. So cross off *C*. What about *D*, *symbolism*? Do you think Oedipus means literally that he's cursed? Yes, he really means this—this isn't figurative speech—he's just found out that he's done a horrible thing. That leaves you with (*B*), apostrophe, even if you're not clear exactly what that is!

Chapter 9

MCAS ELA Practice Test 2

Writing Prompt, Sessions 1A and 1B, Composition

1. WRITING ASSIGNMENT

In literature, as in real life, love sometimes changes a person's life. Choose two novels about characters who are in love. These may be novels that you have read in class or on your own. Compare and contrast how love changed the central characters.

The following selection is excerpted from chapter 9 of the novel Sense and Sensibility, *written by Jane Austen. Following the death of their father, the Dashwood sisters, Margaret, Marianne, and Elinor, have moved with their mother to a new home. Read the selection about how Marianne sprains her ankle while walking with Margaret and meets a handsome stranger. When you have finished reading the selection, answer the questions that follow.*

Sense and Sensibility

by Jane Austen

1 "Is there a felicity in the world," said Marianne, "superior to this?—Margaret, we will walk here at least two hours."

2 Margaret agreed, and they pursued their way against the wind, resisting it with laughing delight for about twenty minutes longer, when suddenly the clouds united over their heads, and a driving rain set full in their face. Chagrined and surprised, they were obliged, though unwillingly, to turn back, for no shelter was nearer than their own house. One consolation however remained for them, to which the exigence of the moment gave more than usual propriety; it was that of running with all possible speed down the steep side of the hill which led immediately to their garden gate.

3 They set off. Marianne had at first the advantage, but a false step brought her suddenly to the ground; and Margaret, unable to stop herself to assist her, was involuntarily hurried along, and reached the bottom in safety.

4 A gentleman carrying a gun, with two pointers playing round him, was passing up the hill and within a few yards of Marianne, when her accident happened. He put down his gun and ran to her assistance. She had raised herself from the ground, but her foot had been twisted in her fall, and she was scarcely able to stand. The gentleman offered his services; and perceiving that her modesty declined what her situation rendered necessary, took her up in his arms without further delay, and carried her down the hill. Then passing through the garden, the gate of which had been left open by Margaret, he bore her directly into the house, whither Margaret was just arrived, and quitted not his hold till he had seated her in a chair in the parlour.

5 Elinor and her mother rose up in amazement at their entrance, and while the eyes of both were fixed on him with an evident wonder and a secret admiration which equally sprung from his appearance, he apologized for his intrusion by relating its cause, in a manner so frank and so graceful that his person, which was uncommonly handsome, received additional charms from his voice and expression. Had he been even old, ugly, and vulgar, the gratitude and kindness of Mrs. Dashwood would have been secured by any act of attention to her child; but the influence of youth, beauty, and elegance, gave an interest to the action which came home to her feelings.

6 She thanked him again and again; and, with a sweetness of address which always attended her, invited him to be seated. But this he declined, as he was dirty and wet. Mrs. Dashwood then begged to know to whom she was obliged. His name, he replied, was Willoughby, and his present home was at Allenham, from whence he hoped she would allow him the honour of calling tomorrow to enquire after Miss Dashwood. The honour was readily granted, and he then departed, to make himself still more interesting, in the midst of an heavy rain.

7 His manly beauty and more than common gracefulness were instantly the theme of general admiration, and the laugh which his gallantry raised against Marianne received particular spirit from his exterior attractions. Every circumstance belonging to him was interesting. His name was good, his residence was in their favourite village, and she soon found out that of all manly dresses a shooting-jacket was the most becoming. Her imagination was busy, her reflections were pleasant, and the pain of a sprained ankle was disregarded.

8 Sir John called on them as soon as the next interval of fair weather that morning allowed him to get out of doors; and Marianne's accident being related to him, he was eagerly asked whether he knew any gentleman of the name of Willoughby at Allenham.

9 "Willoughby!" cried Sir John; "what, is HE in the country? That is good news however; I will ride over tomorrow, and ask him to dinner on Thursday."

10 "You know him then," said Mrs. Dashwood.

11 "Know him! to be sure I do. Why, he is down here every year."

12 "And what sort of a young man is he?"

13 "As good a kind of fellow as ever lived, I assure you. A very decent shot, and there is not a bolder rider in England."

14 "And is that all you can say for him?" cried Marianne, indignantly. "But what are his manners on more intimate acquaintance? What his pursuits, his talents, and genius?"

15 Sir John was rather puzzled.

16 "Upon my soul," said he, "I do not know much about him as to all THAT. But he is a pleasant, good humored fellow, and has got the nicest little black pointer ever saw. Was she out with him today?"

17 But Marianne could no more satisfy him as to the color of Mr. Willoughby's pointer, than he could describe to her the shades of his mind.

18 "But who is he?" said Elinor. "Where does he come from? Has he a house at Allenham?"

19 On this point Sir John could give more certain intelligence; and he told them that Mr. Willoughby had no property of his own in the country; that he resided there only while he was visiting the old lady at Allenham Court, to whom he was related, and whose possessions he was to inherit; adding, "Yes, yes, he is very well worth catching I can tell you, Miss Dashwood; he has a pretty little estate of his own in Somersetshire besides; and if I were you, I would not give him up to my younger sister, in spite of all this tumbling down hills. Miss Marianne must not expect to have all the men to herself. Brandon will be jealous, if she does not take care."

20 "He is as good a sort of fellow, I believe, as ever lived," repeated Sir John. "I remember last Christmas at a little hop at the park, he danced from eight o'clock till four, without once sitting down."

21 "Did he indeed?" cried Marianne with sparkling eyes, "and with elegance, with spirit?"

22 "Yes; and he was up again at eight to ride to covert."

23 "That is what I like; that is what a young man ought to be. Whatever be his pursuits, his eagerness in them should know no moderation, and leave him no sense of fatigue."

24 "Aye, aye, I see how it will be," said Sir John, "I see how it will be. You will be setting your cap at him now, and never think of poor Brandon."

25 "That is an expression, Sir John," said Marianne, warmly, "which I particularly dislike. I abhor every common-place phrase by which wit is intended; and 'setting one's cap at a man,' or 'making a conquest,' are the most odious of all. Their tendency is gross and illiberal; and if their construction could ever be deemed clever, time has long ago destroyed all its ingenuity."

2. The word, *felicity* is best defined as

    A. happiness.

    B. finery.

    C. fine weather.

    D. rainstorms.

3. According to Sir John, Willoughby is

    A. agreeable.

    B. hardworking.

    C. honorable.

    D. ambitious.

4. What does the statement, "But Marianne could no more satisfy him as to the color of Mr. Willoughby's pointer, than he could describe to her the shades of his mind" mean?

    A. Marianne and Sir John are both inarticulate people.

    B. Marianne and Sir John pay attention to what interests them in a person.

    C. Marianne and Sir John are both color blind.

    D. Neither Marianne nor Sir John are interested in Mr. Willoughby.

5. The phrase "setting one's cap at a man" is an example of

    A. figurative language.

    B. symbolism.

    C. irony.

    D. personification.

6. What sort of man is Willoughby? Be sure to draw your answer from the passage itself.

Marie-Antoinette, queen of France (wife of Louis XVI) was tried and beheaded for treason. Read the following account of her trial and execution and answer the questions that follow.

The French Revolution

by Thomas Carlyle

1 On Monday the Fourteenth of October, 1793, a Cause is pending in the Palais de Justice, in the new Revolutionary Court, such as these old stone walls never witnessed: the Trial of Marie-Antoinette. The once brightest of Queens, now tarnished, defaced, forsaken, stands here at Fouquier Tinville's Judgment-bar; answering for her life! The Indictment was delivered her last night. (Proces de la Reine, Deux Amis, xi. 251-381.)

2 At four o'clock on Wednesday morning, after two days and two nights of interrogating, jury-charging, and other darkening of counsel, the result comes out: Sentence of Death. "Have you anything to say?" The Accused shook her head, without speech. Night's candles are burning out; and with her too Time is finishing, and it will be Eternity and Day. Include this: This Hall of Tinville's is dark, ill-lighted except where she stands. Silently she withdraws from it, to die.

3 Two Processions, or Royal Progresses, three-and-twenty years apart, have often struck us with a strange feeling of contrast. The first is of a beautiful Archduchess and Dauphiness, quitting her Mother's City, at the age of Fifteen; towards hopes such as no other Daughter of Eve then had: 'On the morrow,' says Weber an eye witness, 'the Dauphiness left Vienna. The whole City crowded out; at first with a sorrow which was silent. She appeared: you saw her sunk back into her carriage; her face bathed in tears; hiding her eyes now with her handkerchief, now with her hands; several times putting out her head to see yet again this Palace of her Fathers, whither she was to return no more. She motioned her regret, her gratitude to the good Nation, which was crowding here to bid her farewell. Then arose not only tears; but piercing cries, on all sides. Men and women alike abandoned themselves to such expression of their sorrow. It was an audible sound of wail, in the streets and avenues of Vienna. The last Courier that followed her disappeared, and the crowd melted away.' (Weber,i. 6.)

4 The young imperial Maiden of Fifteen has now become a worn discrowned Widow of Thirty-eight; grey before her time: this is the last Procession: 'Few minutes after the Trial ended, the drums were beating to arms in all Sections; at sunrise the armed force was on foot, cannons getting placed at the extremities of the Bridges, in the Squares, Crossways, all along from the Palais de Justice to the Place de la Revolution. By ten o'clock, numerous patrols were circulating in the Streets; thirty thousand foot and horse drawn up under arms. At eleven, Marie-Antoinette was brought out. She had on an undress of pique blanc: she was led to the place of execution, in the same manner as an ordinary criminal; bound, on a Cart; accompanied by a Constitutional Priest in Lay dress; escorted by numerous detachments of infantry and cavalry. These, and the double row of troops all along her road, she appeared to regard with indifference. On her countenance there was visible neither abashment nor pride. To the cries of Vive la Republique and Down with Tyranny, which attended her all the way, she seemed to pay no heed. She spoke little to her Confessor. The tricolor Streamers on the housetops occupied her attention, in the Streets du Roule and Saint-Honore; she also noticed the Inscriptions on the house-fronts. On reaching the Place de la Revolution, her looks turned towards the Jardin National, whilom Tuileries; her face at that moment gave signs of lively emotion. She mounted the scaffold with courage enough; at a quarter past Twelve, her head fell; the Executioner shewed it to the people, amid universal long-continued cries of 'Vive la Republique.' (DeuxAmis, xi. 301.)

7. In paragraph 1 what is an *indictment*?

   A. a verdict

   B. a command

   C. a formal request

   D. an indicator

8. In paragraph 2, Carlyle says that "Night's candles are burning out; and with her too Time is finishing." What does he mean by this expression?

   A. It's almost daybreak.

   B. Time is nearly up for Marie Antoinette.

   C. The hallways will soon be dark, which makes them seem long.

   D. It's dark where Marie Antoinette is standing.

9. In what paragraph does the account of the condemned Marie-Antoinette's journey to the guillotine begin?

   A. paragraph 1

   B. paragraph 2

   C. paragraph 3

   D. paragraph 4

10. According to this account, how much time passed between the end of the trial and Marie-Antoinette's beheading?

    A. about 8 hours

    B. about 24 hours

    C. about one week

    D. about two weeks

11. In paragraph 4 what does *abashment* mean?

    A. haughtiness

    B. self-respect

    C. shame

    D. modesty

12. How does the writer create a vivid image of Marie-Antoinette's trip to the guillotine?

   A. He lets the reader know how much time has gone by since Marie-Antoinette sadly left her homeland at age 15.

   B. He contrasts details of two processions.

   C. He describes the details of Marie-Antoinette's emotional state.

   D. He draws a moving picture of her beloved supporters, prostrate from grief.

13. The main purpose of Carlyle's account is to show

   A. Marie-Antoinette's innocence.

   B. how far Marie-Antoinette had come since her humble beginnings.

   C. the inscriptions on the housefronts and the flowers in the Jardin National.

   D. how Marie-Antoinette comported herself regally, even at her execution.

14. What is the best inference we can make from the pages of the Bulletin Tribunal?

   A. Marie-Antoinette faced an arduous trial.

   B. Marie-Antoinette was given a reprieve by the Tribunal.

   C. Common French citizens refused to believe the charges and supported their queen.

   D. Marie-Antoinette complained bitterly about the treatment she received.

This passage is the "Cook's Tale," from Chaucer's Canterbury Tales, a series of stories told to one another by travelers on a pilgrimage to the shrine of Thomas a Becket. Read the tale and then answer the questions that follow.

Cook's Tale

By Geofrey Chaucer

1 There lived a 'prentice, once, in our city,

2 And of the craft of victuallers was he;

3 Happy he was as goldfinch in the glade,

4 Brown as a berry, short, and thickly made,

5 With black hair that he combed right prettily.

6 He could dance well, and that so jollily,

7 That he was nicknamed Perkin Reveller.

8 He was as full of love, I may aver,

9 As is a beehive full of honey sweet;

10 Well for the wench that with him chanced to meet.

11 At every bridal would he sing and hop,

12 Loving the tavern better than the shop. . .

17 He gathered many fellows of his sort

18 To dance and sing and make all kinds of sport.

19 And they would have appointments for to meet

20 And play at dice in such, or such, a street.

21 For in the whole town was no apprentice

22 Who better knew the way to throw the dice

23 Than Perkin; and therefore he was right free

24 With money, when in chosen company.

25 His master found this out in business there;

26 For often-times he found the till was bare.

27 For certainly a revelling bond-boy

28 Who loves dice, wine, dancing, and girls of joy-

29 His master, in his shop, shall feel the effect,

30 Though no part have he in this said respect;

31 For theft and riot always comrades are,

32 And each alike he played on gay guitar. . .

35 This 'prentice shared his master's fair abode

36 Till he was nigh out of his 'prenticehood,

37 Though he was checked and scolded early and late,

38 And sometimes led, for drinking, to Newgate;

39 But at the last his master did take thought,

40 Upon a day, when he his ledger sought,

41 On an old proverb wherein is found this word:

42 Better take rotten apple from the hoard

43 Than let it lie to spoil the good ones there.

44 So with a drunken servant should it fare;

45 It is less ill to let him go, apace,

46 Than ruin all the others in the place.

47 Therefore he freed and cast him loose to go

48 His own road unto future care and woe;

49 And thus this jolly 'prentice had his leave.

50 Now let him riot all night long, or thieve.

51 But since there's never thief without a buck

52 To help him waste his money and to suck

53 All he can steal or borrow by the way,

54 Anon he sent his bed and his array

55 To one he knew, a fellow of his sort,

56 Who loved the dice and revels and all sport

15. "Brown as a berry" is an example of

    A. hubris.

    B. understatement.

    C. personification.

    D. simile.

16. Which is *not* something the storyteller says the central figure of his tale enjoys?

    A. gambling

    B. cooking

    C. drinking

    D. women

17. The master let the servant go so that he would not

    A. steal any more of the master's fruit.

    B. continue to allow the master's apples to rot.

    C. be a bad influence on the other servants.

    D. keep encouraging the master to get drunk.

18. "For theft and riot always comrades are,

    And each alike he played on gay guitar"

    These lines contain an example of everything *except*

    A. synecdoche.

    B. couplet.

    C. alliteration.

    D. personification.

The following selection is a poem, "The Song of Princess Zeb-un-Nissa In Praise of Her Own Beauty" (translated from the Persian). Read the poem and answer the questions that follow.

The Song of Princess Zeb-un-Nissa

When from my cheek I lift my veil,
The roses turn with envy pale,
And from their pierced hearts,
rich with pain,
5 Send forth their fragrance like a wail.
Or if perchance one perfumed tress
Be lowered to the wind's caress,
The honeyed hyacinths complain,
And languish in a sweet distress.
10 And, when I pause, still groves among,
(Such loveliness is mine) a throng
Of nightingales awake and strain
Their souls into a quivering song.

19. The roses turn pale from

    A. jealousy.

    B. shame.

    C. cold.

    D. fear.

20. In line 3, what part of speech is the word *pierced*?

    A. an adverb

    B. a verb

    C. an adjective

    D. a noun

21. What is the rhyme scheme of the first stanza?

    A. AABCD

    B. ABABC

    C. BBACA

    D. AABCA

22. In lines 6-10, the speaker means that

    A. birds are distressed when the wind pays attention to her instead of to them.

    B. sweet-smelling flowers are jealous of her nice-smelling hair.

    C. the bees mistake her for a flower when she splashes on some perfume.

    D. the flowers complain when she borrows honey to smooth her wind-blown hair.

23. "The honeyed hyacinths complain,/ And languish in sweet distress" is an example of

    A. assonance.

    B. analogy.

    C. allusion.

    D. alliteration.

24. The poet reinforces the meaning of her poem through

    A. use of a first-person speaker.

    B. logical ideas.

    C. informal language.

    D. heroic couplets.

25. How does the speaker feel about the way she looks and the impact she makes on others? Support your answer with details from the poem.

Read the following excerpt from an essay by Jonathan Swift written in 1729. At the time, a great famine was causing enormous poverty and privation in Ireland. Then answer the questions that follow.

A Modest Proposal for preventing the children of poor people in Ireland from being a burden on their parents or country, and for making them beneficial to the publick

by Dr. Jonathan Swift

1 It is a melancholy object to those, who walk through this great town, or travel in the country, when they see the streets, the roads and cabin-doors crowded with beggars of the female sex, followed by three, four, or six children, all in rags, and importuning every passenger for an alms. These mothers instead of being able to work for their honest livelihood, are forced to employ all their time in strolling to beg sustenance for their helpless infants who, as they grow up, either turn thieves for want of work, or leave their dear native country...

2 I think it is agreed by all parties, that this prodigious number of children in the arms, or on the backs, or at the heels of their mothers, and frequently of their fathers, is in the present deplorable state of the kingdom, a very great additional grievance; and therefore whoever could find out a fair, cheap and easy method of making these children sound and useful members of the common-wealth, would deserve so well of the publick, as to have his statue set up for a preserver of the nation. But my intention is very far from being confined to provide only for the children of professed beggars: it is of a much greater extent, and shall take in the whole number of infants at a certain age, who are born of parents in effect as little able to support them, as those who demand our charity in the streets... it is exactly at one year old that I propose to provide for them in such a manner, as, instead of being a charge upon their parents, or the parish, or wanting food and raiment for the rest of their lives, they shall, on the contrary, contribute to the feeding, and partly to the clothing of many thousands...

3 I shall now therefore humbly propose my own thoughts, which I hope will not be liable to the least objection. I have been assured by a very knowing American of my acquaintance in London, that a young healthy child well nursed, is, at a year old, a most delicious nourishing and wholesome food, whether stewed, roasted, baked, or boiled; and I make no doubt that it will equally serve in a fricassie, or a ragout. I do therefore humbly offer it to public consideration, that of the hundred and twenty thousand children,... a hundred thousand may, at a year old, be offered in sale to the persons of quality and fortune, through the kingdom, always advising the mother to let them suck plentifully in the last month, so as to render them plump, and fat for a good table.

4 A child will make two dishes at an entertainment for friends, and when the family dines alone, therefore or hind quarter will make a reasonable dish, and seasoned with a little pepper or salt, will be very good boiled on the fourth day, especially in winter. I have reckoned upon a medium, that a child just born will weigh 12 pounds, and in a solar year, if tolerably nursed, increaseth to 28 pounds. I grant this food will be somewhat dear, and therefore very proper for landlords, who, as they have already devoured most of the parents, seem to have the best title to the children.

5 I have already computed the charge of nursing a beggar's child (in which list I reckon all cottagers, labourers, and four-fifths of the farmers) to be about two shillings per annum, rags included; and I believe no gentleman would repine to give ten shillings for the carcass of a good fat child, which, as I have said, will make four dishes of excellent nutritive meat, when he hath only some particular friend, or his own family to dine with him. Thus the squire will learn to be a good landlord, and grow popular among his tenants, the mother will have eight shillings neat profit, and be fit for work till she produces another child. Those who are more thrifty (as I must confess the times require) may flea the carcass; the skin of which, artificially dressed, will make admirable gloves for ladies, and summer boots for fine gentlemen. As to our City of Dublin, shambles may be appointed for this purpose, in the most convenient parts of it, and butchers we maybe assured will not be wanting; although I rather recommend buying the children alive, and dressing them hot from the knife, as we do roasting pigs.

6 Some persons of a desponding spirit are in great concern about that vast number of poor people, who are aged, diseased, or maimed; and I have been desired to employ my thoughts what course may be taken, to ease the nation of so grievous an incumbrance. But I am not in the least pain upon that matter, because it is very well known, that they are every day dying, and rotting, by cold and famine, and filth, and vermin, as fast as can be reasonably expected. And as to the young labourers, they are no win almost as hopeful a condition. They cannot get work, and consequently pine away from want of nourishment, to a degree, that if at any time they are accidentally hired to common labour, they have not strength to perform it, and thus the country and themselves are happily delivered from the evils to come. I have too long digressed, and therefore shall return to my subject. I think the advantages by the proposal which I have made are obvious and many, as well as of the highest importance...

26. In which paragraph does Swift reveal his 'modest' proposal?

    A. paragraph 2

    B. paragraph 3

    C. paragraph 5

    D. paragraph 6

27. In paragraph 5, the author

    A. contrasts the mother's love for her child with the gentleman's use for the child.

    B. offers calculations to prove the financial benefits of his proposal to mother and squire.

    C. summarizes the financial and ethical pros and cons of his proposal.

    D. explains the cause-and-effect relationship between poverty and thriftiness.

28. What aspect of his society was Swift actually skewering throughout this essay?

    A. English adults who showed compassion for poor Irish children, but hated their parents.

    B. The English who showed a callous disregard for the plight of poor Irish children.

    C. English politicians who were more interested in the welfare of one group of children than the financial stability of their country.

    D. British politicians who were more concerned about the plight of Irish children than the children's own parents.

29. Which underlined word in the following excerpts from *A Modest Proposal* derives from the Latin word *bulla* which means "bubble"?

"These mothers....are forced to employ all their time in strolling to _beg_ sustenance for their helpless infants"

"I shall now therefore _humbly_ propose my own thoughts, which I hope will not be liable to the least _objection_."

"...and seasoned with a little pepper or salt, will be very good _boiled_ on the fourth day"

    A. beg

    B. humbly

    C. objection

    D. boiled

30. According to the author, his proposal is a good one because it

    A. will be cost-effective for the nation as a whole.

    B. has already been adopted and shown to work in America.

    C. will solve the problem of unregulated child labor in Ireland.

    D. will enable more mothers to stay home and care for their children.

31. It is important to recognize that this is a piece of satire and that Swift's *actual* attitude toward the poor is one of

    A. disgust.

    B. rage.

    C. envy.

    D. compassion.

32. Which of the following statements are *not* among the advantages Swift describes to his proposition?

    A. Mothers will profit and be able to purchase more food.

    B. Butchers will get increased employment.

    C. Landlords will not starve.

    D. Society will be alleviated of a pressing problem.

33. Is paragraph 1 an effective introduction to this essay? Cite evidence from the essay to support your answer.

The following selection is an excerpt from Uncle Vanya *by Anton Chekhov. It is a story about what happens when an old professor, Serebrakoff, and his young wife (Helena) come to live at the estate managed by the professor's first wife's brother (Voitski, also known as Uncle Vanya). As you read this excerpt, think about how the writer develops characters and theme. When you are done, answer the questions that follow.*

Uncle Vanya

by Anton Chekhov

1   **MARINA:** [Shaking her head] Such a confusion in the house! The Professor gets up at twelve, the samovar is kept boiling all the morning, and everything has to wait for him. Before they came we used to have dinner at one o'clock, like everybody else, but now we have it at seven. The Professor sits up all night writing and reading, and suddenly, at two o'clock, there goes the bell! Heavens, what is that? The Professor wants some tea! Wake the servants, light the samovar! Lord, what disorder!

2   **ASTROFF (the doctor):** Will they be here long?

3   **VOITSKI. (also known as Uncle Vanya):** A hundred years! The Professor has decided to make his home here.

4   **MARINA:** Look at this now! The samovar has been on the table for two hours, and they are all out walking!

5   **VOITSKI:** All right, don't get excited; here they come.

6   Voices are heard approaching.

7   [SEREBRAKOFF, HELENA, SONIA, and TELEGIN come in from the depths of the garden, returning from their walk.]

8   **SEREBRAKOFF:** Superb! Superb! What beautiful views!

9   **TELEGIN:** They are wonderful, your Excellency.

10 **VOITSKI:** Ladies and gentlemen, tea is ready.

11 **SEREBRAKOFF:** Won't you please be good enough to send my tea into the library? I still have some work to finish.

12 [HELENA, SEREBRAKOFF, and SONIA go into the house.]

13 [TELEGIN sits down at the table beside MARINA.]

14 **VOITSKI:** There goes our learned scholar on a hot, sultry day like this, in his overcoat and galoshes and carrying an umbrella!

15 **ASTROFF:** He is trying to take good care of his health.

16 **VOITSKI:** How lovely she is! How lovely! I have never in my life seen a more beautiful woman. Such eyes—a glorious woman!

17 **ASTROFF:** Come, Ivan, tell us something.

18 **VOITSKI:** [Indolently] What shall I tell you?

19 **ASTROFF:** Haven't you any news for us?

20 VOITSKI: No, it is all stale. I am just the same as usual, or perhaps worse, because I have become lazy. I don't do anything now but croak like an old raven. My mother, the old magpie, is still chattering about the emancipation of woman, with one eye on her grave and the other on her learned books, in which she is always looking for the dawn of a new life.

21 ASTROFF: And the Professor?

22 VOITSKI: The Professor sits in his library from morning till night, as usual—Straining the mind, wrinkling the brow, We write, write, write, Without respite Or hope of praise in the future or now. Poor paper! He ought to write his autobiography; he would make a really splendid subject for a book! Imagine it, the life of a retired professor, as stale as a piece of hardtack, tortured by gout, headaches, and rheumatism, his liver bursting with jealousy and envy, living on the estate of his first wife, although he hates it, because he can't afford to live in town. He is everlastingly whining about his hard lot, though, as a matter of fact, he is extraordinarily lucky. He is the son of a common deacon and has attained the professor's chair, become the son-in-law of a senator, is called "your Excellency," and so on. But I'll tell you something; the man has been writing on art for twenty-five years, and he doesn't know the very first thing about it. For twenty-five years he has been chewing on other men's thoughts about realism, naturalism, and all such foolishness; for twenty-five years he has been reading and writing things that clever men have long known and stupid ones are not interested in; for twenty-five years he has been making his imaginary mountains out of molehills. And just think of the man's self-conceit and presumption all this time! For twenty-five years he has been masquerading in false clothes and has now retired absolutely unknown to any living soul; and yet see him! stalking across the earth like a demi-god!

23 ASTROFF: I believe you envy him.

24 VOITSKI: Yes, I do. Look at the success he has had with women! Don Juan himself was not more favoured. His first wife, who was my sister, was a beautiful, gentle being, as pure as the blue heaven there above us, noble, great-hearted, with more admirers than he has pupils, and she loved him as only beings of angelic purity can love those who are as pure and beautiful as themselves. His mother-in-law, my mother, adores him to this day, and he still inspires a sort of worshipful awe in her. His second wife is, as you see, a brilliant beauty; she married him in his old age and has surrendered all the glory of her beauty and freedom to him. Why? What for?

25 ASTROFF: Is she faithful to him?

26 VOITSKI: Yes, unfortunately she is.

27 ASTROFF: Why unfortunately?

28 VOITSKI: Because such fidelity is false and unnatural, root and branch. It sounds well, but there is no logic in it. It is thought immoral for a woman to deceive an old husband whom she hates, but quite moral for her to strangle her poor youth in her breast and banish every vital desire from her heart.

29 TELEGIN: [In a tearful voice] Vanya, I don't like to hear you talk so. Listen, Vanya; every one who betrays husband or wife is faithless, and could also betray his country.

30 VOITSKI: [Crossly] Turn off the tap, Waffles.

31 TELEGIN: No, allow me, Vanya. My wife ran away with a lover on the day after our wedding, because my exterior was unprepossessing. I have never failed in my duty since then. I love her and am true to her to this day. I help her all I can and have given my fortune to educate the daughter of herself and her lover. I have forfeited my happiness, but I have kept my pride. And she? Her youth has fled, her beauty has faded according to the laws of nature, and her lover is dead. What has she kept?

34. In passage 20, Voitski says he doesn't "do anything now but croak like an old raven." This phrase is an example of a(n)

    A. oxymoron.

    B. soliloquy.

    C. simile.

    D. hyperbole.

35. When Voitski says that his sister loved the Professor "as only beings of angelic purity can love those who are as pure and beautiful as themselves," his expression is an example of

    A. hyperbole.

    B. metaphor.

    C. personification.

    D. assonance

36. Telegin says of his wife, "I have forfeited my happiness, but I have kept my pride. And she? Her youth has fled, her beauty has faded according to the laws of nature, and her lover is dead. What has she kept?" Telegin could have used everyday speech to describe his reaction to his wife's infidelity. Instead, the author chooses formal, elevated language and rhetorical questions, mainly in order to

    A. show that Telegin is highly educated and well-cultured.

    B. emphasize Telegin's belief that his actions represent a higher spiritual plane.

    C. produce an authentic-sounding conversation.

    D. create the atmosphere of a classroom.

37. Which prediction is best supported by this passage?

    A. Vanya will fall in love with Helena.

    B. Telegin will give up alcohol.

    C. Vanya will fall in love with Marina.

    D. The Professor will give up the practice of medicine.

Session 3, Open-response Question

38. Based on this passage, how would you describe the Professor? What kind of person does he appear to be? How does Chekhov show us what these characters think of the Professor?

Read the following excerpt about Abraham Lincoln from Henry Cabot Lodge's Hero Tales from America. *Then answer the questions that follow it.*

Hero Tales from America

by Henry Cabot Lodge

Lincoln died a martyr to the cause to which he had given his life, and both life and death were heroic. The qualities which enabled him to do his great work are very clear now to all men. His courage and his wisdom, his keen perception and his almost prophetic foresight, enabled him to deal with all the problems of that distracted time as they arose around him. But he had some qualities, apart from those of the intellect, which were of equal importance to his people and to the work he had to do. His character, at once strong and gentle, gave confidence to everyone, and dignity to his cause. He had an infinite patience, and a humor that enabled him to turn aside many difficulties which could have been met in no other way. But most important of all was the fact that he personified a great sentiment, which ennobled and uplifted his people, and made them capable of the patriotism which fought the war and saved the Union. He carried his people with him, because he knew instinctively, how they felt and what they wanted. He embodied, in his own person, all their highest ideals, and he never erred in his judgment.

He is not only a great and commanding figure among the great statesmen and leaders of history, but he personifies, also, all the sadness and the pathos of the war, as well as its triumphs and its glories. No words that any one can use about Lincoln can, however, do him such justice as his own, and I will close this volume with two of Lincoln's speeches, which show what the war and all the great deeds of that time meant to him, and through which shines, the great soul of the man himself. On November 19,1863, he spoke as follows at the dedication of the National cemetery on the battlefield of Gettysburg:

1 Four score and seven years ago our fathers brought forth on this continent a new nation, conceived in liberty, and dedicated to the proposition that all men are created equal.

2 Now we are engaged in a great civil war, testing whether that nation, or any nation so

3 conceived and so dedicated, can long endure. We are met on a great battlefield of that war. We have come to dedicate a portion of that field as a final resting place for those who here gave their lives that that nation might live. It is altogether fitting and proper that we should do this.

4 But in a larger sense, we cannot dedicate—we cannot consecrate—we cannot hallow—this ground. The brave men, living and dead, who struggled here, have consecrated it far above our poor power to add or detract. The world will little note or long remember what we say here, but it can never forget what they did here. It is for us, the living, rather, to be dedicated here to the unfinished work which they who have fought here, have thus far so nobly advanced. It is rather for us to be here dedicated to the great task remaining before us—that from the honored dead we take increased devotion to that cause for which they gave the last full measure of devotion; that we here highly resolve that these dead shall not have died in vain; that this nation, under God, shall have a new birth of freedom; and that government of the people, by the people, for the people, shall not perish from the earth.

39. The word *pathos* is best defined as

    A. great despair.

    B. enormous sacrifice.

    C. death.

    D. suffering.

40. Lincoln said: "We have come to dedicate a portion of that field as a final resting place for those who here gave their lives that that nation might live." In these lines, he created a sense of closeness to his audience by

    A. using dialect and slang.

    B. using informal English and colloquial phrasing.

    C. addressing the audience directly as "we."

    D. using vernacular rather than Standard English.

41. The line, "But in a larger sense, we cannot dedicate—we cannot consecrate—we cannot hallow—this ground" contains an example of

    A. repetition for emphasis.

    B. alliteration.

    C. simile.

    D. rhetorical questioning.

42. In the famous line: "The world will little note or long remember what we say here...", the word *little* serves as an

    A. adjective modifying *world*.

    B. adverb modifying *note*.

    C. adjective modifying *we*.

    D. adverb modifying *long*.

43. When Lincoln says that "it is rather for us to be here dedicated to the great task before us," he is alluding to

    A. the consecration of the cemetery.

    B. memorializing the dead.

    C. the cause of the Civil War.

    D. keeping the spirit of his soul alive.

44. Lincoln used the words "birth" and "perish" to describe our nation and government. His statement that: "... this nation, under God, shall have a new birth of freedom; and that government of the people, by the people, for the people, shall not perish from the earth" contains

   A. assonance.

   B. understatement.

   C. irony.

   D. personification.

45. Using information from Henry Cabot Lodge's introduction as well as Lincoln's Gettysburg Address, explain why we have remembered Lincoln—and the message he conveys in the Gettysburg Address—for so long. Include evidence from both to support your answer.

The following excerpt is from Dryden's translation of The Aeneid *by Vergil. The Aeneid is a poem celebrating the legendary origin of the Roman people. In this selection, from Book VI of the poem, it describes Aeneas entering the cave of Hades, or the underworld. Read the excerpt and answer the questions that follow.*

The Aeneid

by Vergil

Deep was the cave; and, downward as it went
From the wide mouth, a rocky rough descent;
And here th' access a gloomy grove defends,
And there th' unnavigable lake extends,
O'er whose unhappy waters, void of light,
No bird presumes to steer his airy flight;
Such deadly stenches from the depths arise,
And steaming sulphur, that infects the skies.
From hence the Grecian bards their legends make,
And give the name Avernus to the lake.

Obscure they went thro' dreary shades, that led
Along the waste dominions of the dead.
Thus wander travelers in woods by night,
By the moon's doubtful and malignant light,
When Jove in dusky clouds involves the skies,
And the faint crescent shoots by fits before their eyes.
Just in the gate and in the jaws of hell,
Revengeful Cares and sullen Sorrows dwell,
And pale Diseases, and repining Age,
Want, Fear, and Famine's unresisted rage;
Here Toils, and Death, and Death's half-brother,

Sleep, Forms terrible to view, their sentry keep;
With anxious Pleasures of a guilty mind,
Deep Frauds before, and open Force behind;
The Furies' iron beds; and Strife, that shakes
Her hissing tresses and unfolds her snakes.
Full in the midst of this infernal road,
An elm displays her dusky arms abroad:
The God of Sleep there hides his heavy head,
And empty dreams on ev'ry leaf are spread.
Of various forms unnumber'd specters more,
Centaurs, and double shapes, besiege the door.
Before the passage, horrid Hydra stands,
And Briareus with all his hundred hands;
Gorgons, Geryon with his triple frame;
And vain Chimaera vomits empty flame.
The chief unsheath'd his shining steel, prepar'd,
Tho' seiz'd with sudden fear, to force the guard,
Off'ring his brandish'd weapon at their face;
Had not the Sibyl stopp'd his eager pace,
And told him what those empty phantoms were:
Forms without bodies, and impassive air.

46. This excerpt is from a type of poem called a(n)

    A. limerick.

    B. epic.

    C. ode.

    D. ballad.

47. What is the rhyme scheme of the first ten lines of this excerpt?

    A. AABBAACCAA

    B. ABCDEABCDE

    C. EEDDCCBBAA

    D. AABBCCDDEE

48. An atmosphere of gloom is suggested by which of the following lines?

    A. "From hence the Grecian bards their legends make"

    B. "By the moon's doubtful and malignant light"

    C. " The chief unsheath'd his shining steel, prepar'd"

    D. "Off'ring his brandish'd weapon at their face."

49. What line marks the end of the exposition, and the beginning of the action?

    A. "Deep was the cave; and downward as it went"

    B. "When Jove in dusky clouds involves the skies"

    C. "The chief unsheath'd his shining steel, prepar'd"

    D. "Had not the Sibyl stopp'd his eager pace"

50. "Before the passage, horrid Hydra stands" contains an example of

    A. alliteration.

    B. assonance.

    C. anapest.

    D. personification.

51. Hydra, Briareus, Gorgons, and the Chimaera are all

    A. men.

    B. gods.

    C. monsters.

    D. angels.

52. In the fourteenth line, what does the word *malignant* mean?

    A. evil

    B. bright

    C. dim

    D. uncertain

Chapter 10

Answer Key for ELA MCAS Practice Test 2

1   If you recall, a superior essay is well structured, draws on good support, and is well written. This essay would surely have received full marks:

> Love changes the lives of two well-known characters for the worse in classic literature—Medea (of Euripides' Medea) and Claire Zachanassian (of Friedrich Durrenmatt's The Visit). Both Medea and Claire Zachanassian are betrayed by their lovers and both exact violent revenge.

> There are many parallels between Medea and Claire Zachanassian, who are both examples of the idea that the uplifting passion of a great love can turn into a destructive force. At one point, the women in Medea compare a great love to a fire that burns the roof beams. That fire engulfs both Medea and Claire as well as the ones they love when the women are betrayed—Medea, when Jason marries Creusa, and Claire, when Anton Schill refuses to acknowledge he has fathered her child.

> Both women experience anger following their lovers' breach of faith. Medea is exiled from Colchis after she assists Jason in killing his father. She flees to Corinth, where she finds herself a stranger in a strange land. Then, after Jason marries Creusa, she feels especially mad.

Claire is furious because she becomes pregnant at seventeen by Anton Schill, and he betrays her by bribing two men to testify that they were her lovers rather than accept responsibility. As a result, she earns a reputation for promiscuity and encounters the harsh judgment of her community. One particularly painful memory she recalls years later is the scene at the cold train station where young boys whistled at her and pelted her with stones as she got on the train to leave Gullen. On that day she vowed to return and get her revenge.

Anger and love changed both these women completely. They want revenge. While Claire pursues her lover directly, Medea exacts her revenge indirectly by killing those who are most dear to Jason.

Both women are consumed by an obsession with justice. In one touching scene, Medea wishes that she could "peel off the flesh" and the memory of what once was. Filled now with self-hatred, she finds her children a bitter reminder of Jason, and she decides to rid herself of that reminder.

Claire, on the other hand, admits that just as she cannot forget her lover's treachery, she cannot forget their love. She observes that Schill's love for her died ago, and admits that her love for him would not die but turned into something evil. Claire's obsession becomes so strong and self-destructive that she spends years carrying out her plan for revenge against Schill. She wants not only Schill but the whole town to suffer, and she plans to buy the town's industries and then let them lie idle. Then she offers one billion marks for the life of Anton Schill, and watches the townspeople lower themselves to kill him.

In the end, both women find that their great loves have eaten them up.

Maybe you've read completely different books, such as *Madame Bovary, Romeo and Juliet, Great Expectations, Pride and Prejudice*, or short stories such as "Wings of the Dove" by Henry James. Or you may pick completely different books in which love transforms a main character.

Remember the seven steps for success?

1) Read the prompt and make sure you understand it.

2) Brainstorm ideas. How were your two central characters changed by love? Start jotting down your ideas.

3) Now you can organize your ideas. Is there a similar way love changed your two characters? A difference in the way they were changed? Maybe your main ideas are that love made your characters similar in one way but different in two others. Great!

4) Line up your details, your supporting information, under these three points.

5) Think of your conclusion. Maybe love is both a positive and a negative force? Maybe love affects one character in a way you admire, but affected another character in a dangerous way?

6) Put your plan into action. Look at your outline. Write out your main idea. Introduce your two books. Write a sentence describing your first point. Present the evidence for the first point. Describe your second idea. Give your support for this second idea. Write out your third supporting idea. Make sure you give good supporting examples that show this point. Write out your conclusion.

Excellent job! Don't forget to revise your composition.

2   **A** If you know *felicity* means great happiness, you would aggressively guess *A*. But if you didn't, you could employ POE to find the correct answer choice. Marianne is in high spirits, and she is asking her sister if she has ever experienced greater joy than this. We can infer that *felicity,* whatever it is, is something nice. Strike out *D, rainstorms.* Try the remaining choices in the context. "Is there a finery in the world greater to this?" Sounds pretty weird, huh? Cross off *B.* You may have to guess between *A* and *C* at this point, but you've increased your odds considerably.

3   **A** An author lets you know what a character is like through what he or she says and does and through what others say about him or her. Look back at Sir John's comments and you will find him saying that Willoughby is "a pleasant, good humored fellow..." You can guess aggressively that one of the choices will be something like "nice" or "friendly" and sure enough—*A* (*agreeable*) is a match. Sir John mentions that Sir Willoughby stands to inherit some property, but says nothing to indicate that the man works hard, is especially honorable, or has big plans for his own future, so eliminate *B, C,* and *D.*

4   **B** Check out the context of this observation, especially what precedes and comes after the narrator's observation that neither Marianne nor Sir John tell the other what they want to know about Willoughby. Put this scenario in your own words—Marianne wants the scoop on his interests ("pursuits") and his talents; Sir John wants to know if that "nicest little black" puppy was with him. The problem certainly isn't that either one is *inarticulate* (*A*), *color blind* (*C*), or *disinterested in Willoughby* (*D*). By using POE, you are left with

247

ANSWER KEY FOR ELA MCAS PRACTICE TEST 2

B—which fits your paraphrase. (They each only pay attention to what they think is interesting in a person.)

5   **A**   This phrase is an expression that means "flirting with a man." In the old days, it often implied trying to win a marriage proposal. Expressions like these contain language that is not meant to be taken literally (figurative language); there are no real hats involved here. The expression does not have some deeper significance, does not mean the opposite of what it says, and does not attribute human qualities to something inhuman, so cross off *B*, *C*, and *D*.

6.   A four-point answer might be:

Willoughby appears to be a gentleman, based on his manners and from his reputation. He recognizes immediately that Marianne is in distress, and he carries her home. Once in the Dashwoods' home, he behaves perfectly. He excuses himself because he's a mess but asks whether he can visit Marianne the next day. Willoughby's reputation is also one of a gentleman. Sir John praises of the young man as "as good a kind of fellow who ever lived," plus he informs the Dashwoods that Willoughby is in line to inherit Allenham Court.

An answer above the call of duty might be:

Although Willoughby is a gentleman, he seems to be a very rash sort of person. His manners are fine—such as excusing himself while he's muddy and dirty, but making sure to be solicitous of Miss Dashwood's health. Sir John emphasizes what a gentleman Willoughby is by describing that he has a "pretty little estate" in Somersetshire and that he's due to inherit Allenham Court. But despite this nobility, Willoughby seems to be a very reckless sort of person. He scoops up Marianne "without further delay" and Sir John also relates a story of impulsive partying. He describes Willoughby as dancing from eight until four.

7   **A**   Skim the passage for the word and study the context clues. The *indictment* was delivered "last night" and now Marie-Antoinette is sentenced to death. Hmmm, definitely not a *request* (*C*) or an *indicator* (*D*). Look at the context for more clues. A verdict implies a jury; a command implies a decree without a jury, summoned by a single person. What does the text say happened here? It plainly mentions a jury, interrogation, and counsel. *A*, *verdict*, makes the most sense in this context.

8 **B** Start by kicking out the wrong answers. *C* is wrong because Carlyle doesn't mention or care that the hallways are long. *D* is also wrong, because the text tells us that Marie-Antoinette is standing near the light. This leaves *A* and *B*. Refer to the context again. Carlyle contrasts the queen with the candle by juxtaposing the two images. How does the paragraph end? "Silently she withdraws from [the light], to die," because when dawn comes, Marie-Antoinette will be beheaded. He's telling us Marie-Antoinette's life will soon be extinguished like the candle. While *A* isn't entirely incorrect, it's too literal—the exam is checking that you can read a figurative image in this paragraph. You can review figurative speech on page 48. Just so you know, this is a difficult passage. You may encounter some selections that are harder than what you are accustomed to—but don't worry. Try your best. Use POE. And keep in mind the selection may be a field-test item, one that does not count.

9 **D** Summarize each paragraph. You might end up with: (1) The author sets the stage for his subject. (2) The death sentence handed down. (3) The author recalls Marie-Antoinette's beloved departure from Vienna (leaving to marry the King of France.) (4) Marie-Antoinette begins another procession—to her death.

10 **A** Read closely for time clues. First we have the indictment, at four in the morning (Ignore how long the jury took to deliberate—the question wants to know between *the end of the trial* and the beheading.). So when is Marie-Antoinette beheaded? "At a quarter past Twelve, her head fell." About eight hours have elapsed.

11 **C** You may know that *abashed* means *ashamed* or *embarrassed*. That eliminates any positive words like self-respect (*B*) and modesty (*D*), and it points to *C* as the correct answer choice. Read the context—"neither abashment nor pride." It tells you that abashment is opposite from pride, which eliminates *A*.

12 **B** Use POE and first strike out all the incorrect facts. *C* is not possible (Marie-Antoinette is very composed and not emotional at all). *D* is likewise wrong (completely opposite of the jeering crowd, cheering for her death). That leaves us with *A* and *B*. Look at the text. Do you think the point of the contrast between paragraphs four and five is to show how many years have passed or to compare two opposite processions; one in which she's the object of adoring crowds that started her life in France, the other in which she's a focal point of a hatred that leads to the end of her life? Guess you've already figured it out—it's *B*.

13 **D** The main idea is the idea that every paragraph underscores. Eliminate answers that are factually incorrect, such as *A* (Carlyle doesn't comment on whether Marie-Antoinette is innocent) and *B* (Marie-Antoinette didn't have humble beginnings.). While *C* is correct, it's a supporting detail, not a main idea. You're left with *D*, an idea emphasized again and again by Carlyle.

14 **A** Start by crossing out the many false statements here. Was Marie-Antoinette given a reprieve? No, she was indicted, the opposite. Nix *B*. Did the French citizens support their queen? The crowd is screaming "Down with Tyranny" and when the executioner holds up her head, they love it. Get rid of *C*. *D* is also the opposite of what the text is saying—Marie-Antoinette was composed up to the end. That leaves *A*, that Marie-Antoinette faced a difficult trial. This makes perfect sense, since the passage mentions she was interrogated for two days and two nights. Yes, we would say this was a strenuous trial.

15 **D** In this description of how the cook looks, the word "as" should set off a familiar little bell in your head. Comparisons like this with the words "as" or "like" are similes. This isn't hubris (the excessive pride for which heroes like Odysseus were punished), understatement (saying less than you mean), or personification (talking about an object or idea as if it were human). Notice that you could probably use aggressive guessing to figure this one out—even if you hadn't read the tale! This shows how important it is to read the question carefully; sometimes the question is all you need.

16 **B** You might think that a story called the Cook's Tale would describe how much the main character likes to cook—but there's no evidence that that's the case here! The storyteller reveals at several points that the apprentice likes to gamble, drink, and party with women ("Who loves dice, wine, dancing, and girls of joy"), so by POE you arrive at *B—cooking*.

17 **C** The reason why the master fires the cook is given in lines 42-46. Ever heard the expression about "one bad apple spoiling the whole basket"? Guess aggressively based on the tale, before you even look at the choices. The boss was worried that this bad-apple servant would make his other employees rotten—by being a bad role-model (*C*). You can use POE to eliminate the other choices. The word "proverb" hints this may be a figurative expression—the master isn't literally worried about fruit, so cross off *A* and *B*. There's plenty in the tale about how drinking gets the cook in trouble—he steals and even goes to prison ("sometimes led, for drinking, to Newgate")—but there's no evidence that he tries to get his master to drink, so *C* is wrong.

18 **A** You may not know that *synecdoche* is a figure of speech in which the part is used for the whole (like "I need some wheels" instead of "I need a car."). If you draw a blank or simply don't know something, don't worry about it. Use your common sense and POE to do your best. Which of the remaining choices *are* found in the given lines. Is there rhyme? Yes—are and guitar. Is there alliteration? Yup, those repeated g's in gay guitar. Is there

personification? Yes—actions (theft and riot) are described as if they were humans ("comrades"). The question asks for the *exception* to the list, so all that's left is A.

19 **A** "The roses turn with envy pale" so you can predict that the word you are looking for means "envy." Only answer choice *A* matches this criteria.

20 **C** Always check the text for grammar. Don't be fooled by the *-ed* ending (which often signifies a verb). In this case, *pierced* describes what kind of hearts the roses have. It's an adjective that modifies a noun (see page 56).

21 **D** Review how to assign letters to end rhymes, if you need to (see page 94). It's very likely that any poems you get on the exam will ask you to chart the rhyme scheme.

22 **B** Paraphrase these lines. You might translate them as something like this: *If a nice-smelling strand of hair blows in the wind, the sweet-smelling flowers complain and act bent out of shape because the hair smells better than they do.* There's nothing here about birds or bees or honey ("honeyed" refers to the sweet smell of the hyacinth flowers), so get rid of *A, C,* and *D*.

23 **D** Did you look for personification? Sometimes there's more than one literary device being used, so you have to pick from the choices they give you. Assonance uses vowels, so cross off *A*. An analogy makes no sense here, so get rid of *B*. An allusion refers to a myth or a biblical story, and there's no reference in these lines. Only *D*, alliteration, is left and what was that again? The repetition of initial consonants such as "If done well, alliteration is a sweetly satisfying sensation." (If you don't remember, review pages 101.)

24 **A** There isn't anything particularly logical or informal about the poet's language, and there are no couplets (two line rhymes). Would you characterize these lines as informal—read them to yourself "…or if perchance" and "…a throng of nightingales awake." This sounds quite formal, hardly casual. Cross off C. The poet has chosen, however, to have this beautiful woman speak for herself, "And, when I pause…" So this answer is definitely possible. Does the poem reinforce its meaning through her voice? Yes, her confidence nicely underscores the point of the poem.

25. Here's a sample good response:

> The female speaker has no doubt that she is beautiful, seeing herself more
> lovely even than nature's flowers. We can almost hear the confidence in her
> voice as she tosses her head. Sounding quite smug, she describes how pained
> the roses are when they see her pretty cheeks. She describes how distressed the

hyacinths are when they smell her perfumed hair wafted by the breeze. Finally, she likes walking among the trees where the nightingales sing of her beauty.

26 **B** To understand the structure of a passage, summarize each paragraph. You might get an outline that looks something along these lines: (1) There's a big poverty problem. (2) Everyone agrees that we need a solution to this poverty problem. (3) I recommend we eat these babies from poor homes. (4) They're quite tasty. (5) Think of the benefits—poor moms get money, rich people are relieved of the burdens of poor people... (6) For all you nay-sayers, just think about the suffering of the poor and reconsider the merits of my plan. Swift describes his 'modest proposal' in the third paragraph.

27 **B** Look at paragraph 6 and you will find Swift figuring what it costs to raise a child; how much money that child could bring when sold, and how many people the child would feed. There is nothing stated or implied about the mother's love for the child, or whether this may not be ethical, so cross off *A* and *C*. Don't fall for *D* because it picks up the word "thrift" from the passage. Swift is suggesting how a particularly thrifty person could stretch the earnings from a single child, not analyzing how poverty causes people to be careful with money, thriftiness.

28 **B** Step back and ask yourself what Swift's purpose is. What does he want his readers to think after reading this essay? Take answer choice *A*, that English adults really disliked Irish parents. Why would Swift satirize this situation? It doesn't really make sense. Take answer choice *B*. Well, this seems to have possibilities. The English are callous about poverty in Ireland, so why shouldn't they just start stewing these babies? Take answer choice *C*, that English politicians care more about babies than financial stability. This seems irrelevant to the essay. What about the idea that British politicians cared more about Irish children than the Irish. It seems unlikely and doesn't explain why Swift wrote his essay. Answer choice *B* is the correct answer choice. He's tweaking the idea of being callous, because can't he claim to be more active and concerned about the poverty problem than the do-nothings? He is after all, looking for a solution, one he might argue (with a wink) that has many merits.

29 **D** Boiling water bubbles. That—plus the resemblance between the words *bulla* and *boil*—should clue you in that *D* is the best answer choice. (And didn't those word parts knock out answers like *beg* and *objection*?)

30 **A** Swift mentions Americans and mothers, but does not make the statements contained in *B* or *D*. He says nothing about child labor, so eliminate *C* as well. That leaves *A* by POE, which is a good restatement of Swift's proposal of how to keep poor children from being a "burden on their parents or country."

31 **D** Tone is the attitude behind the words that are written (see page 68). If you take Swift's words at face value, you miss the point of this satire and cringe. (Ew! Eating babies! Gross!) But Swift doesn't want his words taken literally—he wants you to pick up on the sarcasm of his excessive details. (Babies are tasty when boiled on the fourth day, especially in winter; Rather than using a butcher, consider chopping up the baby yourself.) That's why his title is an understatement; would you say this is a *modest* proposal? More like inflammatory! He wants to create compassion for poor families.

32 **C** Take a look at paragraphs five and six, where Swift describes who he thinks can benefit from this plan. Does he mention that moms will profit? Yes. Does he mention butchers? He says they "will not be wanting." What does he say about landlords? He says landlords will become popular among tenants because they'll be paying for all these babies. And, yes, Swift believes his proposal can relieve England of a pressing problem. The right answer choice is *C*, as he expresses concern that landlords are starving and that this is a benefit to the proposal.

33   Here's a sample four-pointer:

> Swift effectively grabs the reader's sympathy and attention in the opener. By conjuring a vivid image of beggar women in rags with several children in tow, the author engages us in their plight. We want to read on and find out how he proposes to help these poor women and their "helpless infants." Swift also uses the introduction to spark our self-interest. By referring to the future possibilities of these babies, who he predicts will grow up into thieves or expatriates, he indicates that what he is about to say is important to our future as well as that of these children. He implies that the rest of his essay will be crucial to our well-being as well as theirs, and so we are effectively drawn into the piece of writing.

34 **C** Comparisons such as this—with the words *like* or *as*—are similes (see page 48).

35 **A** Hyperbole is gross exaggeration, such as saying that your sister possesses angelic purity. You can cross off *B*, *metaphor*, because this comparison is a *simile*. People can't be personified—they already are people—so cross off *C*. And assonance refers to the repetition of vowel sounds, so say no to *D*.

36 **B** Imagine Telegin's situation. He recalls how his wife betrayed him, but how in the end he kept his pride while she lost her beauty. If anything, his lofty language makes the conversation sound less authentic and more forced, so eliminate *C*. While the language is learned, Chekhov is not depicting a classroom, so get rid of *D*. Using POE, you have narrowed your choices to *A* and *B*. While Telegin may be well educated, that has little to do with his point:

He wants to convey that he took the moral high road (and he uses appropriate lofty, "high" language to express this). *B* is the best answer choice.

37 **A** Use POE and get rid of misleading choices. There is no discussion of alcohol; chances are this is not the prediction. Eliminate *B*. Likewise, there's no reference to medicine (and the Professor is not a doctor, he's an art critic), so cross off *D*. Look at the two remaining choices—who do you predict Vanya will fall in love with? Read Vanya's praises of Helena; he laments that she "has surrendered all the glory of her beauty and freedom" to the Professor. He thinks it's unfortunate how faithful Helena is. It's a good bet that he might fall in love with this woman.

38 A great response might be:

> Chekhov draws attention to how self-centered the Professor is by showing him to us through his servants and through his first-wife's brother, Uncle Vanya. Marina comments that the Professor inconvenienced her quite rudely the night before by ringing his bell at two in morning and demanding tea immediately. But it's Vanya's observations that are more cutting about how pompous the Professor is. By using hyperbole, Vanya makes humorous observations about the ridiculous Professor, telling us his life is "stale as hardtack," and "has been writing on art for twenty-five years, and he doesn't know the very first thing about it." These exaggerations also have the effect of making the Professor seem preposterous, making "mountains out of mole-hills."

A three-point response, that clearly makes good point but doesn't quite get all the details correct, might be:

> Chekhov shows us how self-centered the Professor is by showing us how rude he is. When Telegin, who has been carefully getting the tea ready, proudly tells the Professor that the tea is ready, the Professor says to send it to the study. The other servant comments he woke her in the middle of the night for tea. And Vanya tells us he whines all the time, even though he is a lucky man. He just doesn't care about other people.

39 **D** Check out the context for the word *pathos*. Lincoln personified the "sadness and pathos of the war." Cross off *A*. The context is not that Lincoln personified despair, that belongs in the essay about Lincoln the miserable leader, not an essay on how heroic and majestic Lincoln was. The other three answers seem plausible in the context, so think of words that might help you define *pathos*. What about *pathetic*? Someone pathetic is someone who

gets our sympathy. Hey, what about *sympathy*? These words have something to do with feelings, so get rid of *B, sacrifice*, and *C, death. Pathos* is *suffering*.

40 **C** Whenever an author says *we* instead of *you* he is establishing a degree of intimacy, implying that *we* are in this together. Presidents in the nineteenth century were pretty formal folks, so Lincoln doesn't use informal English (slang or colloquial phrases or vernacular). *A, B*, and *D* are out.

41 **A** Hear these lines in your head and you probably notice that the words "we cannot" are repeated three times. Lincoln was a great speaker and you can bet that this wasn't just an oversight. Rather, he was repeating himself to emphasize how inadequate these gestures (dedicate, consecrate, and hallow) are, because they honor the deeds of dead men and these gestures of respect cannot replace these men. POE leads you to cross off *A*, (there are no repeated initial consonants), *B* (no comparisons with the words *like* or *as*), and *C* (no questions are asked for effect).

42 **B** An adverb is a word that modifies a verb, often telling how or when or how long an action takes place (see page 56). The word "little" tells how Lincoln thinks the world will note his words. (Ironically, Lincoln was wrong. The world, in fact, has long noted his famous speech.)

43 **C** What is the context of Lincoln's words? Sure, he's dedicating a cemetery at Gettysburg, but the entire third paragraph of his speech is about "the unfinished work" of those who will be buried here. What unfinished work is that? You can bet the dead soldiers's unfinished work is *not* building their own final resting place, so cross off *A*. Nor would the soldiers be working to memorialize themselves or keeping Lincoln's spirit alive. This leaves C, that Lincoln is asking his audience to carry on the work of the dead men—by carrying on the work and the cause of the Civil War.

44 **D** Lincoln is speaking of freedom as if it were a human being, a thing that can be born and who needs to be kept alive. Freedom doesn't literally live; this is an example of personification.

45 Here's an example of a four-point answer:

> President Abraham Lincoln has been long remembered for both his fine mind
> and character. The Gettysburg Address demonstrates his gift for finding stir-
> ring words to uplift and unite the people. He was aware of how weary of war
> his audience must be, but managed to energize his listeners by appealing to
> their patriotism and urging them to honor the dead by taking up their cause,
> a "new birth of freedom."

His words reflected the integrity of the man. Many other politicians have been quickly forgotten, but Lincoln has always been a national hero, remembered for his strength, courage, dignity, patience, and his ability to bring out the best in those he governed during the worst of times.

46 **B** Long, sweeping poems about heroes and their adventures—like the *Iliad*, the *Odyssey*, and the *Aeneid*, are known as epics. For review on some types of poems, see page 93.

47 **D** Every successive pair of lines ends in a new rhyme. To review how you figure out rhyme scheme, see page 94.

48 **B** All these lines are in the *Aeneid*, but which one makes you see and feel just how gloomy Hell is? Certainly the image of the moon casting doubtful and "malignant" light is pretty creepy. On the other hand, there's nothing very depressing about telling legends (*A*)— and if anything, the image of our hero taking out his sword (*C*) and waving it around at the bad guys (*D*) is pretty exciting, not dismal, so these choices aren't right.

49 **C** Everything up to the point where the chief, Aeneas, takes out his shining sword is pretty much background (exposition) Up until then, we are get to see and hear and smell and feel how horrible Hell is—but nothing much happens. Sibyl the prophetess slows him down *afterward* by saying, in effect—"Hey, they're just ghosts!"

50 **A** The repetition of the initial "h" sounds in horrid Hydra is an example of alliteration.

51 **C** You may remember from other Greek myths you've read that these are all monsters. Even if you don't, you can figure out that they're something pretty bad by looking at how they're described: "horrid Hydra", "Briareus with all his hundred hands," and "Chimaera vomits empty flame." That eliminates men, gods, and angels (*A*, *B*, and *D*) from the running.

52 **A** Ever hear doctors on *E.R.* talk about malignancies? Not good news, right? If you take Spanish or French, you might also recognize that "mal" means "bad." Then look at how the word is used in context and you see that it's describing the moon's light in Hades. You can guess aggressively, then, that your answer will be something negative—which eliminates *B*. *C* and *D* are weak choices, too. Don't go for *C* just because it's another word that could be used to describe a light or *D* just because it's a word in the passage. This is Hades—it's a really bad place and as you read on in the poem you get some illustrations of just how grim a place it is. So go for a really bad word like "terrible evil" to describe the light there.

Index

Completely darken bubbles with a No. 2 pencil. If you make a mistake, be sure to erase mark completely. Erase all stray marks.

1. YOUR NAME: _____
(Print)   Last   First   M.I.

SIGNATURE: _____   **DATE:** ___ / ___ / ___

HOME ADDRESS: _____
(Print)
                                                                              Number

_____
                    City   State   Zip Code

PHONE NO.: _____
(Print)

IMPORTANT: Please fill in these boxes exactly as shown on the back cover of your test book.

2. TEST FORM

_____

6. DATE OF BIRTH

Month	Day		Year	
○ JAN				
○ FEB				
○ MAR	⓪	⓪	⓪	⓪
○ APR	①	①	①	①
○ MAY	②	②	②	②
○ JUN	③	③	③	③
○ JUL		④	④	④
○ AUG		⑤	⑤	⑤
○ SEP		⑦	⑦	⑦
○ OCT		⑧	⑧	⑧
○ NOV		⑨	⑨	⑨
○ DEC				

3. TEST CODE   **4. REGISTRATION NUMBER**

⓪	Ⓐ	⓪	⓪	⓪	⓪	⓪	⓪	⓪	⓪	⓪
①	Ⓑ	①	①	①	①	①	①	①	①	①
②	Ⓒ	②	②	②	②	②	②	②	②	②
③	Ⓓ	③	③	③	③	③	③	③	③	③
④		④	④	④	④	④	④	④	④	④
⑤		⑤	⑤	⑤	⑤	⑤	⑤	⑤	⑤	⑤
⑦	Ⓖ	⑦	⑦	⑦	⑦	⑦	⑦	⑦	⑦	⑦
⑧		⑧	⑧	⑧	⑧	⑧	⑧	⑧	⑧	⑧
⑨		⑨	⑨	⑨	⑨	⑨	⑨	⑨	⑨	⑨

7. SEX
○ MALE
○ FEMALE

5. YOUR NAME

First 4 letters of last name				FIRST INIT	MID INIT
Ⓐ	Ⓐ	Ⓐ	Ⓐ	Ⓐ	Ⓐ
Ⓑ	Ⓑ	Ⓑ	Ⓑ	Ⓑ	Ⓑ
Ⓒ	Ⓒ	Ⓒ	Ⓒ	Ⓒ	Ⓒ
Ⓓ	Ⓓ	Ⓓ	Ⓓ	Ⓓ	Ⓓ
Ⓔ	Ⓔ	Ⓔ	Ⓔ	Ⓔ	Ⓔ
Ⓕ	Ⓕ	Ⓕ	Ⓕ	Ⓕ	Ⓕ
Ⓖ	Ⓖ	Ⓖ	Ⓖ	Ⓖ	Ⓖ
Ⓗ	Ⓗ	Ⓗ	Ⓗ	Ⓗ	Ⓗ
Ⓘ	Ⓘ	Ⓘ	Ⓘ	Ⓘ	Ⓘ
Ⓙ	Ⓙ	Ⓙ	Ⓙ	Ⓙ	Ⓙ
Ⓚ	Ⓚ	Ⓚ	Ⓚ	Ⓚ	Ⓚ
Ⓛ	Ⓛ	Ⓛ	Ⓛ	Ⓛ	Ⓛ
Ⓜ	Ⓜ	Ⓜ	Ⓜ	Ⓜ	Ⓜ
Ⓝ	Ⓝ	Ⓝ	Ⓝ	Ⓝ	Ⓝ
Ⓞ	Ⓞ	Ⓞ	Ⓞ	Ⓞ	Ⓞ
Ⓟ	Ⓟ	Ⓟ	Ⓟ	Ⓟ	Ⓟ
Ⓠ	Ⓠ	Ⓠ	Ⓠ	Ⓠ	Ⓠ
Ⓡ	Ⓡ	Ⓡ	Ⓡ	Ⓡ	Ⓡ
Ⓢ	Ⓢ	Ⓢ	Ⓢ	Ⓢ	Ⓢ
Ⓣ	Ⓣ	Ⓣ	Ⓣ	Ⓣ	Ⓣ
Ⓤ	Ⓤ	Ⓤ	Ⓤ	Ⓤ	Ⓤ
Ⓥ	Ⓥ	Ⓥ	Ⓥ	Ⓥ	Ⓥ
Ⓦ	Ⓦ	Ⓦ	Ⓦ	Ⓦ	Ⓦ
Ⓧ	Ⓧ	Ⓧ	Ⓧ	Ⓧ	Ⓧ
Ⓨ	Ⓨ	Ⓨ	Ⓨ	Ⓨ	Ⓨ
Ⓩ	Ⓩ	Ⓩ	Ⓩ	Ⓩ	Ⓩ

The Princeton Review
© 1996 Princeton Review L.L.C.
FORM NO. 00001-PR

Practice Test ①

1. Ⓐ Ⓑ Ⓒ Ⓓ   15. Ⓐ Ⓑ Ⓒ Ⓓ   29. Ⓐ Ⓑ Ⓒ Ⓓ   43. Ⓐ Ⓑ Ⓒ Ⓓ
2. Ⓐ Ⓑ Ⓒ Ⓓ   16. Ⓐ Ⓑ Ⓒ Ⓓ   30. Ⓐ Ⓑ Ⓒ Ⓓ   44. Ⓐ Ⓑ Ⓒ Ⓓ
3. Ⓐ Ⓑ Ⓒ Ⓓ   17. Ⓐ Ⓑ Ⓒ Ⓓ   31. Ⓐ Ⓑ Ⓒ Ⓓ   45. Ⓐ Ⓑ Ⓒ Ⓓ
4. Ⓐ Ⓑ Ⓒ Ⓓ   18. Ⓐ Ⓑ Ⓒ Ⓓ   32. Ⓐ Ⓑ Ⓒ Ⓓ   46. Ⓐ Ⓑ Ⓒ Ⓓ
5. Ⓐ Ⓑ Ⓒ Ⓓ   19. Ⓐ Ⓑ Ⓒ Ⓓ   33. Ⓐ Ⓑ Ⓒ Ⓓ   47. Ⓐ Ⓑ Ⓒ Ⓓ
6. Ⓐ Ⓑ Ⓒ Ⓓ   20. Ⓐ Ⓑ Ⓒ Ⓓ   34. Ⓐ Ⓑ Ⓒ Ⓓ   48. Ⓐ Ⓑ Ⓒ Ⓓ
7. Ⓐ Ⓑ Ⓒ Ⓓ   21. Ⓐ Ⓑ Ⓒ Ⓓ   35. Ⓐ Ⓑ Ⓒ Ⓓ   49. Ⓐ Ⓑ Ⓒ Ⓓ
8. Ⓐ Ⓑ Ⓒ Ⓓ   22. Ⓐ Ⓑ Ⓒ Ⓓ   36. Ⓐ Ⓑ Ⓒ Ⓓ   50. Ⓐ Ⓑ Ⓒ Ⓓ
9. Ⓐ Ⓑ Ⓒ Ⓓ   23. Ⓐ Ⓑ Ⓒ Ⓓ   37. Ⓐ Ⓑ Ⓒ Ⓓ   51. Ⓐ Ⓑ Ⓒ Ⓓ
10. Ⓐ Ⓑ Ⓒ Ⓓ   24. Ⓐ Ⓑ Ⓒ Ⓓ   38. Ⓐ Ⓑ Ⓒ Ⓓ   52. Ⓐ Ⓑ Ⓒ Ⓓ
11. Ⓐ Ⓑ Ⓒ Ⓓ   25. Ⓐ Ⓑ Ⓒ Ⓓ   39. Ⓐ Ⓑ Ⓒ Ⓓ
12. Ⓐ Ⓑ Ⓒ Ⓓ   26. Ⓐ Ⓑ Ⓒ Ⓓ   40. Ⓐ Ⓑ Ⓒ Ⓓ
13. Ⓐ Ⓑ Ⓒ Ⓓ   27. Ⓐ Ⓑ Ⓒ Ⓓ   41. Ⓐ Ⓑ Ⓒ Ⓓ
14. Ⓐ Ⓑ Ⓒ Ⓓ   28. Ⓐ Ⓑ Ⓒ Ⓓ   42. Ⓐ Ⓑ Ⓒ Ⓓ

Completely darken bubbles with a No. 2 pencil. If you make a mistake, be sure to erase mark completely. Erase all stray marks.

1. YOUR NAME: _____
(Print)   Last   First   M.I.

SIGNATURE: _____ **DATE:** ___ / ___ / ___

HOME ADDRESS: _____
(Print)   Number

_____
City   State   Zip Code

PHONE NO.: _____
(Print)

IMPORTANT: Please fill in these boxes exactly as shown on the back cover of your test book.

2. TEST FORM

3. TEST CODE

4. REGISTRATION NUMBER

5. YOUR NAME

First 4 letters of last name				FIRST INIT	MID INIT

6. DATE OF BIRTH

Month	Day	Year
JAN		
FEB		
MAR		
APR		
MAY		
JUN		
JUL		
AUG		
SEP		
OCT		
NOV		
DEC		

7. SEX
- MALE
- FEMALE

The Princeton Review
© 1996 Princeton Review L.L.C.
FORM NO. 00001-PR

Practice Test ②

1. Ⓐ Ⓑ Ⓒ Ⓓ
2. Ⓐ Ⓑ Ⓒ Ⓓ
3. Ⓐ Ⓑ Ⓒ Ⓓ
4. Ⓐ Ⓑ Ⓒ Ⓓ
5. Ⓐ Ⓑ Ⓒ Ⓓ
6. Ⓐ Ⓑ Ⓒ Ⓓ
7. Ⓐ Ⓑ Ⓒ Ⓓ
8. Ⓐ Ⓑ Ⓒ Ⓓ
9. Ⓐ Ⓑ Ⓒ Ⓓ
10. Ⓐ Ⓑ Ⓒ Ⓓ
11. Ⓐ Ⓑ Ⓒ Ⓓ
12. Ⓐ Ⓑ Ⓒ Ⓓ
13. Ⓐ Ⓑ Ⓒ Ⓓ
14. Ⓐ Ⓑ Ⓒ Ⓓ

15. Ⓐ Ⓑ Ⓒ Ⓓ
16. Ⓐ Ⓑ Ⓒ Ⓓ
17. Ⓐ Ⓑ Ⓒ Ⓓ
18. Ⓐ Ⓑ Ⓒ Ⓓ
19. Ⓐ Ⓑ Ⓒ Ⓓ
20. Ⓐ Ⓑ Ⓒ Ⓓ
21. Ⓐ Ⓑ Ⓒ Ⓓ
22. Ⓐ Ⓑ Ⓒ Ⓓ
23. Ⓐ Ⓑ Ⓒ Ⓓ
24. Ⓐ Ⓑ Ⓒ Ⓓ
25. Ⓐ Ⓑ Ⓒ Ⓓ
26. Ⓐ Ⓑ Ⓒ Ⓓ
27. Ⓐ Ⓑ Ⓒ Ⓓ
28. Ⓐ Ⓑ Ⓒ Ⓓ

29. Ⓐ Ⓑ Ⓒ Ⓓ
30. Ⓐ Ⓑ Ⓒ Ⓓ
31. Ⓐ Ⓑ Ⓒ Ⓓ
32. Ⓐ Ⓑ Ⓒ Ⓓ
33. Ⓐ Ⓑ Ⓒ Ⓓ
34. Ⓐ Ⓑ Ⓒ Ⓓ
35. Ⓐ Ⓑ Ⓒ Ⓓ
36. Ⓐ Ⓑ Ⓒ Ⓓ
37. Ⓐ Ⓑ Ⓒ Ⓓ
38. Ⓐ Ⓑ Ⓒ Ⓓ
39. Ⓐ Ⓑ Ⓒ Ⓓ
40. Ⓐ Ⓑ Ⓒ Ⓓ
41. Ⓐ Ⓑ Ⓒ Ⓓ
42. Ⓐ Ⓑ Ⓒ Ⓓ

43. Ⓐ Ⓑ Ⓒ Ⓓ
44. Ⓐ Ⓑ Ⓒ Ⓓ
45. Ⓐ Ⓑ Ⓒ Ⓓ
46. Ⓐ Ⓑ Ⓒ Ⓓ
47. Ⓐ Ⓑ Ⓒ Ⓓ
48. Ⓐ Ⓑ Ⓒ Ⓓ
49. Ⓐ Ⓑ Ⓒ Ⓓ
50. Ⓐ Ⓑ Ⓒ Ⓓ
51. Ⓐ Ⓑ Ⓒ Ⓓ
52. Ⓐ Ⓑ Ⓒ Ⓓ

Gloria Levine graduated from Mt. Holyoke College, and received a master's in education from the University of California at Berkeley. She has taught grades 6-12 and has written several test-prep books on getting ready for the GED, the PSAT, and the SAT. Currently she lives in Potomac, MD, with her husband, a daughter and a son, and two computer-loving cats.

The Princeton Review

Find the Right School

BEST 331 COLLEGES
2002 EDITION
The Smart Buyer's Guide to College
0-375-76201-9 • $20.00

COMPLETE BOOK OF COLLEGES
2002 EDITION
0-375-76202-7 • $26.95

COMPLETE BOOK OF
DISTANCE LEARNING SCHOOLS
0-375-76204-3 • $21.00

POCKET GUIDE TO COLLEGES
2002 EDITION
0-375-76203-5 • $11.95

AFRICAN AMERICAN STUDENT'S
GUIDE TO COLLEGE
Making the Most of College:
Getting In, Staying In, and
Graduating
0-679-77878-0 • $17.95

Get in

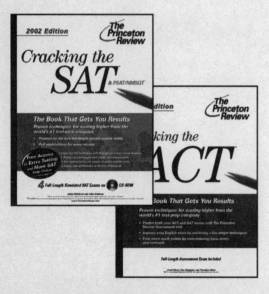

CRACKING THE SAT & PSAT/NMSQT
2002 EDITION
0-375-76207-8 • $18.00

CRACKING THE SAT & PSAT/NMSQT
WITH SAMPLE TESTS ON CD-ROM
2002 EDITION
0-375-76192-6 • $29.95

MATH WORKOUT FOR THE SAT
2ND EDITION
0-375-76177-2 • $14.95

VERBAL WORKOUT FOR THE SAT
2ND EDITION
0-375-76176-4 • $14.95

CRACKING THE ACT
2002 EDITION
0-375-76233-7 • $19.00

CRACKING THE ACT WITH
SAMPLE TESTS ON CD-ROM
2002 EDITION
0-375-76234-5 • $29.95

CRASH COURSE FOR THE ACT
10 Easy Steps to Higher Score
0-375-75326-5 • $9.95

CRASH COURSE FOR THE SAT
10 Easy Steps to Higher Score
0-375-75324-9 • $9.95

Get Help Paying for it

DOLLARS & SENSE FOR COLLEGE STUDENTS
How Not to Run Out of Money by Midterms
0-375-75206-4 • $10.95

PAYING FOR COLLEGE WITHOUT GOING BROKE
2002 EDITION
Insider Strategies to Maximize Financial Aid
and Minimize College Costs
0-375-76211-6 • $18.00

THE SCHOLARSHIP ADVISOR
5TH EDITION
0-375-76210-8 • $26.00

Better Students, Better Scores, Better Schools

Designed to improve standardized test scores.

Parents

- Stay involved with child's classwork and test performance

- Access resources to use at home to help child succeed in school

- Spend quality time with child while directly affecting test scores

Students

- Diagnose which skills are strong and which need improvement

- Work with Homeroom's tailored resources to master each and every weak skill

- Work at their own pace, on their own level

Educators

- Keep track of whole class and individual student progress

- Individualize students' learning

- Maximize school's technology investment

For Math and Reading in Grades 3–8, Homeroom covers:

- CTBS/TerraNova
- ITBS
- SAT-9
- VA: SOL

- FL: FCAT
- TX: TAAS
- NY: ELA and Math
- MA: MCAS

For more information:
- Visit www.homeroom.com
- Call 1-877-8Homeroom or
- E-mail info@homeroom.com